TAKING AMERICA

TAKING AMERICA

*How We Got from
the First Hostile Takeover
to Megamergers, Corporate Raiding,
and Scandal*

JEFF MADRICK

BANTAM BOOKS
TORONTO • NEW YORK • LONDON • SYDNEY • AUCKLAND

TAKING AMERICA
A Bantam Book / April 1987

Library of Congress Cataloguing-in-Publication Data

Madrick, Jeffrey G.
   Taking America.

   1. Tender offers (Securities)   2. Consolidation and
Merger of corporations—United States.   3. Insider trading
insecurities—United States.   I. Title.

HG4028.T4M33   1987   338.8'3'0973   87-928
ISBN 0-553-05229-2 (U.S.)

Published simultaneously in the United States and Canada

_____

Bantam Books are published by Bantam Books, Inc. Its trademark, consisting of the
words "Bantam Books" and the portrayal of a rooster, is Registered in U.S. Patent
and Trademark Office and in other countries. Marca Registrada. Bantam Books,
Inc., 666 Fifth Avenue, New York, New York 10103.

_____

PRINTED IN THE UNITED STATES OF AMERICA

FG   0 9 8 7 6 5 4 3 2 1

FOR MATINA

ACKNOWLEDGMENTS

If an author gets sole credit for writing a book these days, it is probably only by virtue of tradition.

My sincerest gratitude goes to the following people.

Jane Berkey and Don Cleary, my agents, championed the book long before takeovers were the talk of the town.

Linda Grey, Bantam's extraordinary editor-in-chief, bought the book, patiently accepted its delays, and edited it with great fidelity and caring.

Alex Rich made it accurate. In the final stretch to meet the deadline, she researched and corrected it, and found new material. She did a wonderful job.

Three other researchers provided invaluable services: Vicki Contavespi, Maggie Peters, and Patricia Neering.

My colleagues at WNBC-TV were very understanding, both of my need for time to write and of my sour moods as deadlines approached.

Special thanks go to those people who answered my many questions with forthrightness and, above all, patience; and to the staff of Bantam who rushed to get the book to publication.

Finally, my family continually urged me on and so did several close friends. I only hope I am as good a friend to them.

And, to my daughter, who must have asked me every weekend for several years how work on this book was going, I answer: Thanks for worrying about your father.

TAKING AMERICA

INTRODUCTION

The announcement, on a late Friday afternoon in November 1986, that Ivan Boesky would personally pay a penalty of $100 million for illegal insider trading seized the nation's imagination. It no doubt fed a public fantasy. The rich really did make hundreds of millions of dollars—and sometimes they stole it.

But few on Wall Street were taken aback by the sum. Never before in modern times had trading securities been as profitable to a select few as it had become in the 1980s. The truth was that audacity had always been at the heart of this hostile-merger movement. Big, unfriendly takeovers had begun long before famous mavericks like T. Boone Pickens, Carl Icahn, and Ivan Boesky made headlines. The history of this modern takeover movement was one of an endless series of precedents and of rising levels of aggressiveness, leading to by far the largest mergers of all time. The rewards had long been going to the boldest.

It started in 1974, when a public bid was made by an old-line industrial giant for a large Philadelphia battery company which wanted none of it. It began, then, with the establishment—the first hostile bid ever made by such a company. If one could have looked forward from 1974, the results would have seemed the stuff of the most far-fetched fiction. Carl Icahn, back then an options broker, now controlled TWA. Ted Turner, the iconoclastic businessman who built a broadcasting company out of an Atlanta TV station, could bid for CBS and indirectly drive it into the hands of Laurence Tisch, a man who had made his money in tobacco, hotels, and insurance.

Men who had made their fortunes in real estate or drilling for oil could now bid for long-established paper manufacturers or legendary movie companies or retailers with illustrious names like Neiman-Marcus and Marshall Field. General Foods itself was now a subsidiary. Kennecott Copper was gone to the highest bidder, as were Carnation and Nabisco and Norton Simon and scores of industrial companies such as Garlock and Microdot.

A small retail company could acquire Revlon and all its glamorous trappings. Through acquisitions, U.S. Steel largely became an oil company called USX. General Motors and General Electric would eventually make giant acquisitions they would regret, as would Exxon. Schlumberger, which had always seemed infallible—at least back in 1974—would stub its toe on Fairchild Electric. Even IBM made a major acquisition. And the biggest industry of all, oil, was transformed by the driven man who traced his ancestry to Daniel Boone. Conoco, Getty, Gulf, and Marathon now belonged to others—were, really, no more.

The bonanza for Wall Street was that most of these mergers had to pass through the hands of a relative few: the dozen or so major banking houses which through contacts, experience, and tradition had learned how to engineer these mergers best. A small percentage of a merger that was valued in the billions of dollars produced fees unheard-of before. The good fortune for arbitrageurs like Boesky was that the prices paid for companies were bid very high, and that the nation's largest corporations would be gathered into the swirl. In the mid-1970s, the money paid for a hostile acquisition sometimes reached as high as $500 million. In the early '80s, the amount would top $1 billion. In 1984 a single hostile acquisition was valued at $13 billion. Twenty-five-year-olds made $200,000 a year. Thirty-year-olds made $1 million. Forty-year-olds made $10 million. Every chief executive officer in the nation, no matter how large his corporation, eventually quaked in fear at the prospect of being taken over. But the chief executives, too, learned how to get rich. Golden parachutes entitled them to millions of dollars if they were taken over. And they learned how to borrow money and buy their own companies. Macy's and Storer Communications and Metromedia were taken private by their managements, and probably would soon make them wealthy. Metromedia was ultimately sold to publisher Rupert Murdoch, who set it side by side with Twentieth Century-Fox, which he bought from oil man Marvin Davis, who later bought the Beverly Hills Hotel from Ivan Boesky.

And one consequence, of course, was the fall of Boesky, the biggest of the arbitrageurs and the man who probably made more money directly from hostile takeovers than anyone else. Boesky egregiously overstepped the bounds. He paid systematically to find out what companies were targets of corporate bids. With that information he could buy stocks from unsuspecting investors, then sell after a takeover offer was announced and the price had gone up. The Securities and Exchange Commission said Boesky stole $50 million this way, and the agency fined him another $50 million. At this writing, it is not yet clear who else Boesky brought down with him, but a younger crop of men has been implicated already. Money had become the first objective of this takeover movement, and gamesmanship came to rule. The line between right and wrong blurred badly.

The spark for the takeover movement was low stock prices, which made corporations appear to most businessmen as rare bargains. The American economy was also shifting emphasis, away from its industrial traditions to service and high-technology businesses. Older companies were withering and seeking new business in other areas. The tax laws strongly influenced the incentive to merge. But men do not operate automatically, unanimously, or immediately on economic interest. The growth of takeovers over this period demonstrates that fallacy of economic thought all too well.

This is a story of how events build on each other, grow larger, bolder, and take on a life of their own. The maverick corporate raiders of the mid-1980s were only the latest stage in a long progression. The links, of course, were men. Those trained in the 1950s passed on their lessons to younger men in the 1960s. In the 1970s, the mantle was taken by the experienced men of the earlier decade, and pushed further by those who learned from them. Most of the men of the takeover movement were shaped by their times, even the best-known of them, especially the raiders later in the movement. But a handful stood above the pack: the lawyers Joseph Flom and Martin Lipton, investment banker Robert Greenhill of Morgan Stanley, and executive Charles Baird (for one deal alone),

Harry Gray of United Technologies; oil man T. Boone Pickens; and finally arbitrageur Ivan Boesky, even before the scandal that toppled him. They molded the system more than they were molded by it.

But in every movement, there are also differences. Most of those who drove mergers in the 1970s and 1980s were money men. They were rarely dreamers, or builders, or even men who could run a business. They were men who wanted, and knew how to make, money. And throughout the history of this movement, mergers were often made for the wrong reasons. That is the message that stands out so clearly and alarmingly. As making deals took precedence over doing real business, merger activity got busier and mergers bigger, and the debt incurred to finance them grew dramatically. Outrageous prices were paid for companies. And one criticism was never satisfactorily answered: Billions of dollars inflated the value of existing business but did not find its way into new investment. Money spent on acquisitions could instead have been used to drill for more oil or to build modern steel plants or to support basic research and development. Businessmen took the easier way out and bought what already existed. Yet even that seemingly easier kind of business decision turned out badly time and again.

Insight into this movement's lack of value is best found in the motivation and thinking behind the individual deals themselves. Each deal is a story of men, not economic necessity, and when stripped of business rhetoric, the thinking behind many mergers becomes distressingly clear. A deal borrowed from the one that preceded it, and the power of this history lies in its progression. Such are the stories of fads.

It is easy to forget that an investment banking house was once satisfied with a fee of only a couple of hundred thousand dollars, or that a giant merger was anything over $100 million. Only a handful of years ago, an arbitrageur's big killing was half a million dollars. Few remember that in 1974 no one believed a new round of corporate mergers could get under way at all. Bursts of merger activity had never followed one another in quick succession before. There had been only three such movements in the century, each separated by a couple of decades, at least. And the last wave of mergers had ended bitterly. The conglomerates, many of whom acquired literally hundreds of companies each in the 1960s, collapsed in the market crash beginning in 1969. Many blamed that crash on the excesses of these conglomerates, and no one thought the veil of business shame would be raised quickly. An article published in *Fortune* magazine in 1973 stated: "A repetition of the Sixties could not occur. . . . Merger movements of dramatic intensity have occurred only three times since the 1890s. The phenomenon is infrequent, some economists contend, because it requires a rare conjuncture of events."

By the end of the 1970s, and certainly by the mid-1980s, it had become clear that very much the opposite was true. The impulse of the modern corporation was to grow and acquire. Mergers would occur in great numbers unless they were stopped by special events—a deep recession, a war, strong government policy. The renewal of shame brought by the Boesky scandal probably would not stop them, either. The beginning of the merger wave can be exactly traced to twelve days in July 1974, only five years after the last merger movement had ended.

J. M.
January 1987

1

Judged by his photographs, Frederick Port did not have an innocent face. It was assuredly not the storybook face of a victim, either. If anything, it was an innocuous face—even friendly. It was pudgy, perhaps kind; it might have a good smile. It was decidedly not the face of a businessman. There was no lean determination in it. It could be the face of a comedian from the '50s, or even an intellectual. It had softness, and maybe a tendency to self-pity.

Because Port had died in 1978, one dwelled on his photographs and tried to put together the pieces of the man who had to fight the first hostile tender offer undertaken by the cream of the establishment. There was nothing ironic in his death. He did not die of a disease that could reasonably be related to his difficult years of trying to turn a profit at his once-independent company. Port was taken suddenly by cancer of the bladder. There was little of the classic victim in his life. He enjoyed the fruits of being a corporate president. He even liked a good fight.

What he was not was a businessman's businessman. He had earned a doctorate in engineering from MIT. He loved to hunt, and he was also given to long walks alone at his Maryland farm. He occasionally grew a beard that his chairman, Edward Dwyer, would poke light fun at. He was said to be the first to wear colored shirts at the Union League in Philadelphia. Some say he was aloof, even artsy; it was more that he was diffident and introspective. He stood nearly six feet tall but was no athlete. He was slightly overweight and gave the impression of being even heavier than he was. He was married three times, but was not a ladies' man. It was more as if the ladies claimed him. But he did look forward to running the company; he enjoyed it, had been successful at it. His widow, Rolanda, says he was very ambitious. What everyone else conceded about him was that he was very intelligent. But his was an inward-looking and occasionally brooding intelligence, not the kind businessmen are typically comfortable with. Another man in his position might have perceptibly altered the course of the merger movement that followed. Another man almost certainly could have altered the course of ESB.

In 1972, Port at fifty-seven was named president and chief executive officer of ESB, Inc. (formerly Electric Storage Battery Co.), an old, respected Philadelphia company. By 1974 he was firmly in charge. He had been picked by his predecessor, Ed Dwyer, now chairman of the board, but it was not a completely sympathetic choice. A lawyer by training, Dwyer was far more outgoing than Port. And he was far more social. Not brought up on Philadelphia's Main Line, Dwyer, who had been an undergraduate at St. John's in Annapolis, seemed to enjoy his acquired status in Philadelphia. He had become chairman of the United Way, and served as president of the Union League. He once headed the National Association of Manufacturers. Port joined these organizations only reluctantly. But Dwyer did believe Port was a good manager. Port had turned around the automotive division, the most important in ESB. Dwyer might have preferred a different sort of man, but Port was really the only one for the job.

ESB was founded in 1888 and had paid a dividend every quarter since the turn of the century. It had been a close member of the Philadelphia community. It was the eleventh-largest company in the city. On its board sat a member of the Widener family, as Main Line a family as there was. And Dwyer had risen to social prominence as its former president. In 1974, ESB was the largest battery maker in the world, specializing in auto batteries sold under the Willard and Exide names. Under Port, it had just ended its most profitable fiscal year. It earned $20 million after taxes on sales of more than $400 million in the year ended March 31, 1974. Port, son of a country doctor in South Dakota, a scholarly engineer who had put himself through college and graduate school, had come a long way.

The phone call that would initiate the surprise of the decade came during a meeting Port was holding with several of his executives. It was around noon on Wednesday, July 17, 1974. Port's secretary interrupted, saying a man from Morgan Stanley was on the phone and insisted on speaking with Mr. Port. The caller had told her it was very important. Port instructed his secretary to tell him he would call back in a few minutes.

What Robert Greenhill of Morgan Stanley wanted was to arrange a meeting between Port and representatives of International Nickel Company of Canada for the next day. Port protested that he and his wife were leaving for Africa that Thursday evening for a vacation and he would prefer to postpone the meeting until his return. Greenhill assured him that that was impossible. International Nickel wanted to discuss a major investment in ESB. Port agreed to receive them.

Port had been through similar discussions with companies interested in acquiring ESB in recent months. While profits rose at the company, the stock had dropped, in line with the rest of the stock market. Where it had stood at nearly $30 a share in early 1974, it was now hovering below $20 a share. ESB's book value— assets less liabilities—was nearly half again as high as its current market value at these deflated prices.

Even in 1974 there were few concrete signs of the business slowdown that was under way. Port probably believed, as did most observers of the time, that the stock market would soon turn back up. What's more, the oil embargo imposed by the Arab oil countries in the fall of the preceding year had placed the role of energy front and center. Power sources like batteries looked more desirable now that the supply of oil had been curtailed, and could again be curtailed in the future. The multiple increases in the oil price made energy derived from batteries that much cheaper comparatively. If anything, the Arab nations had conferred a bit of glamour on ESB.

Among the companies that had approached Port before, the most notable was United Aircraft, bigger than International Nickel if not as old-line. He had turned it away. He would listen carefully to what International Nickel and Morgan Stanley had to say, and while he may have sensed that this time it might be different, he had every intention of sending them packing as well. Port looked forward to that summer vacation on safari in Kenya. He told his wife,

Rolanda, about the meeting, but he still believed it would not interfere with the trip.

Four men arrived by helicopter in Philadelphia that Thursday, July 18, with their plans well laid out. They were Samuel Payne, the lordly senior partner of Morgan Stanley, and Robert Greenhill, a young Morgan partner in charge of new mergers business. International Nickel was represented by its chief financial officer, Charles Baird, who made his headquarters in New York. Finally, there was Joseph Flom, managing partner of Skadden Arps Slate Meagher and Flom, a New York law firm that Dwyer cannot remember ever having heard of before.

The New Yorkers were greeted by Port and his financial officer, Benno Bernt. Dwyer was in Washington for a meeting with the National Association of Manufacturers. Flom waited in the hotel. Baird presented his case immediately and, he says, in the friendliest light possible. Inco, as International Nickel was generally called, proposed to make a complete acquisition of ESB. Baird and his colleagues had no intention of replacing any ESB management. They believed that at this stage in ESB's development, given both its competition and its potential for new growth, ESB could use a rich parent. Port, of course, had heard similar arguments before. But what made Baird's significantly different was this: The giant nickel company said it would go ahead with a public tender offer whether or not Port and Dwyer agreed to be taken over.

Greenhill says that Port's face turned red when he heard the news. But Port apparently knew enough not to respond immediately. He told them that if he and his board decided to accept the merger, he would call them at their hotel that afternoon. But Port probably already knew what he was going to say. And Dwyer, once Port found him in Washington, would agree. "They threw down the gauntlet," Dwyer recalls, years later. Port began to arrange a board meeting for the next day. He called his wife just as she was about to leave and told her to cancel the plans. The babysitter had arrived to take care of the two children. In fact, Rolanda Port remembers that the cab was already waiting to take her to the airport. And Port arranged for the call to Baird of Inco. Baird describes the call as cryptic, but not so obscure as to be misleading. ESB would not agree to a takeover.

After the close of stock trading in New York, Inco announced its tender offer with a press release in Toronto, where it was headquartered. It had already filed the necessary documents with the Securities and Exchange Commission, having had lawyers standing by in Washington. Inco would pay $28 a share to all holders of ESB stock. The offer would expire in two weeks. An hour or so earlier, ESB shares had closed on the New York Stock Exchange at $19.50. Port did not get home until about nine that evening. Dwyer says that both he and Port were calm. But Rolanda says that Port was angry. This just wasn't done, he would think. Who did they think they were? Coming in here like that, with no warning and giving us an ultimatum. This just wasn't done.

In fact, no hostile tender offer had ever been undertaken by a full-fledged member of the corporate elite before.

A decade later, Charles Baird stood conspicuously trim compared to the image of his one-time antagonist Fred Port. He reveled in being in excellent physical shape for a man in his early sixties. He was nothing if not confident, and certainly imposing in personality and charm. He was proud of an Episcopalian background that stressed honesty, discipline, and hard work. "You work hard and keep your word," he said. Baird has a directness that suggests he does indeed abide by those principles. He made the odd claim that his mother, a Christian Scientist, had imbued her children with upper-class moral values. He did not elaborate. His father, he said, was middle-class, and he grew up accustomed to a middle-class income. Baird used to commute on the Long Island Railroad to Freeport High School, the public school that served the neighboring farm communities on Long Island's south shore. His résumé notes that he was born in Southampton, farther east of Freeport, and much farther up the social scale.

In 1980, Baird was named chairman and chief executive officer of Inco, the same year that Inco put ESB up for sale. Baird said he had no instinct for running a business like ESB's. He was not comfortable dealing with ESB's salesmen and customers. "Our salesmen are college-educated," he said. The many small marketers of electric batteries, the retailers, were alien to Baird. The small favors, the socializing, were not easy for him or his company. "It's a gutsier business than they're used to," said Robert Kent, a former ESB executive. "It's more down to earth. I never bought a distributor a woman or a TV set, but I'm not saying some of my men didn't."

"Our business is so much cleaner" is the way Baird put it. As one Inco officer said: "Lorillard is a great company. But Baird would be uncomfortable running a cigarette company. He wouldn't be able to deal with all those wholesalers."

Since the early years of the century, Inco had been one of the great monopolies of the world. High-mindedness came easily to it. A Canadian company, Inco controlled about 85 percent of the nickel available in the free world well into the 1950s. It also mined copper, the ore of which is commonly found with that of nickel. Since the company started operations in 1902, it had lost money in only two years, the Depressions of 1922 and 1932. In 1974, it stood number 122 in size among industrial companies outside the United States. In that year, Inco still controlled some 40 percent of the market. Its closest competitor had less than half of that.

It says much about modern industrial life that a mining company considers itself a business with clean hands. What businessmen typically mean is that they are not forced into the gracelessness of having to sell their products or win over their customers. Moreover, their customers are large and dignified companies.

It was lack of sales, however, that began to bring Inco down in the world, beginning in 1961. Demand for nickel soared throughout the '60s. Almost uninterrupted economic growth in the United States created most of the demand, and the United States was Inco's biggest single market. The fast growth in demand, unfortunately for Inco, attracted many new competitors who could often pry away customers. Though the quality of the nickel they produced was lower, it was still entirely suitable for new products, notably stainless steel. Inco found that it was losing market share rapidly.

What really jarred Inco was a sudden drop in demand for nickel in 1971. Rapid growth during the '60s had allowed for a lackadaisical attitude. There had been no recession in the United States since 1960, and the rest of the world was enjoying fast, if more sporadic, growth. In 1970, however, a recession at last settled on Western economies. In that year, nickel demand remained strong, but by 1971 the amount of nickel mined dropped from more than 500 million pounds the previous year to less than 350 million pounds. The business cycle, by and large dormant in the lucky '60s, would leave its mark on most basic industries as the '70s began. The drop in nickel demand, coupled with encroachment on its territory by a host of new competitors, forced the old-line company to act.

The long, successful history of Inco had bred a management that was self-satisfied. Inaction was a sign of grace. By 1972, Inco clearly knew it needed action. It installed L. Edward Grubb as its new chairman. Grubb was fresh from a success for Inco in England. He had cut costs and employee rolls enough at a British subsidiary to turn the sluggish business into a moneymaker. Grubb had spent his whole career at Inco and his principal task now would be to cut costs across the board. His second task: to change the selling practices of the company. In its complacency Inco had offered itself as the seller of last resort to its customers, while its competitors locked in sales by means of one-year (and even longer) contracts. Grubb now demanded contracts as well. At first he settled for one-year agreements. Soon, he requested three-year contracts from his customers. They bridled, but accepted them.

Henry Wingate, Grubb's predecessor, was talked of with great respect by those who worked for him, but he was not a cost cutter. Under the reign of Grubb, condescension surfaced in the notion that Inco could accomplish whatever it wanted to. In ways akin to John F. Kennedy's taking over after the sleepy Eisenhower years, Grubb and his team felt they could remake Inco. In fortuitous confirmation of this view, the economy bounced back strongly soon after Grubb took over. Nickel demand was again high; the long-term contracts were falling into place. Grubb already looked good. In 1973, Inco would produce both record sales and record earnings. Sales would hit $1.2 billion. The coffers were filling with cash—which Grubb needed to implement another piece of his plan.

Grubb and his second-in-command, J. Edwin Carter, another longtime Inco employee, were determined to protect Inco from the new instability of the nickel market. Long-term sales contracts would help. He started searching for new nickel sources and even-

tually even drilling for oil. But principally, Inco management agreed
that they wanted to buy into an entirely different business, one that
was less cyclical and with more opportunities for growth. A new
minerals tax in Ontario made Grubb all the more determined. That
diversification was a relatively new business concept, requiring more
than casual justification, was not acknowledged. Despite the spectacular failures of the conglomerates in the previous decade, it had
become an accepted, if unproved, principle that one set of managers
could handle a variety of businesses. Grubb reached for this idea as
easily as he did for basic cost cutting. He said later that he was so
busy closing plants he did not think about it much and left it to his
president, Ed Carter. In fact, other metals companies had done it.
By late 1973, Grubb had the cash to buy the company that would
provide Inco with a new avenue of growth.

What transformed a gentlemanly, old-style company into the
engineer of the first hostile takeover of its kind was just this confident activism. But opportunity was also required. Inflation, in its
diverse ways, created opportunity. In the '70s, inflation was the
dominant fact of economic life. More than any other single factor, it
explains the many lines of the merger movement of the period. To
the acquiring company, it made new investment very expensive, and
created great value in standing assets. It also helped to provide
seemingly extraordinary bargains in the stock market. Inflation became the principal justification for the giant mergers of the '70s and
'80s.

In retrospect, it seems implausible but true that inflation was as
much on people's minds in 1970 and 1971 as it would be after the
oil price increases of 1973 and 1974. In the early '70s, for example,
an inflation rate of nearly 6 percent was enough to cause President
Nixon to adopt price and wage controls. By the end of the decade
the United States was suffering inflation rates that ran well into the
teens, without a thought of adopting controls. By 1974, inflationary
fears had already permeated the economic and business discourse of
the day, and within a few years, most acted as if inflation were here
to stay.

Until 1965 the growth of inflation had been imperceptible. In 1966 it jumped to a nearly 5 percent annual rate. After a brief drop during the 1966 slowdown, it would rise gradually to the end of the decade. It was the era of high military spending for Vietnam and the argument over whether the nation could afford both guns and butter. In 1968 inflation had become a central campaign issue for the first time since the end of World War II. By 1971 a Republican President, ideologically opposed to tampering with the free market, felt compelled to impose a version of wage and price controls that, when lifted months later, resulted in a spurt in prices. The business community had a taste of the anti-inflation medicine it deplored, and from the political party of its choice.

Nowhere was the distaste for inflation more evident than in the stock market. An accepted tenet back then held that stocks were the best inflation hedge—in other words, that they should rise in value with inflation. The logic was impeccable: Inflation can take hold only if businesses raise prices, so business profits will always keep up with prices. Stocks should then go up. The much-respected idea ignored the destabilizing effect of inflation on overall economic growth, and therefore on profits. Beginning in 1974, the nation suffered the worst recession since World War II, and growth would remain sluggish compared to the 1960s. Through the decade, stocks would not nearly keep pace with inflation.

As measured by the Dow Jones industrials, stocks had attained their peak in 1966. The broader Standard & Poor's 500 Index, however, did rise higher through 1969. After the precipitous 1970 fall, the S&P 500 again reached a higher peak in 1972. But when the rise is discounted by inflation, the S&P 500, even in 1972, was still below its 1968 level. Comparing the average level of the S&P 500 in constant 1966 dollars, stock prices in 1970 fell to an average of 80 percent of their 1966 value. An average investor, even looking back from the vantage point of the 1972 bull market, when prices rose sharply, would still see that after inflation he was only as well off as he was in 1966. But it would get much worse. By the bear market of 1974, stocks adjusted for inflation stood at less than 65 percent of their 1966 value. Investors accustomed to making handsome profits on their stocks in the bull markets of the 1960s were more than a little frustrated. And so were the corporations that could produce no returns for their investors.

In low stock prices, however, there should be opportunity. What businessmen deduced was that inflation and slow economic growth had produced bargains. While stock prices had fallen, the cost of building new plants, buying new equipment, and starting new businesses soared along with inflation. Economists developed an approximate measure of this, called the Q Ratio. Toward the end of the 1970s, the President's Council of Economic Advisers started computing the figure. The Q Ratio compares the cost of new investment to the market value of corporations' stocks and bonds. If the ratio rises above one, the implication is that it is cheaper to buy a company on the stock market than to build one from scratch. The Q Ratio is such a rough measure that the Council has since abandoned it. But the direction of the ratio in the '70s was clear. It became cheaper and cheaper to buy rather than to build, at least when measured by the current cost of replacing an old plant. "Cheaper to buy than to build" became the explanatory slogan for the merger movement to come.

The rise in the book value of corporations compared to their stock prices demonstrates the same point. The book value is the measure of all the assets on the corporation's books, at the price originally paid, less their liabilities. These assets include cash, accounts receivable, and inventories, as well as plants and equipment. In 1966 the book value of Standard & Poor's 400 industrial companies was only about 50 percent of their stock prices. Investors valued companies at twice what they originally paid for their assets. During the bull markets of 1967 and 1968, the proportion fell well below 50 percent. But after 1969, stock prices fell sharply compared to book value. In 1973, as stock prices slid, book value rose above 50 percent of stock prices. At the low point of the bear market of 1974, book value reached more than 90 percent of stock market values. Even as the stock market rose sharply in 1975, the book value averaged 70 percent of stock prices. In the late '70s it would rise to the 90 percent level, and remain there through the early '80s.

If stocks on average were selling at about the value of a company's assets, there were many cases where stocks were selling well below that value. And most of these assets were bought before rising inflation. A virtual industry grew on Wall Street, seeking out stocks that were selling not merely below book value, but frequently below the value of *current* assets less *all* liabilities. Stock prices got so low that if all the debt were paid off, many companies had cash and accounts receivable enough to exceed the market value of their companies trading in the stock market.

But on a still more meaningful scale, stocks looked cheap. Assets were only as good as the earnings they generated. The stock price in relation to earnings per share—the price-earnings multiple—fell to levels not seen since just after World War II. After the early 1950s, price-earnings multiples of the S&P 500 seldom traded lower than ten and gradually climbed to the mid-teens. A company earning $1 a share, then, was selling on average in the stock market for a price of about $15. In the '60s, the average multiple rose to the high teens and low twenties. Its peak was reached in 1961, but the multiple did not fall as low as fifteen again, except briefly in 1966, until the 1969 collapse. The multiple rose again in the early 1970s for what proved a temporary respite. In late 1973, the average multiples of the S&P 500 dropped to around twelve. By late 1974, in the depths of the stock market decline, the multiple stood at about seven. Stock prices compared to earnings were at their lowest levels since the frail years just after World War II.

Low stock prices could not fail to impress businessmen. By any conventional standards, stocks were selling at bargain levels. Or so twenty years of business experience in the United States told them. The numbers literally stared them in the face. On the basis of the most elementary analysis, it looked better to buy a public company than to build from scratch. At no time, before or since, was this argument more compelling than in 1974. But that did not necessarily make it right.

Charles Baird was Edward Grubb's point man. He would eventually run the takeover. In Baird, Grubb knew he had a fighter. Baird proved to Grubb that he was willing to make the tough decisions necessary to trim the fat from Inco. In his attention to physical fitness, the ex-marine lieutenant also thrived on competition. When Baird turned sixty, eight years later, he was ranked number one in the United States in platform tennis for his age group. He kept in shape and he still cared about winning.

Yet Baird was an organization man. He had served with Exxon, the former Standard Oil of New Jersey, or Esso, for seventeen years, rising to assistant treasurer before joining Inco at the age of forty-seven. He had spent most of his time overseas for the company, which added some worldliness to his natural charm. For much of his tenure he was the only American in Esso France. In 1967, he became Under Secretary of the Navy. Baird had graduated from Middlebury College in economics, and also put in some time at Dartmouth which was interrupted by World War II. He lived in very acceptable Short Hills, New Jersey. By every conventional criterion, Baird was part of the establishment. An interesting combination of propriety and competitiveness marked this man who would defy precedent and become the spark behind the hostile tender offer.

But Baird was not in charge of the committee that was looking for a takeover candidate. The planning committee was headed by Ed Carter, Inco's president. It agreed on a strategy which was very much a part of the conventional wisdom of the day. There was much talk of future oil shortages well before the Arab oil countries' embargo in 1973. After the embargo—and the subsequent tripling, then quadrupling of the oil price—new sources of energy seemed the key to the future. By the end of 1973, Inco's management had decided to concentrate their search on energy companies. The availability of computerized information on thousands of companies— even back in 1973—makes such searches far less mysterious than they may seem to the outsider. The committee first narrowed the screen to a handful of fast-growing industries, which they divided between resource companies—those with commodities such as oil— and all other energy companies. Then Carter's team searched out individual companies according to a variety of financial criteria. Morgan Stanley proposed candidates as well; they had long been Inco's investment bankers, and Baird had developed a close relationship with the firm during his years with Standard Oil of New Jersey, one of Morgan's most important clients. Baird and Robert Baldwin, one of Morgan's most prominent partners, were close friends and platform-tennis competitors. Baldwin had brought Baird to Washington as assistant Navy Secretary. The two men are remarkably alike, both physically and in manner.

Baird's first choice for an acquisition was an oil company, but Inco management eventually sided with the recommendations of staff consultant Raymond Schaefer. No doubt what the acquisition team called "packaged energy" had the ring of a good concept. Schaefer's first choice was Chloride Ltd., in Great Britain, a car battery maker. Baird went to London for discussions with the firm in the spring of 1974. But Chloride's strong-minded chairman, Michael Edwards, who later went on to resuscitate the giant British Leyland, would not agree to merge. The takeover laws in Great Britain are more rigid than those of the United States, especially for a foreign firm. After consultation with lawyers and investment bankers there, Baird concluded that the chances of winning a take-over contest were slim if Edwards objected.

The second choice was ESB, the U.S. battery maker. ESB enjoyed a solid if staid reputation in its field, and was the largest battery maker in the world. Its principal source of business was the lead-acid batteries used in cars. The faster-growing business, however, was in the long-life dry-cell batteries in which Duracell and Eveready would emerge as leaders. ESB's Ray-O-Vac was behind in the development of these products. Baird believed the cash-rich Inco could help ESB. For one thing, it seemed to Baird that ESB needed capital to supplement both its research and its marketing efforts. "ESB had no marketing," said Baird. All these conclusions were based on public information only, however. Baird was not about to talk to the company, and no top Inco executive had had any experience in the industry. Inco, in fact, had very little experience in marketing of any kind, a fact they would conveniently overlook.

There were also seeds for promising longer-range projects. In 1974 an electric car seemed feasible to a petroleum-short world. Batteries would be integral to such a car, of course. Inco also owned the patent on a new medical device that could make use of ESB's products and technological know-how. The prospects, though long shots, added glamour to the acquisition. "We were accustomed to thinking long-term," said Baird. "After all, we were involved in jet engines back in 1936."

Baird did not have to work hard to convince Grubb that ESB was the best buy available. But his case was greatly strengthened by the eroding stock market. The devastating bear market of 1974 would touch bottom in the late summer. Stocks in general would drop nearly 50 percent from their early 1973 highs. ESB started the year at $28 a share, some nine times earnings. By June, it was down to $20 a share, six times earnings, and falling. Book value was recorded well above that. In a time of inflation, book value was undoubtedly understated. To replace the manufacturing facilities of ESB would cost perhaps twice its value on the books. Baird argued that, with stock prices so low, there would be no more opportune time to make a bid for ESB. Grubb and Carter agreed.

After his unsuccessful talks with Chloride in Great Britain, Baird was also convinced that Inco should take no chance of losing ESB. He did not hesitate to propose that Inco make a hostile tender offer. Grubb, the activist, and a man who trusted Baird's judgment, did not take long to concur. Baird realized he was defying convention for a company with Inco's long-standing reputation. He also suspected that ESB would ultimately give in under pressure, making the hostile tender unnecessary.

Grubb, Carter, and Baird decided they would not approach ESB beforehand. It might jeopardize their chances of winning. They also believed they knew enough about the company and the industry based on public information to go ahead with a bid. Now, they had to line up their bankers and their board of directors. Baird did not know whether he would have a difficult fight on his hands. Morgan Stanley, the most respected firm in investment banking, had never represented a client in a hostile takeover before. On Inco's board sat representatives of some of the oldest institutions in North America. But Baird seemed to have been exhilarated by the fight and the prospect of success. He had the support of his chief executive. He was a savvy enough infighter to know that once the campaign was under way, the odds were high that Inco would win. He believed he had the conviction and the strength of personality to win over his board and his investment bankers. Baird was seldom short on confidence. In all these matters, he was right. Most who know him consider him a formidable man.

2

The cash tender offer was a relatively new phenomenon even in the early '70s. In the 1950s and early '60s, the only widespread technique for gaining control of a business from its management was the expensive and cumbersome proxy contest. Every year, public companies are required to have their shareholders elect a board of directors. Outsiders can buy stock and propose their own slate of directors to replace the current board. In turn, new directors can name a new management.

The disadvantages of the proxy contest were overwhelming. The cost to mount what is in effect a political campaign was very high. More to the point, proxy contests usually did not work. Shareholders almost invariably voted for the incumbent management. Of the fifty-six proxy contests for control between 1956 and 1960, forty-two failed to overthrow management.

The tender offer was an appealing alternative. It is a publicly made offer to all shareholders to buy all or part of a company's shares, usually at a substantial premium above the current price of the shares. Until the late '60s, tender offers were unregulated. If undertaken as aggressively as possible, the tender offer was a technique of speed and sure grip. There need be no warning to management. Shareholders could be compelled to tender their shares quickly for fear of being left out if they waited. Offers could be made to expire in very little time so that management, or another bidder, had little opportunity to respond. The acquiring company was not required to disclose information about its finances or intentions. A bid could even be made anonymously, and occasionally was.

What the tender offer was *not* was a generally acceptable business practice. Corporations frowned on a technique that seemed at the time a version of highway robbery. Banks would rarely lend to corporations who undertook these tender offers. And it was in the banks, conventionally the stodgiest of all businesses, that the financial power ultimately lay. Their identity, too, would evolve in the late '60s and '70s into something fundamentally more aggressive than it had been in the earlier years.

But as confidence in the effectiveness of cash tender offers built in the 1960s, more companies undertook them. They had become a common practice in Great Britain. By the mid-'60s, they would grow popular in the United States because they were so effective. The New York and American Stock Exchanges had adopted rules restricting the tender procedures to some degree. Some states adopted rules regarding tenders. Yet in 1965, there were forty-four tender offers compared to only eight in 1960.

The popularity and effectiveness of the tender offer necessarily caught the attention of the federal government. The speed, pressure, and lack of adequate information was unfair, it was widely felt, to both shareholders and target companies. The odds of success were too much in favor of the acquiring company. Senator Harrison Williams's banking committee proposed legislation in 1967 that would circumscribe many tender practices, and provide procedures and disclosure requirements for the acquiring and acquired companies. In 1968 the Williams Act passed. It required the acquiring company to accept all shares tendered, or a pro rata share from each shareholder in the case of a partial tender. Then, shareholders would not be forced to tender shares immediately. The law also required that a tender offer be kept open to all comers for at least seven days. Further, it gave the Securities and Exchange Commission (SEC) broad powers to establish new takeover rules.

One important section of the Williams Act was aimed at the acquirer who bought up shares of a company quietly in the open market. A buyer could purchase a large percentage of a company, without the company's or other shareholders' knowledge. With that chunk, the buyer would have a significant leg up in trying to acquire the rest of the company, or simply to gain control through a proxy contest. Typically, in the 1950s and '60s, acquirers bought up only part of the shares of a company and then tried to take control through a proxy contest. The majority of the shareholders would be left in the cold. The Williams Act, in its section 13D, provided that anyone who accumulated 10 percent of a company must make that information and future intentions known. In 1970 the threshold was reduced to 5 percent. The filing is called Schedule 13D.

The establishment of federal regulations where none have existed before typically has the unintended consequence of making the previously unregulated activity respectable. Years later, most lawyers would agree that the Williams Act served to make tender offers legitimate. And while it reduced takeover abuses, and did a better job of protecting all shareholders, it made almost no dent in the level of tender activity after it was passed. In fact, respectable companies now considered using it. The law made far clearer than ever before the procedure for undertaking a tender offer, friendly or hostile. It legalized a theretofore dubious financial practice.

No lawyer was more familiar with the implications of the tender law and hostile takeovers in the early 1970s than Joseph Flom. No one individual would contribute more to the merger movement of the following years. Once the size of the bid was determined, hostile takeovers were almost all legal jostling and ingenuity. Flom had cut his teeth on the proxy battles of the '60s and had become one of the two most prominent attorneys in the field. His counterpart in those days was George Demas of the small law firm Demas & Hall.

Flom is a man of few indulgences and little pretension. Born to what he calls a lower-middle-class family, and what a close friend calls downright poor, like many of his generation he went to City College of New York. But he entered Harvard Law School three years later, and made the Law Review. His hero, like that of so many of his peers, was Clarence Darrow, the eloquent litigator and defender of individual rights. When Flom graduated in 1948, he avoided the large firms that had sought him out because of his excellent record as a student. He wanted opportunity, he thought, and he joined a small firm—Skadden, Arps & Slate—with only a handful of lawyers, as Flom puts it, and virtually no clients. If he had known the risks, Flom said, he would not have done it. One longtime Skadden partner, Barry Garfinkel, says Flom was the first associate hired by the firm. "It turned out to be a stroke of genius," says Garfinkel.

Years later, after Flom had become a wealthy man, he hung two paintings in his office. They immediately bring to mind Rembrandt's time and place. "I found them while walking along a street in Rome," said Flom. "They are Dutch. The painter is known, but not a valuable name. I just liked them." Flom has not moved from the apartment he and his wife have lived in since they were married in 1959, and in which his two sons were raised. He is a small man of reticent personality. His wife, Claire, a strong-willed woman in whom some of his friends say Flom finds his strength, is actively involved in charities. Flom appears to be especially proud of her. It is best said that Flom is a man of content rather than form. That the paintings on his wall are good, if without special provenance, well represents the man. He is universally thought to be a superb lawyer.

There were few proxy contests in the '60s that Joe Flom was not involved in. The first was brought to his firm by a new partner, William Timbers. He had been general counsel to the SEC and had represented the agency in a proxy contest. When United Industrial, Inc., needed an attorney to defend it in a proxy battle in 1959, they turned to Timbers. Flom's career as a takeover specialist was launched. In the '60s, there were few proxy contests in which he and George Demas did not square off against each other. The more prestigious law firms avoided such work. "We did not have the luxury then of choosing our business," said Flom. "We were small. We had about fifteen lawyers. We didn't have time to study an area and get into it. We just got into it."

One contest in particular brought Flom to public attention. American Hardware Corp., later to be called Emhart Co., was being challenged by a wealthy individual, a well-known corporate raider of his time whose group owned one third of the voting stock. Most believed that American Hardware was vulnerable. But with Flom on the defense, American Hardware prevailed. It turned out that Flom was on the defense, by his own estimate, 90 percent of the time. He would eventually work with such companies as Studebaker, Elgin

Watch, and Gulf & Western. He successfully defended Chemical Bank against the controversial acquisition effort by Saul Steinberg's much smaller Leasco. And handling the new tender offers was a natural offshoot of the proxy contests. Flom is particularly proud of having successfully defended Bath Williams, later called Congoleum, by citing for the first time a disclosure violation of the Williams Act by the acquirer.*

The role of lawyers back then was not nearly so well publicized as it would be later in the '70s. In a long article in *The New Yorker,* Flom's role in the Chemical Bank defense against Steinberg was not discussed. His name was not even mentioned. Nevertheless, in business circles Flom's reputation was high. It was natural that Morgan Stanley would gravitate to him when the time came. The legal business of Morgan Stanley, the preeminent firm on Wall Street, was handled by the equally prestigious and long-established Davis, Polk & Wardwell. But in 1968, Morgan, under the direction of William Sword, a partner, managed a takeover of Gallaher Limited, the English tobacco maker of the Benson & Hedges brand, by The American Tobacco Company, later called American Brands. Philip Morris was also bidding, and Sword recommended that American Tobacco, who was the white knight, simply buy up the shares necessary for control on the London Exchange. But the lesson for Sword was that he needed experienced legal counsel if he was to do more such deals. Introduced to Flom by another Morgan partner, Sword, who was in charge of Morgan's mergers business, hired Flom as a special counsel, ruffling the feathers of Davis, Polk & Wardwell, who Sword believed did not have the experience for the job. "The chemistry with Flom was perfect," says Sword, who left Morgan at the end of 1975 to start his own firm. "He did great work for us," remembers Robert Greenhill, then a young member of the mergers group.

In 1970, Flom represented Morgan Stanley when one of its clients, Warner Lambert, acquired Parke Davis. What never became public was that the prestigious Morgan had agreed to represent

---

*Among the less predictable consequences of the Williams Act was that it provided more defensive possibilities because there were now rules that might have been broken.

Warner Lambert in an unfriendly acquisition earlier that year, and long before Inco had arrived with its controversial proposal for ESB. Warner wanted to buy the wet-shave business of Eversharp, who resisted. Ultimately, after first complaining loudly to the Morgan clients, Eversharp management gave in. But Sword and others say Morgan was ready to make a hostile bid if necessary.

The relationship between Flom and Morgan Stanley over the next few years would be critical to the development of the takeover movement that followed. Because of its old-line prestige, no firm would have a greater influence in legitimizing the hostile takeover than Morgan Stanley. Now the banking firm was teamed with probably the best takeover lawyer in the business. When Inco management decided to approach Morgan to represent them, they did not know how much they already had going for them.

Charles Baird's aggressiveness—from Bob Greenhill's perspective, it was "guts"—would constantly surprise both Greenhill and Flom. "I had the quickest hands in the West," said Baird. He persuaded his superiors at Inco that they could make a hostile bid with or without Morgan Stanley. He was also determined to keep the tender plan a secret, not even to divulge it to the board of directors until the last minute. Nevertheless, he wanted Morgan Stanley on his side. The relationship between the blue-chip investment bankers and the blue-chip mining company was a close one. Inco had been so rich over the years that it seldom had to raise money in the capital markets. The one time it did, in the 1960s, it had chosen Morgan. Henry Wingate, Grubb's predecessor and the longtime chief executive of Inco, had a close friendship with Samuel Payne, long head of Morgan's corporate finance department. Baird knew Baldwin well, on and off the platform-tennis courts. Baldwin had recently been named president of a newly incorporated Morgan Stanley. Baird presented his proposal directly to Ray Gary, who then headed corporate finance at Morgan, and whom Baird knew from his days at Exxon. But Baird was firm. Inco would do it with or without Morgan. For a man in Baird's position, it was a decision of extraordinary boldness.

Baird met with Gary on July 2, 1974, and Gary ultimately took the proposal to Frank Petito, Morgan's chairman and former head of corporate finance. This was a matter the entire firm would have to discuss, although the decision rested with a management committee. Petito knew that Morgan's standing in the financial community could be on the line. Morgan's preeminence in the financial world was unchallenged even to 1974. The company was originally the investment arm of the former J.P. Morgan & Co., by far the most prominent financial firm of its time. Morgan Stanley was formed as a distinct entity in 1935, when the securities laws passed during the Great Depression required that commercial and investment banking be separated. But it never lost the legendary romantic aura of its association with J. Pierpont Morgan. Morgan's clients included many of the largest companies in the world: Exxon, American Telephone & Telegraph, General Electric, and General Motors.

By 1974, however, the world of investment banking was changing. The privilege of the brokerage community was tied directly to fixed brokerage commissions. Underwriting an offering by General Motors at a substantial commission, not subject to competition, was enormously profitable. In 1969, Congress took the first step toward outlawing fixed commissions. In stages, beginning with the largest trades, commissions were unfixed. They could be cut as much as necessary to win business. By May 1975, no commission on any size trade was fixed. Now, all prices charged by an investment firm were set competitively. That competition became intense and would fundamentally change the way Wall Street did business. Relative upstarts in investment banking such as Salomon Brothers and Merrill Lynch were competing hard against Morgan Stanley and the older guard. Firms like Morgan, First Boston, and Dillon Read were feeling the competition. Morgan expanded its emphasis on marketing in 1971, no small compromise for a firm that had always stood above the crowd. By the mid '70s, it, like most of its less privileged peers, was hungry for new business.

In some men, ambition grows with opportunity and a talent that needs to be fulfilled. In Robert Greenhill, ambition seemed to have risen full grown. He was born in Minneapolis, and while he was young, his father, son of a Swedish immigrant, moved the family to Baltimore, where he became president of Stuart & Co., a retail clothing company. From a Baltimore day school, called Gilman School, Bob Greenhill entered Yale with every intention of studying nuclear physics. In 1955 it was many a boy's dream. The promise of atomic energy was not merely exciting, it had the glamour of the new and unlimited. Greenhill gravitated, as he would in the future, to where the glamour and action were. But he lost interest in physics in college and switched to liberal arts. An excellent student, he planned to enter Harvard business school and follow his father into the retailing business. He married, as he says, "a girl from Vassar" just after graduation. After service in the Navy, Greenhill did enroll at Harvard. The size of his ambition was no secret there. One classmate called him impetuous and aggressive, not very sensitive to others in the class. Later, an investment banker who occasionally sat opposite him said of him that he "always liked being against Greenhill. It was better to have a strong opponent. I liked him. But I doubt I was in the majority."

In the summer between his two years at Harvard, Greenhill worked for the Baltimore investment banking firm Alex Brown. There he learned what he wanted to do. He did not wait to pass through Harvard's orderly job recruitment process. He started to call on the best-known investment bankers on Wall Street, and landed a job at Morgan in the fall of his graduation year. He was named a partner in 1970.

No one would deny Greenhill's intelligence. It is described as fast off the mark, sharp especially under pressure. But the quality that stands out, aside from his sheer tense aggressiveness, is his ability to motivate others, not only those who work for him, but his clients as well. There would be others to follow Greenhill who were particularly good salesmen, excellent at presentations to the board or the president. Martin Siegel, a young, driven investment banker at Kidder, Peabody, would break new ground for that firm with his smooth, comprehensive presentations several years later. Bruce Wasserstein of First Boston was imposing and intellectual, a style that proved influential. But Greenhill's energy and excitement were contagious. Few could come away from a meeting with him without a slightly quickened pulse. Greenhill rarely reached the office later than 7:30 A.M. His merger team wore beepers on their belts so they could be contacted at any time. His aggressiveness created enemies,

but his energy was compelling, and those who were not directly
competitive with him usually found it attractive.

Part of this attraction was his clear-eyed ambition. There is
power in not having doubts. Greenhill communicated that. He also
knew that Morgan Stanley, the grand old name of Wall Street, had
to find and perhaps fight for new sources of growth. No precedent
was sacrosanct for Greenhill. Not only would he recommend that
Morgan undertake hostile deals, but he and his key subordinate,
Yerger Johnstone, another Harvard graduate, along with the senior
William Sword, would also help change the way Morgan earned
fees. Until then, the banking firm had performed all kinds of
services for their existing corporate clients without compensation.
Sword argued that the bank could not afford this largesse. He
proposed, and it was accepted, that if Morgan studied a possible
merger for a client, a minimum fee would be charged. But Greenhill
and Johnstone, soon to be dubbed the *enfants terrible* of the firm,
also eventually changed the fee schedule for undertaking a merger.
The industry-wide scale to date, known as the Lehman formula,
after the investment firm of Lehman Brothers, was outmoded, designed
for small mergers. It would pay handsomely on acquisitions up to
$25 million or so, but became meaningless after that. Greenhill and
Johnstone created a new schedule beginning at 2 percent of the first
$20 million and decreasing in quarter-percent adjustments after
that. The fee would be 1.5 percent on a $50 million deal, or
$750,000; 1 percent for $100 million, or $1 million; down to .4
percent or less on the very largest deals. The schedule was more or
less taken up throughout Wall Street, with slight adjustments over
the years. It would transform the potential for profits on mergers
for Morgan, and eventually run fees into the many millions.

The Greenhill revolution would not have gotten very far without the patronage of Frank Petito, then chairman of Morgan. He
had grown fond of Greenhill when Greenhill was a junior member
of his department, and believed that the younger man was among
those who would provide a new direction for the firm. Greenhill
always went to Petito when he needed support. His team would
soon say, when a Morgan executive stood in their way, that they
needed someone "fapped." The word was derived from Petito's
initials: F. A. P.

The Morgan management had already discussed the possibility of a hostile takeover when Warner Lambert acquired part of Eversharp in 1970. But Petito said it never became as important as the Inco matter. When Inco's Baird approached Morgan with his proposal, the discussion over whether to represent Inco took place among Morgan partners. Greenhill would argue that not representing Inco flew in the face of the new reality. Yerger Johnstone argued that the hostile deal had long been a part of corporate life in England, that not to accept it was deliberately looking backwards. But what probably most influenced the management to accept the assignment was its relationship with Inco. Petito said that if it had been another company, the partners might not have gone through with it. Petito threw his weight to Greenhill's cause. He argued that it was a matter of serving a client of the greatest respect, and that that was Morgan's principal business. The discussions went on for two days, but the dissenting Morgan managers eventually relented. Ray Gary called Baird with the news that Morgan would represent them. Inco had the most prestigious investment firm on its side, and the best takeover lawyer in Joseph Flom. It was quite a way to start.

There was little doubt, Petito said, about how momentous a decision they had made. In fact, in an important sense, they refused to make it. Accepting hostile deals was still not official Morgan policy. Petito says that Inco was regarded then merely as an exception to the standing policy, which was not to undertake such deals. When Morgan undertook several other hostile acquisitions after Inco-ESB, Petito again insisted it was to be regarded as an exception. But after that, the firm drew up guidelines for a new policy. As usual, official policy would play catch-up to reality. By then, Greenhill and his team were well under way.

Baird said the procedure that Inco followed in setting up their tender offer for ESB was basically a plan devised by Joe Flom and Bob Greenhill. Almost certainly, the essentials were laid out by Flom. The entire tender could be set up and ready to go without anyone but a handful of people knowing about it. Flom and Greenhill worked on preparing the disclosure documents that had to be filed with the Securities and Exchange Commission under the Williams Act. They also prepared advertisements for placement in *The New York Times* and *The Wall Street Journal* with the aid of the proxy solicitors, D.F. King & Co. The Williams Act provided guidelines for what the advertisement should include. The papers could be filed with the SEC on very short notice, once Inco decided to go ahead with the tender.

Inco's plans never leaked apparently, not even to its own board of directors. Some ten days after Baird approached Morgan Stanley, the tender offer was ready to go. Inco management would make a careful presentation to the board on the same day that they would advise ESB of their intentions. The Inco executives at last gave the go-ahead, and Greenhill called Fred Port that Wednesday, July 17. They made their appointment for Thursday at two P.M. Then Inco called an emergency board meeting for Thursday morning at Inco's New York headquarters in a new skyscraper at the tip of lower Manhattan.

Inco's board of directors was appropriately illustrious. It included Ellmore Patterson, chairman of Morgan Guaranty Trust; Kenneth Jamieson, chairman of Exxon; Samuel Woolley, former chairman of The Bank of New York; Robert Bonner, former chairman of MacMillan Bloedel; and Allen Lambert, chairman and CEO of the Toronto Dominion Bank. Inco needed board approval to make the acquisition. That approval was fairly certain to come. The board had never yet overruled an action Grubb had proposed. Still, undertaking an unfriendly acquisition was more out of the ordinary than most actions Grubb had proposed.

Baird prepared diligently for the morning meeting. The day before, he, Grubb, and Carter rehearsed their presentation. No one approached the board beforehand. Secrecy was foremost in the Inco officers' minds. Baird remembers the meeting as tense. The board was fully aware of Inco's decision to diversify and to seek an acquisition. They were in full agreement with the objective. But several members were surprised by the decision to launch a hostile tender offer. Baird presented the case carefully, Morgan Stanley by his side. He reminded the board of Inco's need to diversify. He recounted their efforts at searching for a suitable merger candidate. He insisted that Inco did not want to lose this one. He proposed to make a tender offer for all of ESB's shares at $28 a share. The total cost of the acquisition would come to $154 million, plus $4.5 million in various legal and underwriting expenses. They were ready to launch the tender offer that afternoon if ESB management resisted the proposal. The board was told that Baird, along with the Morgan bankers, had an appointment with Fred Port.

Discussions went on for several hours. The board was apparently uncomfortable. But when the discussions were over, the board unanimously voted in favor of the action. There were two abstentions. Ellmore Patterson of Morgan Guaranty Trust, once Morgan Stanley's first cousin, did not vote, officially claiming a conflict of interest because he sat on Union Carbide's board, and they were direct competitors of ESB. Allen Lambert also abstained, because he sat on the board of General Motors, a major buyer and manufacturer of car batteries.

After the board vote, Baird, Samuel Payne, Greenhill, and Flom, who had been standing by all morning, climbed aboard the helicopter that had been waiting for them in lower Wall Street. It got them quickly to Philadelphia for their two o'clock meeting with Fred Port.

By about eight o'clock the night of his fateful meeting with Inco, Fred Port was ready to go home. He had reached Rolanda just before she was to leave for the airport to cancel their flight. He had arranged for a directors' meeting the next afternoon. He had filed the papers with the Securities and Exchange Commission to fight the Inco offer. He called the stock exchange to halt trading in ESB the next day. But he was still furious. Rolanda remembers that he got home about nine o'clock that night. His favorite expression when he was angry was *goddammit*. "We heard a lot of goddammits that night," she says.

When Baird had received his rejection in the hotel room that afternoon, he put his plan in operation. The lawyers filed the papers with the SEC. Inco in Toronto issued its press release, which would run in Friday morning's papers. The Monday papers would carry Inco's formal announcement. The tender offer would expire August 2. Baird was quite certain that he would win.

In a competition with only two sides, there is generally room for only two main players. In Inco's bid for ESB, attorney Joe Flom would not yet find his counterpart, but Bob Greenhill would. Goldman Sachs, the respected investment banking firm, had a thriving mergers business in the 1960s, when many family businesses were acquired. In 1966, Stephen Friedman joined the firm. He had graduated from Columbia Law School and joined a law firm. But he found, he says, that "investment banking had more action, more fun." He applied for a job at Goldman and was hired. He quickly gravitated to the mergers department, where he became chief of the department in the early '70s.

Friedman is a tense man with curly hair and a muscled body. As an undergraduate at Cornell, he was the American Athletic Union champion wrestler in his weight class. But perhaps his impatience showed even then. It was 1961, and he did not want to wait three years for a try at the Olympics. Under the influence of his father, an insurance broker, he decided to enter Columbia Law School, where he made the Law Review. While at law school, he married. His new brother-in-law was a student at Harvard Business School, and Friedman's reading of his cases—summaries of actual business situations—prompted his interest in investment banking. It was L. Jay Tenenbaum, an influential partner at Goldman, who hired him. Friedman fit in well. Trim, quick-thinking, hardworking, he enjoyed the collegial atmosphere at Goldman. At Morgan the investment bankers were more individual. At Goldman, they were team players. They shared the work, the credit, and the profits. They are a noticeably straightforward group, who work very hard. Friedman could work harder than most of them, and he liked a fight.

In 1973, Ronson was threatened by a takeover bid from an Italian firm. Goldman Sachs represented Ronson. During the Ronson battle, Friedman had visited Fred Port and ESB's vice-president for operations, Robert Kent, near Philadelphia. Along with Ronson executives, he hoped to persuade ESB to buy Ronson. Port and Kent liked what they saw but said they would need more time to study the question. Friedman had only four days. But an acquaintanceship, and some level of trust, were established.

In 1974, Port was aware that ESB could be a possible takeover target because its stock was so low. He asked his investment bankers, Merrill Lynch, to study the prospects and prepare a report. Port and several of his executives came to New York, and Merrill assured them it was unlikely they would be taken over. But Port had decided that some advance preparation would make sense. He had his financial officer, Benno Bernt, search for a takeover specialist so that ESB could be prepared. Bernt hired William Chatlos, of Georgeson & Co., the proxy solicitation firm. Just a month before Inco's raid, Chatlos wrote what was then commonly called a black book, a set of defense guidelines for ESB in case of a hostile bid. The guidelines provided a list of papers to be filed with the SEC, discussed ways to communicate with shareholders, and proposed a variety of other defensive possibilities, including antitrust suits. Eventually, black books would be outdated. The written rejections of bids, before they were even proposed, were construed by courts as evidence that management was not viewing a takeover proposal seriously. Chatlos later said, "I continued to do exactly the same thing, only we didn't write it down."

Port also had doubts about Merrill Lynch's savvy. By what would turn out to be an extraordinary coincidence, Port lunched with Robert Hurst of Goldman Sachs on Monday of the very week that Inco launched its bid. Hurst was a young investment banker who was now working on getting new business for Goldman. He had recently moved from Merrill, where he was a vice-president. He had worked on the ESB account and had known Port as a result. What he had to say to Port that Monday was that ESB was very likely a takeover target. Its stock price was very low. At about $19, ESB was selling well below book value and not very much above working capital per share. Working capital is the amount by which short-term assets like cash, inventories, and accounts receivable exceed short-term debt and liabilities. You might have been able to buy ESB, sell off the factories and equipment, and still make a lot of money if you bought it at this stock price.

That Friday, the day Inco's announcement appeared in the papers, Hurst had taken the day off and was relaxing in Nantucket. He did not get around to the newspapers until afternoon. When he read of Inco's bid, he immediately called the office. Port had been trying to reach him all morning. Hurst flew back to New York immediately. But Steve Friedman was on business in Oklahoma City. A call was waiting for Friedman when he arrived home late that Friday night. By Saturday, Friedman, Hurst, and a junior member of Goldman's mergers department, Geoffrey Boisi, were on their way to Philadelphia to meet ESB.

Besides defending ESB, Friedman would have two additional problems. First, he had to deal gingerly with Merrill Lynch, which was clearly being pushed aside. Eventually, Goldman and Merrill agreed to share the job, as well as the fees. Perhaps more important, Friedman had to convince the ESB management that most of the preconceived defensive tactics they planned to adopt were nearly worthless. Friedman concedes that merger defense was a new science back in 1974, but he argues that some of ESB's tactics were simply a waste of time. For example, Port wrote a strongly worded letter to Inco, which he made public, in effect calling them ungentlemanly in their conduct. He repeatedly called them a foreign company, although Inco was typically accused by Canadians of being too American. ESB also moved up the release date of their latest quarterly earnings, which hit a record high.

Friedman was fairly certain that public relations would prove useless. Goldman Sachs was a good school for the hard and unsentimental tactics of a takeover fight, having long run one of the best, most aggressive risk arbitrage operations on Wall Street. Risk arbitrageurs invest in takeover targets and merger candidates when they believe the merger will be consummated. They must be thoroughly familiar with the tactics of the battle, and the likelihood of success and failure. The highly regarded head of Goldman at the time, Gus Levy, had been the firm's risk arbitrageur earlier in his career. The man who hired Friedman, L. Jay Tannenbaum, had succeeded Levy in the role. In 1974 a respected younger man, Robert Rubin, was the firm's arbitrageur, and one of the most successful in the field.

With tutelage from his arbitrage department, Friedman had no illusions about the difficulty of defending ESB. He believed only one defense could succeed, an antitrust lawsuit, but saw no serious grounds for an antitrust action that would be strong enough to win an injunction in the courts to delay Inco's tender. The only other alternative was to seek a friendly third party to outbid Inco, one of whom ESB management approved—a white knight. Friedman and his staff analyzed ESB's financial accounts and markets with an eye toward ascertaining an acceptable price at which to acquire the company. Friedman proposed that $34 a share was a price high enough and fair enough to satisfy shareholders. He then asked Port's permission to find a white knight bidder at that price. Port not only gave the go-ahead, he recommended United Aircraft.

3

The best man at Harry Gray's third wedding was Frank Murphy, United Aircraft's public relations man. Murphy had been a reporter on the *Hartford Times* when he was hired by United Aircraft in the 1950s. By all accounts, he was an excellent PR man. He was also probably a good reporter. Down to earth, he speaks what is on his mind. He makes no pretense to social standing. For most, he would be an unlikely choice as confidant to the chairman of what would be the nation's twentieth-largest industrial company. Unless you knew Harry Gray. Murphy was even a Democrat.

Harry Gray was no Democrat. On his board has served Alexander Haig, once his second-in-command and President Nixon's chief of staff, who left United to serve as Secretary of State under President Reagan. Clark MacGregor, one of Nixon's presidential campaign managers, was Gray's lobbyist in Washington. In Gray's office stands an American flag. A flag also flies high in front of his home in a Hartford suburb. It is a comparatively modest home. Gray was born poor, the son of a truck farmer in Georgia, who eventually left him with his sister after his mother died. He studied journalism and marketing at the University of Illinois in Urbana. After being decorated in World War II, he returned for a master's degree. Until he was thirty, he was a successful salesman of trucks. He would always be a successful salesman. His acquaintances say he believes very much in what he is selling, and that he is a born promoter.

To the philosopher's eye, Gray may appear naïve. Fleeing from poverty, he is concerned about money but seemingly less so about social prestige. He married three times, for example, far from the middle-American convention. He tolerates iconoclasm and differences of opinion, but he sponsored simple messages about free enterprise, competition, and patriotism, placed in advertisements around the country. He talks very directly, and he wanted very badly to run one of the largest companies in the nation. And in the 1970s, the man who once wanted to be a reporter became the most successful acquirer of companies in the country.

Gray may have realized his ambition in a variety of business ventures. But had he chosen not to join Litton Industries, soon to be a successful conglomerate, the shape of the merger movement a quarter of a century later would have been different. Few swallowed optimism whole as did Tex Thornton and Roy Ash, the chairman and president of Litton. Thornton bought Litton in the early 1950s, when it was a small electronics company. With the advice of Myles Mace, a Harvard professor, the company started acquiring other firms. By the late '50s it had developed an image for modern, decentralized management. Everything from its plush, sprawling headquarters in Beverly Hills to its plush, expensive annual reports bespoke this idea of the new free-thinking, independent management. And it won high stock prices on Wall Street. More to the point, the high stock price enabled Litton to make acquisition after acquisition cheaply. In 1967, one observer calculated that Litton made a new acquisition every three weeks. The most glamorous of the conglomerates, Litton would increase sales ten times, to $1.8 billion between 1960 and 1968; its stock price by ten times as well; and earnings by nearly eight times.

Litton became the training ground for several of the most prominent conglomerators of the time, all of whom would leave because their rise to the top was blocked by the fact that Thornton and Ash were already there. George Sharffenberger resigned to run City Investing. Fred Sullivan eventually became chief executive officer of Kidde, Inc. Henry Singleton left for Teledyne. When, in 1954, Gray joined Litton from Greyhound Corp., where he was its executive vice-president, he was to run their components operations. He would soon acquire many more companies. Litton's star began to sink in 1968, when earnings stalled. Its stock price would fall from $90 in 1968 to $30 in the market slide of 1969.

Acquisitions became much more difficult to make. Gray had risen to the number three spot in the company. But by 1971, Gray, now fifty-one, realized he could not gain the top spot from Thornton or Ash. He joined United Aircraft as president. His skill was that he knew how to build a diversified company through acquisitions. His luck was that Litton's recent failures had taught him to be very cautious.

In 1971, United Aircraft—whose name was changed to United Technologies in 1975—would post its only loss in history: $92.5 million. It was clear that United Aircraft's main business, aerospace, and its main customer, the U.S. government, were not the cornerstones of a stable, growing business. In its nongovernment business, United Aircraft had trouble producing the engine for the Boeing 747. Arthur Smith, United's chief executive, wanted to diversify. Harry Gray, with experience in electronics and aerospace at Litton, as well as a successful acquisitions man, looked like the ideal candidate for the job. Within a year, Gray was named chief executive officer.

Gray took over a company with $2.3 billion in sales, its most prominent businesses the Pratt & Whitney Aircraft jet engine division and Sikorsky helicopters. While Chairman Smith had diversification in mind, the Litton-trained Gray probably saw something more far-reaching. Gray claims to see a fit in every acquisition he makes, and as old businesses mature, he seeks thriving ones to rejuvenate them. But Gray's record shows him to be at heart a conglomerator, although a much more careful and measured one than the men who failed in the 1960s. Harry Gray may have talked about the fit of companies; he acted as if he were building an empire. He wanted to be big, and he would succeed. Ten years and six major acquisitions later, his company had $13.7 billion in sales and ranked twentieth in the country. In 1982, he claimed to have a goal of $20 billion in sales. By 1986, the year he stepped down as chairman, he had reached $16 billion. It says much about the merger movement of the '70s that with only a handful of acquisitions, compared to hundreds made by conglomerators in the previous decade, Gray became the most emulated chief executive of the time. He was the takeover king.

Harry Gray did not do it alone. In 1972, just at the time Gray was promoted to the chief executive position, Smith and Gray hired a new senior vice-president for finance and administration. Edward L. Hennessy was a senior executive for Heublein, Inc., in Farmington, Connecticut, but he had trained with Harold Geneen at ITT. Hennessy says he was "there at the beginning, when ITT New York was just a mail drop." A graduate of Fairleigh Dickinson College in New Jersey, Hennessy, who was once a seminary student at Notre Dame, joined ITT in 1958. Like Geneen, he was trained as an accountant. From Geneen, Hennessy learned not only how to make acquisitions, but also the application of financial measures and controls. Geneen required fastidious reporting from his managers, and indeed managed himself by examining the endless, carefully prepared financial information that tracked the course of each subsidiary and division. And he stressed return on capital, a criterion Hennessy would stick by. Hennessy was hired to join "the aircraft company across the river" from Heublein. And Hennessy was wooed hard. He was given the title of senior vice-president, a seat on the board of directors, and a salary and bonus plan that ranked him third behind Smith and Gray.

The relationship between Gray and Hennessy would become a subject of controversy over the years, and eventually develop into a rivalry. Hennessy was more conventional than the down-to-earth Gray. Hennessy was still married to the woman he met at twenty-two. Hennessy was a financial man, diffident and methodical. Gray was a salesman who liked to deal with people. By 1979, Hennessy would leave to run Allied Corp., the former Allied Chemical, and embark on an acquisition campaign of his own. In 1982, Gray and Hennessy would square off in the drama between Bendix and Martin Marietta, certainly the one episode that qualifies as absurdist theater in the dozen-year history of the takeover movement. Most agreed with Hennessy's assessment of their working roles years later. "I laid the groundwork," says Hennessy. "He did the final negotiations and had the final say." Those who sat across the table from them would say that Harry Gray was the nice guy, Hennessy the tough guy. Years later, Bob Kent of ESB said Hennessy looked like a son of a bitch. But maybe Hennessy was the honest man, Gray the sweet talker.

By 1973, Gray and Hennessy were actively looking to acquire

companies tied to energy. Already, United Aircraft had approached
Signal Co., and had come to terms over an acquisition. Signal was
looking for a friendly buyer because the Bronfman family of Seagram
was pursuing it. But Signal was finding more oil in its North Sea
wells, and the two companies ultimately could not come to agreement on a fair price for Signal. And Gray was not yet willing to
undertake a hostile deal.*

The first acquisition Gray and Hennessy completed together
was Essex International a Cleveland company with $250 million in
sales. The company manufactured wire and cable, but was also
active in the fuel cell business, and United saw it as a good way to
enter the energy area. The merger was consummated on a friendly
basis, the chairman of Essex seeking to retire in any case. The
acquisition would turn out to be one of the most successful United
Aircraft would make.

A few months later in 1973, Gray and Hennessy called on Fred
Port and Bob Kent at ESB's headquarters in Philadelphia. They
wanted to talk about what they believed were similar technologies at
the two companies. At the least, they could share research and
exchange certain kinds of technical information. Pratt & Whitney's
chief engineer thought in particular there were potentially profitable
overlaps in technology between ESB and aspects of the work Pratt
was doing on the space program. Gray and Hennessy also, of
course, had an acquisition of ESB in mind, but the subject did not
come up directly. The two companies informally agreed to exchange
ideas. But when it became clear to Port that Gray was eyeing ESB,
Port politely said no. Gray, who had apparently not yet a stomach
for the hostile bid—and few were being undertaken at the time—
bowed out gracefully, but relations were left on warm terms.

Late Saturday night, July 20, 1974, the day that the Goldman
Sachs advisers arrived in Philadelphia, Hennessy got the call from
Hal Berry of Merrill Lynch, who was also in Philadelphia. Fred Port
had recommended United Aircraft as a white knight. Would he be
interested? Hennessy knew what Gray's reaction would be; he
immediately said yes. By Sunday, he and Gray were on their way to
Philadelphia. They had to weigh whether they wanted to pay the

*Allied and Signal eventually merged in 1985, under the helm of Hennessy.

$34 price Steve Friedman had come up with. ESB's earnings could be as high as $4 for the year, which would make the $34 price a multiple of earnings of about eight and a half. That was below the market average of the time, which was about eleven. But the $34 price was also about 20 percent above book value. Gray and Hennessy had to decide quickly or ESB would go elsewhere. By Sunday evening, ESB and United Aircraft had come to terms. Port and Dwyer agreed to support the bid.

Representatives from ESB, Goldman Sachs, United Aircraft, and Merrill Lynch met in the offices of Shearman & Sterling, United's lawyers, in New York City that Monday. It became a race against government deadlines to have every detail in place. United and ESB had to file papers with the Securities and Exchange Commission before the tender could be announced. But there were still various details to be ironed out, and then the cumbersome legal documents had to be drawn up, typed out, and completed in time to get them to Washington. The final arrangements had to be approved by both boards of directors. United and ESB were determined to make the bid by Tuesday. They feared Inco would have too much of a head start if they did not. The scene would prove typical: A taxi parked outside Shearman & Sterling, waiting for the completed papers. The taxi would bring the filings to a helicopter, waiting at the nearby pier. A private jet waited at La Guardia Airport, refiling its flight plans frequently in order to be prepared to leave at a moment's notice. In Washington, a limousine was at the ready, the driver equipped with a telephone. A police escort was summoned to get him through traffic. The SEC would close at 5:30 P.M.

The boards gave their approval by about three o'clock. But shortly afterward, the lawyers discovered that not all the changes were carried over from a previous draft. Two pages had to be retyped. Then another problem. Both ESB and United were filing 14D schedules, and both had to attach each other's schedules to their filings. There were not sufficient copies. Everyone, including senior executives and lawyers, was busy copying, collating, and stapling the additional copies. Then it was discovered that more copies of a particular letter were needed. Another delay. The Dispatch Team of four lawyers did not leave the building until 3:55; in addition, in their haste they left by the wrong door. They had just over an hour and a half to file the papers in Washington.

At 5:25, the limousine at National Airport in Washington called and reported no trace yet of the United Aircraft plane. A Shearman & Sterling partner had had some dealings with a young man at the SEC who was new at his job. He had been requesting information from the SEC and it had been delayed for several weeks. He decided to call, and the young man was apologetic. But the partner got what he wanted. The young official agreed to keep the SEC doors open for a few minutes until the papers arrived. At 5:35, the limousine reported that the Dispatch Team was on its way to the SEC, although the lawyers had discovered a handful of mistakes in the papers. They corrected them in the back of the car, and arrived at the SEC at 5:45.

At about six Monday night, both ESB and United Aircraft issued press releases announcing United's bid for all shares of ESB at $34 a share, for a total of $187 million. ESB announced that it believed the offer was "fair" to shareholders and that its board unanimously agreed to accept United's proposal. The ESB management said it would tender all its own shares to United. At both United and ESB, there was elation. Edward Large, chief counsel for United, recalled that they believed there was a 75 percent probability that they would win. No doubt, in the elation of the new bid, and in the heat of meeting their SEC deadline, most of the participants believed the tough part was behind them. Certainly, it seemed a sufficiently high bid to deter Inco from going further.

That day, Inco filed suit against ESB and Fred Port, accusing them of making misleading statements about the value of the Inco bid. Most took the suit as merely another obstacle Inco was throwing in the way, although Port was piqued that the suit named him personally. In the early days of the takeover movement, such tactics still looked like dirty pool. Soon, they would become mere conventions to buy time and wear down the opposition. And the suits, no matter how tough the charges, would always be dropped when the bidding ended. The $6 increment to Inco's bid, however, they still thought, would probably be enough to send Inco home to Toronto.

There was no reason why ESB and United should not have underestimated Chuck Baird, Bob Greenhill, and Joe Flom. This offer was a first of its kind. None of the participants had gone up against these men in this way before. But of the three—Greenhill, the eager young Morgan banker; Flom, the experienced, calm lawyer; and Baird, the competitive organization man—it was Baird who probably made the difference. "If it had been the right company, it wouldn't have mattered whether we paid fifty dollars or sixty dollars a share," he said ten years later. Baird did not like to lose. He did not like to contemplate what Wall Street would think of Inco if it walked away. Somehow, Inco believed its credibility was on the line. CEO Grubb makes the same point. Greenhill urged Baird on. Throughout the bidding contest, says Baird, Greenhill encouraged Inco to bid higher. But it was Baird who surprised both Greenhill and Flom with his willingness to raise the stakes. "Baird was very gutsy," said Greenhill.

Inco had one other asset going for it: plenty of cash. As Baird said: "We made more in the first half than all of ESB's market value. We had the ass to swing it." As it turned out, Inco had considerably more than $300 million lying unused in its banks. The years 1973 and 1974 had been very good ones for the company, and 1974's earnings the highest they would report over the next decade. During the bidding contest, Baird had a copy of the new financial statements with him as he commuted in from Short Hills, New Jersey. He ran into Todd Chrystie, a Merrill Lynch executive, on the train. He deliberately showed him the cash total: $340 million. "Chrystie was amazed," said Baird.

It took Inco less than twenty-four hours to respond to United's $34 offer. On Wednesday, July 24, Inco announced a new, higher bid for ESB of $36 a share, which would put the total value above $200 million, nearly $50 million higher than Inco's original bid.

The optimistic glow at ESB and United was short-lived. Not only had Inco bid higher, but they acted very quickly. Port and his executives were disappointed. They were fairly certain United had won, and they had already begun to envision a healthy working relationship with Harry Gray, who was known to let good managements run themselves with little interference. Now, they had their doubts. Would Gray go higher?

The United forces huddled that day. By late afternoon, they decided to stay in the contest. They did not believe they had to outbid Inco. The terms of Inco's deal were to pay the seller of the shares the $36 price. The shareholder would receive $36, minus the commission to the dealer, which could amount to as much as seventy cents a share. By contrast, United's offer would go straight to the shareholder. The company would pay the commission. United wagered that that difference was enough to give it an advantage if it merely matched Inco's per-share offer. In addition, because its proposal was a friendly one, United believed that, too, was on its side. The next morning, a week after Inco's first bid, the announcement appeared. The night before, United had upped its bid to $36 a share. ESB management was elated.

It took only a few hours for their hopes to be dashed. Baird immediately called all the members of the executive committee. He wanted to raise the bid by another $2 a share. His argument was like the one any wide-eyed consumer uses to purchase a pair of shoes or an automobile that is priced higher than he wants to spend. What's another $2 a share? What's another $11 million? Morgan Stanley strongly supported Baird's point of view. It's the company we want, and in the long run it does not matter. The executive committee gave its approval. "The board never resisted the higher bids," says Baird. Within only a few hours, Inco's announcement was on the news wire. The company offered $38 a share, less the selling commission.

That day, ESB was one of the most actively traded stocks on the New York Stock Exchange. Events were moving faster than anyone had anticipated. Now, United had to respond quickly, and it was clear that Inco would not back off easily. United now also knew what Todd Chrystie of Merrill Lynch had found out on his commuter train: Inco had plenty of cash. But United was game for one more try. Later, on Thursday, United matched Inco's bid of $38, payable directly to shareholders. From an arbitrageur's point of view, the United offer was slightly more desirable. To Greenhill, however, the new offer looked halfhearted. He smelled victory. The offer was also accompanied by an antitrust suit by ESB, which the company had been planning. Greenhill reasoned that if ESB felt it necessary to bring the lawsuit, their resolve must be weakening. He recommended that Inco now top the offer by $3, not $2, in order to show its determination. He thought Inco could be the winner. Baird was quick to agree. Again, he had to get the approval of the executive committee, and again they did not resist. That afternoon, after the stock market closed, Inco upped the ante to $41 a share, some $226 million in total, or $70 million above their original offer. United did not reply that afternoon. Harry Gray had his limits.

The next day, Friday, Ed Grubb asked for a meeting with ESB management for the coming Sunday. Grubb put the request to ESB chairman Edward Dwyer. According to some accounts, Dwyer accepted without contacting Port. Apparently, there had been a quiet schism between Dwyer and Port during the contest, one that Dwyer later denied. Port clearly wanted United Aircraft to win. Dwyer was less concerned with ultimate control, more with the ultimate price to be paid. Grubb freely conceded that he found Dwyer far easier to deal with than Port. And Dwyer, former head of the United Fund and the Union League, was certainly more an Inco man than Port was. On the other hand, Port and Harry Gray were more likely to get along. Port was eventually reached. A mark of his personality, he had been at a horse show that afternoon with his wife. He agreed hesitantly to a meeting with Inco for Sunday afternoon at the Bellevue Stratford in Philadelphia.

Greenhill's information was that Harry Gray wanted to bid higher, but that his board dissuaded him. This is roundly denied by Gray and other United executives. Whatever the reasoning, Gray decided the price had gone too high. It is not clear when they informed Port that they would not bid higher, but by the Sunday afternoon meeting with Ed Grubb, Port was fairly certain he belonged to Inco. On Monday, United announced tersely that it had dropped out of the bidding for ESB. Was it that the experienced acquirer, Gray, had kept his head during the bidding? Several times over the decade, Gray would fold his cards when the bidding got heated. "When they raised their bid by three dollars, I figured something else was motivating them," says Gray. "If their strategy was to scare me off, it worked."

At the Sunday meeting, only two representatives from Inco were present: Grubb, the chairman, and Carter, the president. From ESB came Dwyer and a friend from Bethlehem Steel as an adviser; Port; Kent; and Harry Knoll, a senior vice-president. Grubb's

purpose was clear. He wanted to reassure ESB that they would not
be restricted by the new management. Grubb told them how highly
they thought of ESB and how carefully they had searched for
candidates. He claimed that out of the entire search, ESB was the
number one candidate. Some time later, Kent said that Port would
find out this was not true from Michael Edwards, the head of
Chloride, whom Inco had previously pursued. Ironically, ESB once
owned nearly half of Chloride. But Grubb's intention was to prove
that Inco's motives were pure. They assured ESB that more money
would be available for research and expansion. They said they were
very excited about the prospects for the dry-cell battery that companies like Duracell would be so successful at.

Grubb and Carter basically succeeded in their mission. Dwyer
was convinced. Port, a little skeptical, knew that he at least had
done a good job for the shareholders. And with assurances from
Grubb and Carter, he was now less pessimistic about ESB's doing
well under Inco. After United's announcement on Monday, ESB
issued a press release saying it supported Inco's bid. ESB also
dropped the antitrust suit. Financial analysts and observers in both
Toronto and New York had been skeptical of the price Inco was
willing to pay. A Toronto financial analyst said that at this price,
someone must know something about ESB that nobody else did.
When the antitrust suit was suddenly dropped, an analyst with
Drexel Burnham Lambert said: "At thirty-eight dollars a share it's
antitrust. At forty-one dollars a share it's not. That's a new standard."

"These are tactics," replied an Inco public relations officer.

Port remained optimistic for a while. Later that week, he wrote
his employees a letter. ESB will retain "a high degree of independence," he wrote. "I see no reason at all to doubt the sincerity" of
Inco, he went on. "Their high regard for our enterprise is certainly
demonstrated by their having paid our former shareholders over
twice 'market value.'" And finally, Port wrote, "I see no reason you
should be concerned about your job security, your working atmosphere. . . . To the contrary, with Inco as our partner, the technology resources and financial resources available to us are substantially
increased."

Frank Schaeffer, vice-president for employee relations, wrote
the employees a similar letter, reassuring them about their pension

rights and claiming that "we will operate essentially as before."

By Thursday, August 1, Inco had received nearly 4.5 million shares of ESB, or 80 percent of the outstanding stock. By August 6, it had received more than 5 million shares, or 90 percent. One month later, Inco had been tendered 5.535 million shares, or more than 99 percent of the shares outstanding.

Seven weeks after the first Inco offer, ESB was no longer a public company. It belonged to Inco. Almost no share remained untendered.

Nine years later, there would be virtually no ESB at all.

4

Happy mergers are successful, each in its own way. Unhappy mergers are all alike. Many, if not the majority, of big mergers in this era would be unhappy.

It is striking in looking back over the variety of mergers and acquisitions that have taken place in the years since 1974 how each significant merger contained so many of the elements that characterized the takeover movement. Most hostile mergers were similar in objective, in the nature of the battle, and in the ultimate outcome. Most failed for precisely the same reasons. Inco's takeover of ESB, the very first of its kind, presaged almost every important theme of the takeover wave that was to come. But most noticeable was how these acquisitions floundered in the same waters over and over again. They were all put through the same highly general financial sieve, the inevitably distant and quantitative analysis that investment bankers, Wall Street brokers, and business consultants specialize in. It is shocking and arguably irresponsible that businessmen who knew so well their own business would underestimate how hard it is to learn another. And those who engineered hostile takeovers operated at a still greater disadvantage. Because of their secrecy, any information learned by the raiding corporation about a target company was generally from public documents only. Moreover, because of the speed of the assault, there was little time to make even surreptitious inquiries. A few weeks, and in some cases only one week, leave only enough time to run a few numbers through a calculator. And on that basis alone, many hostile acquisitions were made.

Inco's consultants, the ones who recommended the ESB purchase, were essentially correct about the battery business. It was not so much an energy shortage, however, that would cause an explosion in battery sales. It was miniaturization, which made possible small battery-operated radios, the Sony Walkman, and the pocket calculator. The consumer market for batteries would boom over the next ten years into a business with sales of $3 billion. There would also be a revolution in automotive batteries. ESB participated little in either of these opportunities. The failure to capitalize on this growth highlights a theme that would repeat itself again and again in the takeover movement: U.S. management consistently underestimated the difficulty of running a business. Most startling, they were willing to make decisions worth several hundred million dollars and more in a matter of weeks or less, and on the basis only of publicly available information. Ed Hennessy of United Aircraft, as chairman of Allied Corporation years later, bought a diversified manufacturing firm called Eltra. He would eventually lament his decision. "I read an article in *Business Week* on how well-managed the company was," he surprisingly concedes. "I learned a lesson there." Eltra was probably Hennessy's most unsuccessful acquisition.

The question Ed Grubb, Ed Carter, and Chuck Baird must have asked themselves time and again in the four years that followed their successful raid of ESB was why they thought they could understand a battery company. In addition, Inco believed it could develop a marketing expertise it conceded it did not yet have. Again, another common and rarely challenged bit of business wisdom was that you could hire the talent you needed, one of the most common mistakes of this takeover movement. Finally, Inco undertook an acquisition in which it agreed to take little managerial part. To be fair, that was not entirely Inco's fault. A Justice Department antitrust suit would deter them from involvement in the first few years. Nevertheless, in an effort to mend fences and maintain ESB's morale, Inco management went a long way toward maintaining a hands-off approach.

Inco formally took control of ESB at the beginning of August 1974, almost all the stock having been tendered. Only a few days earlier, however, the U.S. Justice Department had announced that it was investigating the antitrust implications of the merger. Nickel,

Inco's principal product, of course, was an important ingredient in the manufacture of batteries. Justice would examine the issues to determine whether there was indeed a "lessening of competition" due to the merger of the two companies. Of most importance to Inco, the government demanded that Inco not make "any changes in the business and operations of ESB for a period of 60 days" without notifying Justice of those changes ten days in advance. Inco interpreted this directive as a bar to taking any serious action at all. One executive said Inco's counsel advised them to keep hands off. The problem was that the investigation, which originally sounded routine, lasted seventeen months. Then, on January 19, 1976, the Justice Department filed suit to stop the merger. Inco immediately entered negotiations to make the necessary changes that it hoped would satisfy the Justice Department and persuade them to drop their suit.

On November 11, 1977, some thirty-nine months after it had acquired ESB, Inco was at last given a free hand to manage its acquisition. Grubb, Carter, and Baird place a lot of the blame for the ultimate failure of the merger on this more than three-year hiatus, but Lawrence Driever, an Inco personnel executive who ultimately shut down ESB, says that the management probably could have exercised more control earlier. "They were conservative people who listened to conservative lawyers," he says. "The lawyers told them they couldn't do a thing."

But there was another element to Inco's inaction, one that would arise in other forms in other mergers that followed. Baird says, "Grubb believed that after the wounds of the contest, the best way to run it is not to interfere." Grubb was intent on calming any fears among ESB employees that their jobs or their management were in jeopardy. It would be a typical response by raiding managements who feared they might alienate their victims. And no doubt some layer of guilt played a role as well. Bob Kent says Grubb made a very plain promise to allow Fred Port and his team free rein during that Sunday meeting in Philadelphia, just before United Aircraft threw in the towel. Grubb also formalized the promise in a letter to Port written the day Inco took over the company:

Dear Fred:

I am writing to allay as best I can any misgivings that may exist among your employees, customers or the communities in which you operate about Inco's purposes and plans in acquiring ESB's outstanding stock. . . .

It is our intention that you would continue to direct ESB out of your Philadelphia headquarters as you have done in the past. We want you to have the authority to select your own management team and to operate the company as you did when working for the best interests of your many stockholders. While on this subject, I wish you would reassure all of your locations that we have no plans for asking you to move or close any of them. You and your managers will continue to determine how many plants and offices you need and where they should be located.

According to Bob Kent, probably the most vociferous of Inco's critics, Grubb and his management stuck by their word. For whatever combination of reasons, they did not interfere in the first few years. The legal restrictions notwithstanding, Larry Driever says, "If you make a hostile tender, you can't sit around on your hands."

There is no evidence that even if Inco had taken control, they would have known what to do with ESB. While the opportunities in several kinds of battery markets was growing, so was the competition. New products and aggressive marketing were clearly what was called for. Under Fred Port, ESB seriously lagged behind its competitors, though ESB had a consumer battery maker, Ray-O-Vac. It was the time of the hand-held calculator and soon a craze for electronic games would sweep the country. The Sony Walkman would eventually take America by storm. Small radios and TVs were everywhere. But a relatively new alkaline battery with a copper top would dominate the growing market. And while Ray-O-Vac had such a product, it continued to push its traditional lead-zinc battery.

The success of Duracell copper-top battery is one of the nation's great marketing stories. Putting the Duracell battery at supermarket checkout counters turned the product into what marketers call an impulse item. In the meantime, Inco stuck by its old battery while Duracell's market share started to rise.

ESB was even to lose out in its strong automotive market. The maintenance-free battery was introduced by Delco and Sears. ESB had a low-maintenance battery of high quality, but it would turn out that American consumers did not want to bother even with a minimum of maintenance. ESB had been left behind again.

For all that lost opportunity, ESB's profits would hold up throughout Fred Port's reign. Sales reached almost $500 million in 1975. In 1976, they would grow to nearly $600 million. And in 1977, they would set another record. But if profits were holding up, they did not rise much. Then, in 1977, sales were up but profits dropped sharply. Only then, nearly four years after the acquisition, did Inco act.

Most at Inco had no doubt why ESB failed. Fred Port was the wrong man for the job. Bob Kent, a staunch Port ally, sees it another way. ESB was doing just fine until 1977. Then, when the battery subsidiary needed the money to develop and market new products, Inco was having troubles of its own and couldn't provide it. Kent also implies that Inco hadn't the least notion what this business was all about. Both he and Dwyer say that Inco had too much staff and too many layers of management. During the take-over, Baird reported to both Grubb and Carter, for example. Nevertheless, there's little doubt that under Port, ESB was not on the path that could have taken it as far as Duracell or Eveready. Baird says he wishes he had removed him sooner, though he adds that the seeds of problems had been planted before Port's reign. He says Port was the only one Inco ever dealt with, and Baird had no idea how Port communicated Inco's concerns to the rest of his staff. Kent says Port never kowtowed to Inco, and that Inco resented his compensation package, which was larger than that of any Inco executive.

Some conjecture about Port is necessary. Highly intelligent and with business success behind him, he had as his main goal, even his friends admit, to retire to his farm in Maryland. That he was not an Inco man goes without saying. He was distinctly not an aspirant to the establishment. He also may have bridled, if quietly, even sullenly, at having a boss, however distant. One other fact must be brought out. Port earned about $250,000 when Inco bought ESB. Such financial incentives would affect decisions made by the managements of target companies in many of the deals to come. Given these facts, it is possible Port lost his drive. Kent denies it vigorously.

What it does do is highlight the tenuous relationship between raider and target. For at the core of many a good business is a well-motivated and knowledgeable management. Again, any hostile takeover heightens the probability that good management may not stay with a company, or may not act in the company's best interests if it does. On the other hand, a takeover can provide the opportunity to bring in better management. Inco waited until 1977 to try to do that.

If Port can be blamed for being too late with the maintenance-free automotive battery and the long-life alkaline battery, he cannot be blamed for not getting any money from Inco once the Justice Department restrictions were lifted. The alkaline battery did not take off until the second half of the '70s and ESB wanted to make a big push with its own consumer batteries. ESB management also had several other battery products that they would have liked to pursue. If independent, perhaps they could have raised some money on their own. There is every likelihood the stock price would have risen over its 1974 lows. As a subsidiary of Inco, however, ESB would run out of luck. Inco was about to have a very bad year.

Inco was still entirely a victim of the ups and downs of the nickel market. Between 1976 and 1977, earnings would drop by half from $207 million to just over $100 million. The number of pounds of nickel the company would deliver fell to its lowest level— 312 million—since 1958. In 1978, nickel prices hit their lowest point since 1975. And Inco's profit would fall again, now to $78 million. Earnings would begin to pick up after that, but by then it was too late. Inco reached record earnings of about $300 million in 1974, the confident year they bid for ESB, and would never top it again.

Port would die of cancer in July 1978. In 1977 he presented his plan for management changes to Baird. He proposed that Bob Kent succeed him as chief executive. It was a choice Baird called "ridiculous." If Port was not an Inco man, Kent was not even close. Probably Port's best friend, Kent stood on no ceremony, was clearly one of the boys. And he had no doubt why Inco was having troubles: too much staff at the top making decisions. Proposing

Kent as his next in command was probably going to prove the last straw for Port. And it is hard to believe Port did not know that. It suggests that all along, Port might have been spiting Inco. Kent would never be acceptable to them. Only a few days after Baird told Port he had chosen his own man to succeed him, Port called Baird to tell him he had cancer of the bladder. "I had no idea events would go as they did," says Baird.

After Port's death in the summer, Inco named to the presidency the marketing specialist they thought they needed. To most outsiders, David Dawson could not have looked like the right man. Marketing, yes, but his experience was in selling nickel, not consumer products. The company would not enjoy even one encouraging year under Dawson. In 1979, Inco's annual report contained a paragraph stating that the Ray-O-Vac unit was adversely hurt by "severe competition," although operating earnings were up. That would be the last decent showing for ESB. By 1980, ESB would report an operating loss, due to a "depressed North American automotive battery market...." That year Baird became Inco's chairman and chief executive officer, and he changed ESB's name to Inco Electro Energy Corporation. Inco's metals business was again strong. But by the next year, nickel demand again turned very soft. In 1981, Inco would report its first operating loss in fifty years. That year, it wrote down its investment in ESB by about $250 million. Inco could no longer afford ESB; it had problems of its own. It did what a distant parent company would find easiest. It tended to its own business and put the orphan company up for sale.

Not only did Inco decide to sell ESB. From its vantage point, the best price for the whole company would be gained by selling it piecemeal. The former ESB was dismantled and sold in four parts. Ray-O-Vac was shrunk and sold to a group of private investors. Exide Electronics, maker of emergency power systems and related products, was sold and did thrive. Foreign operations were sold to private investors. The Exide battery operation was hardest to sell. It eventually got out of the auto battery business and now concentrates on industrial batteries. Before the parts were sold, Inco had closed down nearly twenty individual plants. In 1974, before Inco took over ESB, the company had about eighteen thousand employees worldwide, twelve thousand of them in the United States. Once sold, the units of the former ESB had only three thousand employees left.

No remaining sign of ESB can be found in Philadelphia or its environs. There is no plant, no sales office. There are memories, however. And there are people who claim the company would still be there if Inco hadn't pirated them away. Wouldn't an independent ESB have made every effort to retain its employees? Wouldn't an independent Port have run the company with more vigor? Could he have raised money when he needed it? Couldn't the company have survived if it had been kept intact? "I have a point of view," says former chairman Ed Dwyer, who basically supported the acquisition. "But I think there would still be an ESB if there had been no raid." The simple fact is that troops fight much harder on their own soil, for their own family and property. Tired of an investment that never paid off, that always caused headaches, Inco found the decision to sell difficult but necessary. If an investment goes bad, get rid of it. But if the employees are yours, if the company has been your life, belongs to your city, then that decision would have been harder to make and might well have been foregone by a management that realized its life depended on its decisions and hard work. Inco's stake in ESB was necessarily smaller than ESB's stake in itself. Driever says he thinks Dawson's real assignment, when he took over as president in 1978, was to ready ESB to be sold. Inco's takeover of ESB has no heroes, on either side of the battle. That would be true of many of the mergers that would follow.

The decision to acquire another company is deceptive. The investment community has done its best to keep the criteria simple. Price compared to the book value of assets is a favorite. So is price as a multiple of cash flow. Historical comparisons are especially enticing. Price-earnings multiples in the 1970s, compared to their heights in the late 1960s, looked very low. The cost of replacing a company's assets was higher for just about every public company than the cost of buying that company in the stock market. But such measurements say little about the nature of a company's business.

Probably the most surprising assumption to be made by busi-

nessmen was that the stock market's low valuation of these companies was fundamentally wrong. Chief executives by the score would
in effect be saying that the stock market was collectively misjudging
the value of at least half the companies in America. The academic
evidence, unfortunately, very strongly supports the case that at least
on average, the stock market's assessment is more correct than
anyone else's. Everyone concedes that to beat the market averages
as an investor is very difficult to do. Yet chief executive officers
thought they should pay 30 percent and 40 percent more than
investors in the stock market were willing to pay for the same
company—though it should be noted that buying control should be
worth more than buying a mere one hundred shares of a company,
but not that much more. Sometimes the premiums would rise to
100 percent.

What seems to have escaped the organization man's grasp time
and again was that acquiring and managing a new company are
almost as hard as starting one up. Yet a start-up will be far more
closely scrutinized than the takeover of an ongoing company. Most
organizations are best at maintaining businesses anyway—not starting up new ones. But these same managers will not hesitate to
acquire a company in a business with which they are completely
unfamiliar. It may be overstating the case to compare an acquisition
to a start-up. There is the matter of market position, name-brand
awareness, lines of distribution—much of the entrepreneurial risk is
gone. But those attributes are usually built into the price of the
acquisition; they are fully paid for. An executive must have realized
that he had to do more than rest on the laurels of the company he
acquired. That the difficulty of the task was so easily ignored in the
hostile takeover movement is a testimony to a financial community
that repeatedly makes taking the easy way out look like the right
way.

Morgan Stanley's Bob Greenhill would soon succeed again
at a hostile takeover. The Netherlands' N.V. Philips was the
third-largest industrial company in the world outside the United
States in the early '70s. Including the United States, it was the

fourth-largest electronics company in the world. In 1973 its sales were $8 billion. In Europe, Philips had 20 percent of the color television market and manufactured all kinds of other electronics products, both for the consumer and for industry. But the European company had long wanted to branch out to the rest of the world in an aggressive way. Competition from Japanese companies was growing in Europe. Philips, not content to wait for them to attack their own shores, wanted to meet the Japanese challenge head-on in other territories. And the United States was the most attractive market. Early in 1974, Philips had tried to buy the American television manufacturer Admiral, but was outbid by Rockwell International in a friendly round of competitive bidding. Now Philips's appetite for an American TV manufacturer had been whetted.

In the early '70s, Magnavox, a diversified manufacturer headquartered in New York, was riding high. In 1971 it sold 10 percent of the color TVs bought in the United States, a respectable distance behind the top two U.S. manufacturers, RCA and Zenith. It earned $35 million that year. But soon Magnavox found itself behind in the race to develop the latest technology. Sony's Trinitron was just catching on. Portable sets were becoming much more popular. And Magnavox, long a respected consumer name, was even having problems maintaining the quality of its basic product. In 1973 its earnings collapsed, coming in at only $7 million. By 1974 its share of the American market dropped to 6 percent. And its stock price would fall from a high in the $60 range several years before to a low below $4 a share earlier in 1974.

To Philips, hungry for an American presence, Magnavox's troubles looked like an opportunity—especially, no doubt, for its low stock price. In the spring of 1974 the Dutch company, through its American subsidiary, North American Philips, a little larger than Magnavox, held discussions about an acquisition of the struggling TV company. The discussions were inconclusive, but Philips's bankers, Morgan Stanley, knew by now that they had a potent weapon in hand: the hostile tender.

Philips, as blue-chip a company as Inco, witnessed the nickel company's success in taking over ESB. Philips was smarting because it had lost Admiral to Rockwell. A swift, bold stroke could secure them Magnavox. Shortly after Inco had taken control of ESB,

Philips launched a hostile tender for Magnavox. It offered $8 a share for Magnavox's nearly 18 million shares, a substantial premium over the price of about $4 at that time. The total cash offer came to $142 million, but was still below their book value per share of about $11.

Following almost exactly the pattern of the Inco-ESB confrontation, Magnavox management saw only one way out. Publicly, it said it was shocked. Privately, it started looking for a white knight to take it away from Philips and agree to maintain the current management. Lazard Freres and Merrill Lynch were signed up to do the job.

A white knight was not necessary. About a week later, Philips upped its bid $1 a share to $9, another $18 million in total. Magnavox management agreed not to oppose the new offer. Did one dollar's increase make that much difference to shareholders? Over that week, Magnavox and Philips had come to a controversial agreement. Sixteen top executives at Magnavox were offered two-year employment contracts.

Morgan Stanley was now launched on a campaign of hostile takeovers. It had completed two major hostile tenders by blue-chip companies that summer. Its competitors stood up and noticed, but could not duplicate the feat yet. Joe Flom, who again represented Morgan in the Magnavox acquisition, remembers that he traveled back and forth from his vacation in Spain four times that summer. It was the last time, he says, that he was able to schedule a vacation for ten years. Morgan earned several hundred thousand dollars in fees from both Inco and ESB. And in the changing, more competitive, and bear-market days on Wall Street, Morgan needed the money.

Morgan could also point proudly to its client and say Philips was happy. But over time, the Philips acquisition was almost as unfortunate a decision as Inco's takeover of ESB. Philips could not revive Magnavox. Magnavox's contribution to Philips's bottom line, in fact, would become a serious disappointment. Philips could not stop the Japanese foray simply by acquiring an American company that was already in the doghouse. Looking back, it is surprising the giant Dutch firm ever thought it could. The stock market's low valuation for Magnavox had proved right.

In the eyes of Greenhill and Yerger Johnstone, the Inco transaction was an astonishing success. Greenhill would speak of it years later with a twinkle in his eye, relishing the victory. But Petito, without whose patronage Greenhill would not have gotten his start—and indeed, perhaps the entire hostile takeover movement would not have taken off—would eventually speak of hostile tenders with a strong sense of regret. "Many did not work out," he says. "But you've got to remember what the times were like. And it was always management that wanted to do them." Petito is a sincere man, but Marty Lipton, the takeover lawyer, saw it differently. "Deals are not bought," he says. "They are sold by investment bankers." Counters Petito: "Most of these chief executives knew what they were getting into."

The truth is there is not much evidence of the last point. History is replete with examples of leaders who command well in war and know nothing of governing during peace. Many a politician campaigns well for office, then finds he has given very little serious thought to the difficulty of doing the job once he's won. For corporate acquirers, the acquisition itself too often became the goal, and the satisfaction was in the winning. Only the wisest looked with equal caution to the task of making the acquired business work. In the 1970s and '80s, acquiring companies were clearly better at waging battle than at ruling after the peace. The Wall Street investment bankers must bear much of the responsibility for this. But while it was true at the beginning, it became still more the case as the takeover movement grew bigger and bolder.

5

Inco's swift takeover of ESB was not heralded in the press as the beginning of a new wave of hostile mergers. Its importance could not have been understood. Had anyone even suggested at the time that something new was now happening, the idea probably would have been met with ridicule even by the investment bankers themselves. At the time, the early stages of this movement were seen more as the last vestiges of the conglomerate period of the 1960s. Bob Greenhill and Steve Friedman, younger men with unthrottled ambition, would add energy as well as youthful optimism about how much business these big hostile tender offers could bring them. But the early forays of this next wave were mostly taken by men who were active in the 1960s as well: chief executives, lawyers, public relations men, proxy solicitors. They were less given to acknowledgment that this time it was any different. The foundation of the new movement was already built. The new younger men overlapped their older, more experienced predecessors. But they had them to learn from. Every thread of the merger movement of the 1970s was directly traceable to the 1960s. The new men, who in many ways would become different kinds of investment bankers, would take it further than the older guard imagined possible. But at the start, it was the old guard who still dominated the way of thinking. Before and during the Inco contest, these men were busy at work making money for themselves and their clients in less-well-known deals that did not involve the so-called establishment. Soon enough, their individual efforts would come together in what eventually looked like an inevitable direction. It did not have that appearance in 1974.

What makes the rise of the movement in the mid-1970s all the more remarkable was that the conglomerate merger wave of the 1960s failed embarrassingly, and a lot of money was lost. Certainly, few who worked on the mergers of the 1960s believed that sort of frenzy could repeat itself. In the 1960s, more giant corporations— mostly the conglomerates—were built in a shorter time than anyone working then had ever seen. The merger movement also coincided, fed, and fed off of, a rampaging bull market that saw the average price of a stock nearly triple over the decade. Some individual issues would rise by ten times or more, reaching heights that seemed to bespeak no conceivable end to fast growth.

The dance did end, however. In 1969 the lights came up, and first embarrassment, then contempt, followed. The crash that came was enervating and sobering. By the bottom of the stock crash, the Dow Jones Industrials Average had lost a third of its value. A far broader measure, the Value Line index, which included 1,400 stocks at the time, fell to one third of its December 1968 high. Some of the major companies would also fall by two thirds of their value. In retrospect, conglomeration was not merely excessive; much of it was ridiculous, and by the early 1970s, most observers believed the conglomerates got what they deserved. Wall Street, it was generally thought, would not make this mistake again.

There was also very good historical reason to believe a new merger movement could not quickly get under way in the 1970s. The three previous merger movements of the modern industrial period each became overheated and ended in a stock market crash. The great trusts were created in the first wave of modern mergers in the late nineteenth century. These were the giant oil and steel companies that gobbled up their smaller competitors and gained efficiency in manufacturing and marketing as they got larger. A national market and rapid strides in manufacturing technologies made such large corporations much more efficient and profitable. But they were also fast becoming pure monopolies, which could raise their prices with impunity, and which gave rise to the trustbusting of the turn of the century, led by President Theodore Roosevelt. The first merger wave ended in the severe panic of 1903, which was preceded by a deep stock-market crash. Out of the debris survived such giants as the offshoots of Standard Oil and U.S. Steel, now USX.

The next wave of mergers was comparatively calm. The passions aroused by the big trusts were not reproduced by the less sweeping nature of mergers in the 1920s. In this period, companies in the same or related businesses would combine to form one large entity. But typically, no one company that resulted dominated a market the way they had in the previous century. The federal legislation that had resulted from the last takeover wave prevented it, as did the general public distaste for the monopolies. The new market structure was called oligopoly—a handful of major firms dominating a market. Here, too, a market crash and depression ended the movement—this time the crash of 1929 and the Great Depression. Out of this period of merger activity came such companies as General Foods and Allied Stores.

Out of the third would come ITT and Gulf + Western, LTV and Litton, Northwest Industries and Teledyne. These companies, built through acquisition in the 1960s, were a relatively new form of business entity, the conglomerate. They housed dozens, and sometimes hundreds, of unrelated businesses under the same corporate roof. By the 1960s the major markets were already dominated by their oligopolies; there was less room for expansion within one's own market. Expanding across markets was the logical next step.

The very idea of conglomerates strained the rationalizing powers even of American big business. As the ambitious executive scanned the list of admired corporations, each enjoyed a dominant position in its own marketplace. After all, what more was there left to do but to collect these companies in one entity? If it required a new conventional wisdom, the business imagination created one, with the all-too-willing help of academia. Professional managers could manage just about anything, went the reasoning. Moreover, business success now demanded not merely the skills of a good engineer, operator, or marketer, but the ability to finance most advantageously, to leverage every investment through borrowing until it reached its maximum return on invested capital. Big business was most akin to a portfolio of investments, each subsidiary a separate stock or bond, so to speak. Professional management had come far enough to be able to take on any number of different kinds of businesses. Like a portfolio of stocks, these businesses could be traded, leveraged, expanded, or shrunk as necessary.

In easy times the taste for elaborate abstraction always rises. The United States had no official recession during the decade of the '60s. Businessmen, even those weaned during the Depression and World War II, began to take the future for granted. The notion that growth would continue unabated was soon the guiding principle of Wall Street, and eventually of big business. Conglomeration became about as abstract a business practice as there would ever be, alienated by definition from manufacturing and marketing. When reality descended with unambiguous authority during the stock market crash of 1969 and 1970, the embarrassment was all the greater because of the absurdity of the claims. At least the mergers of the previous two decades had had a sensible objective. To become a monopoly, or a big corporation in an oligopoly, makes sense for the profit-minded business, even if the consumer is gouged or the overall economy runs less efficiently as a result. The individual businessman would do better if he could get away with it. But why become a conglomerate?

If that were all, perhaps the sudden start of a new merger movement as early as 1974 would be more understandable. But at the heart of the most aggressive conglomerator's strategy were also financial intricacies—funny money. Fast-rising stock prices supplied conglomerators with a cheap medium of exchange. As long as the stock market believed in their story and supported their stock, these businesses could acquire company after company by exchanging that stock. What the high stock prices allowed was not merely an addition to earnings, but an addition to earnings per share for these conglomerates. Earnings per share—total earnings divided by the number of shares owned by the stockholders—represent the amount of profit allocable to each share of stock, and are the best way of assessing a shareholder's value. Overall earnings might grow, but if the number of shares outstanding grows faster, then the original owners see the value of their own shares become diluted. If a company exchanged too many of its own shares to acquire another, it would reduce its earnings per share.

"A growth company worries about one thing," said one corporate president back then: "increasing its earnings per share by twenty percent to forty percent a year." A high stock price allowed a company to do just that almost automatically. The target company could be bought for fewer shares if a stock price was high. To pay $20 a share for a company requires that only one share be exchanged, if your stock price is $20. But it will require two shares if your stock price is $10. Whatever earnings the company was making would then be allocable to fewer shares outstanding. Earnings per share would go up, all due to a high stock price and accounting.

Because the conglomerates' stock prices were high, they automatically raised earnings per share every time they acquired another company with a lower price-earnings multiple. And investors rewarded the earnings-per-share pump with ever-higher stock prices, which in turn allowed still more acquisitions to be made. Teledyne, for example, the Los Angeles conglomerate that started as a small electronics company, made seventy-two acquisitions between 1962 and 1967. Its earnings per share grew by more than 90 percent on average each year. The stock market rewarded this earnings-per-share surge with a rising stock price. Teledyne's shares rose from a low of $9 in 1962 to $143 five years later. *Fortune* magazine concluded that eighteen companies had climbed onto its list of the 100 largest industrial companies during this period through acquisitions alone.

If this was not funny money enough, conglomerators and investment bankers devised a complicated series of bonds, bonds convertible into stock, a variety of stock issues, warrants, and options, all of which served to make acquisitions still cheaper—that is, to keep the earnings-per-share pump going. Jimmy Ling of LTV Inc., formerly Ling-Temco-Vought, was the master of these financial intricacies. Overall earnings for his company would actually decline in 1964, but Ling worked enough paper magic to produce a rise in earnings per share. The stock market rewarded him with a rising stock price that year, anyway. Eventually, Ling built LTV into one of the twenty largest industrial companies in the country, a conglomerate that encompassed electronics, copper, meat packing, and a steel company, Jones & Laughlin.

What the stock market wanted to believe was not that this was merely financial trickery, but that these conglomerators knew how to manage companies better, combine them to gain efficiency, and utilize leverage so that the once-stodgy companies they acquired would now become strong and healthy. *Synergy,* the word adopted to describe why a combination of companies was better than each standing alone, became a ubiquitous part of business jargon. But soon acquisitions were being made merely to raise earnings per share in the short run. Bad companies were being bought. And a few years later, no one would let the word *synergy* trip from his tongue.

The stock market crash began in December 1968. On the Friday after Thanksgiving, the Dow Jones industrials climbed slightly to 985. The following Monday, December 2, they would rise a few points in early trading, then drop swiftly on the surprising news from Chase Manhattan that the bank had raised its prime rate half a point to 6.5 percent. On Tuesday the Dow rose to 985 again, which would prove its high for the next four years. But the market slide took time. By the end of December the Dow was off only thirty-five points. In the late winter of 1969 it staged a temporary rally that almost brought it back to 985. It was June 1969 that was the telling month. The Dow sank below 900. The Dow ended the year below 800. It would not stop until May 1970, when it touched bottom at 631. In one year, it had fallen nearly 340 points, more than one third its value.

The decline of the conglomerates had begun earlier. Ling was among the first to feel the effects. In 1968, LTV's stock tumbled from a high of $136 a share to $80. Ling would lose the chairmanship of the company in 1970. The bubble burst for most of the other well-known conglomerate giants in 1968, as well. First profits fell; the companies were not producing the synergistic magic. Stock prices followed. Gulf + Western's stock nearly halved in 1968 to $38. Textron, which had literally invented the idea of the conglomerate in the 1950s, fell by a third in price to $40 a share.

In 1969, when most stocks had just begun their descent, the conglomerates already lay flat on their backs, gasping for air. Litton started 1969 in the $60 range and ended the year near $30. G+W slid further to $17. Textron halved in price, now down to $23. LTV eventually hit $24 a share. For many of the major conglomerates, the 1969 low price was between one third and one fifth of their 1968 highs. Soon, further acquisitions were impossible. The conglomerates' stock prices were just too low. And as investors realized the earnings-per-share pump was broken, they drove the stock prices down still more. It could come to an end after all.

*   *   *

Of the hundreds of conglomerate mergers in the 1960s, many were hostile, the acquired company's management fighting the takeover and, typically, losing. Of these, several were spectacular battles. Gulf + Western under Charles Bluhdorn provoked bloody battles for Paramount Pictures and South Puerto Rico Sugar. ITT launched a hostile bid for Hartford Fire Insurance, delayed by the antitrust authorities. Ultimately, ITT was allowed to take them over. Some of the failures were as noteworthy. Leasco Data Processing, under a twenty-nine-year-old Saul Steinberg, attempted to acquire Chemical Bank, then the nation's sixth-largest. Bluhdorn at G + W unsuccessfully went after Allis-Chalmers, Sinclair Oil, and even Pan American Airways, and eventually A&P. Fireworks and publicity aplenty accompanied these failed attempts.

The unfriendly takeover in the 1960s had no respectable reputation, tarnished still more in the eyes of most of the business world by the audacious likes of Steinberg and Bluhdorn. These men who initiated unfriendly takeover bids were for the most part outsiders, mavericks at best, uncouth in the eyes of their established competitors. The crash of the conglomerate movement was ample proof to the business world that the hostile deal was not a way to do business.

Ironically, the leaders during the early stages of the next movement, when hostile tenders became common even among the oldest of old-line companies, were by and large trained in the 1960s. Joe Flom would tutor Bob Greenhill. Steve Friedman's seniors had learned their trade in earlier years, as had his arbitrage department. Two other leading investment bankers of the period were groomed in the 1960s.

Felix Rohatyn was the most prominent investment banker in mergers and acquisitions during the mid-1970s. He had built his reputation as the investment banker to Harold Geneen, chairman of ITT. He had been made a partner of the prestigious investment banking firm Lazard Freres in 1960, at only thirty-two years of age. ITT's success added immensely to Rohatyn's status. What also added to his image were Rohatyn's thoughtful ways and European traditions. Lazard was a French bank; its senior partner, and Rohatyn's mentor, André Meyer, was one of a handful of the most respected bankers on Wall Street at the time—and certainly one of the richest. Rohatyn's demeanor was attractive. He was pensive, where many mergers and acquisitions specialists were brash; he seemed modest and unpretentious, where most of his competitors were fast-talking and proud of the money they made. Rohatyn was also a political liberal and shared sympathies with the New York press. By the mid-1970s, as manager of the New York City fiscal crisis, his name was one to conjure with. When Martin Siegel, then a young investment banker, came up against Rohatyn in a takeover contest for the first time, he remembers his awe. "I just tried to imagine him on the crapper, like everybody else," he says. "That was the great equalizer."

On the other hand, those who knew Rohatyn at an earlier age see the more insecure, striving side. Geneen remembers Rohatyn as "always running around, working hard, always bringing me deals, most of which I didn't do." The young Rohatyn was notably ambitious, according to some accounts. And surely he did not shy away from helping ITT launch its controversial bid for Hartford Fire Insurance. There were accusations in 1972 that the Justice Department eventually let the Hartford acquisition by ITT go through because of company campaign contributions made to the Republican National Convention. Rohatyn was called to testify about the donations before Congress. No charges were ever brought against ITT.

At the beginning, in 1974, the movement benefited by the senior presence of Rohatyn, a man then of the establishment, who could generally be trusted by businessmen, who had been with the best of them. If this was a man who had been a mere student at the knees of Meyer and Geneen in the 1960s, he was a wise, experienced, and imposing figure by the time the next merger movement began, the senior man of his time. Rohatyn's interest in mergers occasionally flagged during this period when his public activities were busiest, but in the mid-1980s he was still among the most active of the merger makers.

At Salomon Brothers, a hungry, thriving brokerage firm whose principal strength was its ability to trade bonds in large volume, a gruff, cigar-puffing investment banker from Chicago, Ira Harris, would also prove a major takeover force in the mid-1970s. Harris learned the merger business at Blair & Co. in Chicago. Salomon hired him away in 1969, and he completed a big deal when IC Industries, a Salomon client, bought Pepsi-Cola General Bottlers in 1970. In 1973 he engineered Walter E. Heller's acquisition of American National Bank & Trust for more than $100 million in cash. Many of his deals arose out of personal contacts, which Harris carefully cultivated. But Harris did not build an active mergers department. He was more of a one-man show. Jay Higgins, a Princeton and University of Chicago graduate, and Harris's right-hand man in Chicago, did not come to New York to start a mergers department until 1978.

Well before the Inco-ESB breakthrough, two new bankers had begun to build merger specialties at investment banks that almost certainly would have played small roles in the takeover movement without them. Martin Siegel was a handsome MBA from Harvard Business School, a chemical engineering undergraduate at Rensselaer Polytechnic Institute. A dogged worker and a man of clear-eyed ambition and few doubts, Siegel made honors at Harvard in his second graduate year. With the honor in hand, he landed a job at Kidder, Peabody & Co. In 1972, Kidder Peabody represented Charles Bluhdorn in his unsuccessful raid of A&P. Siegel was the young banker on the team.

After Inco's bid for ESB, two years later, Siegel was sure his instinct that mergers could get hot was right. The investment firm could not compete with Morgan or Goldman; it had a much smaller and less prestigious list of clients. But as hostile mergers began to catch on, Siegel would find his niche. He built a department whose specialty would be defense. And eventually Kidder would be second only to Goldman at it.

Joseph Perella was a very different person from Siegel in every way save a drive to succeed. Where Siegel was handsome and systematic, Perella would scatter a meeting with ideas and act with a kind of bluff coarseness that was probably designed to shock. Nervous and constantly moving, Perella would burp out loud or kick his shoes off at meetings. The son of an economist who immigrated from Italy to the United States, Perella entered the prestigious First Boston Corp. after having graduated from Harvard

Business School. As a trainee, Perella worked on the takeover defense for a First Boston client. He was made the sole man in First Boston's fledgling merger operation in January 1973. Perella interested a First Boston client, Cargill, the giant private grain company, to make a hostile bid for Missouri Portland Cement. Cargill only got twenty percent of the shares, and the bid was enjoined on antitrust grounds. Cargill eventually sold its shares to Thomas Mellon Evans' Crane Co., which took over Missouri Portland. Perella says that was his first encounter with Joe Flom, who was representing Missouri. He also proudly points out that his first hostile bid pre-dated the Inco-ESB contest, having been undertaken in December 1973.

There were other important investment bankers at work in the mid-1970s. Lehman Brothers and White Weld & Co., both eventually acquired by larger firms, were active. But the most influential newcomer to takeovers in the 1970s was a corporate lawyer. He would get his first taste of the action in 1973, again in a merger initiated by men groomed in the aggressive ways of the 1960s, and in no way part of the corporate establishment.

Martin Lipton was an established securities lawyer in the 1960s. Scholarly, but with a taste for the action and publicity of the corporate world, he would help build a firm made up of many of his classmates from New York University's law school. And it was his association with NYU that would get him involved in one of the hardest-fought takeover battles of the decade. Joe Flom would find his counterpart in Lipton.

Laurence and Robert Tisch inherited a small hotel in the Catskills from their father in the 1950s. They later bought Laurel in the Pines, a resort in Lakewood, New Jersey. But the Tisch brothers would set their sights higher. In 1959, Tisch hotels bought the Loew's theater chain when MGM was forced to divest it by the Justice Department. In the early 1960s, the daring brothers would go on to build hotels that were among the first new ones in years in New York City, the Summit and the Americana. By the late 1960s, the Tisches were ready to acquire. They were outbid by Control Data for Commercial Credit Corp. in 1968, but they made about

$30 million on the shares they accumulated, a war chest they would put to work the next year. They then succeeded in purchasing Lorillard Co. The giant cigarette company had nearly $1.5 billion in assets and earned $63 million. The Tisches would spend the next few years digesting the company and selling off unwanted divisions.

Not until the early 1970s were the Tisches ready to strike again. They had still never made an unfriendly bid. But they had been losers two more times since Commercial Credit escaped them. In early 1973, they made a friendly pass at Talcott, only to lose it to Michele Sindona, the Italian financier subsequently convicted for fraud. They also made a bid in 1973 for Gimbel's, the New York department store, but British American Tobacco made a big offer. They would not let their next target get away so easily.

CNA Financial Corp. was an insurance and real estate company with assets of several billion dollars. Its stock had fallen to low levels because of recent financial difficulties. CNA owned two insurance companies, Continental Assurance and Continental Casualty, and the casualty business was faring poorly. CNA's aggressive expansion into real estate had turned sour. The stock, which traded in the mid-twenty-dollar range in 1971 and 1972, had fallen to below $10 a share in 1973, when earnings per share had dropped from $2.66 the previous year to only 20 cents.

After two recent losses, Larry Tisch, the elder brother, chairman and chief decision maker at Loew's, was willing to undertake an unfriendly bid if necessary. His bid for Commercial Credit was essentially hostile. His right-hand man was Lester Pollack, another NYU lawyer, who had risen to senior vice-president at Loew's and who had been instrumental in the Lorillard takeover. Loew's started buying CNA stock as early as late 1972 and filed a Schedule 13D in March 1974, stating that it now owned more than 5 percent of the company. Pollack says Loew's first offered to make the deal on friendly terms, but that CNA adamantly refused. Moreover, Winterthur, a Swiss insurance company, whose formal name was Accident & Casualty Insurance Co. of Winterthur, already had a big stake in CNA and was interested in acquiring it as well.

What developed would be probably the longest-running takeover battle up to that time, the proceedings lasting nine months. Because CNA was an insurance company, several state regulators would have to give their approval to a change in management. Second, Winterthur proved a formidable opponent when CNA management sided with a bid they had made. Marty Lipton handled both fronts in the takeover battle. Pollack had known Lipton at NYU. Larry Tisch was also an alumnus of NYU. The Tisches would become big donors to the university, in fact, and Lipton would eventually serve as chairman of a fund-raiser for the law school. The NYU bond would remain important over the years.

Larry Tisch and Lester Pollack had hired Lipton to handle the Talcott bid, Lipton's first major hostile deal. They again hired him for CNA. Lipton and local counsel had to fight contests with six state insurance commissions who had to give their approval for the acquisition. Pollack also gives Lipton and his co-counsel credit for winning a court injunction that ultimately stopped the determined Winterthur. The injunction was based on a violation of the Williams Act. Loew's won in December 1974, and bought CNA for $5 a share. Lipton came up a big winner.

Pollack says that Joe Flom welcomed the coming of Marty Lipton. Arthur Fleischer, a scholarly lawyer from Fried Frank Harris Shriver and Jacobson, would eventually become number three to Lipton and Flom. But though he had written about tender offers in the 1960s, and handled some hostile deals, he did not rise to competitive prominence with these two until 1977, when he represented Humana in a competitive contest for Medicorp. In Lipton, Flom now had someone he could recommend to corporations on the other side. A more equal battle can encourage the participants, of course. Lipton would only pay Flom compliments, calling him "the genius who started it all." But the two men were very different. Flom was a hands-on lawyer. Lipton thought of himself as a thinker. The restless Lipton would marry three times; Flom stayed married to the same woman and lived in the same apartment for years. In the end, Lipton was probably bolder and quicker to draw; some would say he occasionally shot from the hip. Flom was more ambitious about building his firm's business. Both liked publicity, but Lipton cultivated it, seeming to enjoy the company of the press. Always admirers of each other, they would eventually have a serious falling out over an aggressive takeover defense, devised largely by Lipton, the poison pill.

But that was much later. In the mid-1970s, the takeover movement had its opposing knights, and these two men would contribute
more to the ensuing hostilities than any others. The tide of history
would no doubt have moved in the direction of a massive round of
takeovers anyway. But without Joe Flom it would almost certainly
have taken longer to spiral into the extraordinary whirlwind it did
become, if it would have happened at all. And with Lipton, Flom
had his worthy adversary, a man who could fight back hard enough
to raise the stakes of the battle. Lipton, a creative lawyer willing to
test the boundaries of the law, was probably more innovative. By
any standard, however, these two were considered the best.

   The excessive mergers of the 1960s aroused even a Republican
administration to antitrust action in the late '60s and early '70s.
Under tenacious Assistant Attorney General Richard McLaren, the
Justice Department challenged many of the major acquisitions of the
time. And if several of them got through anyway, most notably
ITT's purchase of Hartford Fire Insurance, the agency's scrutiny of
so many mergers put a damper on activity.

   The Supreme Court established a clearcut and stern antitrust
policy in several key cases during the 1960s. In separate cases, three
companies in particular were kept from merging with others, even
though the combination would result in a relatively small increase in
their share of the market. In what was probably the most important
case, Von's Supermarket Chains sought to merge with a smaller
chain. Their share would amount to only about 8 percent of the
California retail market, yet the Court back then disallowed the
merger.

   In the 1970s, that would change markedly. By 1974 there were
four new appointees sitting on the Supreme Court, all of President
Nixon's more conservative persuasion. When General Dynamics
sought to acquire a coal company, United Electric Coal Cos., the
Justice Department immediately challenged the combination. The
new Court, however, refused to define market share in the old
sense. Now, other factors should be taken into account, such as the
international size of the market. Given the broader definition, the

Court ruled that the merger could be completed. The antitrust laws have generally been interpreted more leniently ever since. Over the duration of the takeover movement, the attitude of the courts would serve to encourage still more acquisitions, as would a far more lenient Reagan administration. "It was much easier to do acquisitions later," says Harold Geneen. "We always had McLaren looking over our shoulder."

Yet the skepticism that a new takeover wave could take hold was still high even as the stage was being set for just the opposite that year. Stock prices were very low. The antitrust laws were being interpreted more loosely. The investment community had an active coterie of specialists ready and willing to do mergers. But most of all, mergers were an obvious, and relatively easy, way to fulfill important needs among big corporations, to provide a way to grow, to reorient a business, to expand an organization, to adapt to changing times. Making altogether new investments, starting new businesses—these were much harder to accomplish, especially in a time of high interest rates and slow economic growth. The impulse to merge was alive and well, even after the excesses of the 1960s.

6

"Mergers are done today because they make business sense." So *Institutional Investor* magazine quoted Richard Rosenthal, a leading arbitrageur for Salomon Brothers, at the end of 1975. The statement reflected the conventional wisdom of the time. The takeover movement was now more than a year under way. Several furious bidding contests had taken place. The hostile cash tender was continually gaining acceptance, with more corporations feeling less guilty about using this method to make a run for a company. But surely no one believed it was anything but a temporary phenomenon compared to the takeover mania of the 1960s. The movement was small by comparison. In 1975, 12 billion dollars' worth of acquisitions would be made, compared to $40 billion in 1968.

Moreover, the key participants, like Rosenthal, believed these takeovers were fundamentally different from those of the '60s. No doubt Rosenthal had every reason to claim that they made more sense, especially to a reporter. Arbitrageurs make money by investing in takeover targets. The more competitive the bidding, the higher the rewards. But equally without doubt, Rosenthal believed what he was saying. The conventional wisdom was probably necessary to give the takeover movement succor in its early days. Any comparison to the excesses of the '60s would have brought criticism, not merely from government but probably also from Wall Street itself, which had been badly stung by the movement that ended only a few years earlier. Logic, this time around, seemed to be on the side of acquisitions, however. For one thing, they pointed out how low stock prices were. Companies could be bought below

book value. The price-earnings multiples paid for them at ten or
even fifteen were meager compared to acquisitions made only five
or six years earlier at fifty and sixty times earnings. Another factor
was that high-flying technological companies were not the typical
takeover target of the time. The targets of choice were more often
stodgy industrial companies like ESB. The raiders were sticking
with basic industrial America, went the argument, not buying go-go
stories of untold profits based on technological breakthroughs that
were so common in the 1960s.

But most important to these men, most supportive of what
would turn out to be a myth every bit as unfounded as the one that
drove the takeover wave of the '60s, was that corporations were
now paying for their acquisitions in cash. No funny money in this
takeover bubble, they would point out: no stock, or convertible
shares, or warrants and options. Companies were bought not for
paper but for good old American greenbacks. A few lines later in
that same December 1975 *Institutional Investor* article, John Gavin
of the stock soliciting firm D.F. King is quoted: "Cash makes you a
better buyer."

In truth, neither economists nor Wall Street completely understood how transformed the economy had become since the Arab oil
cartel had quadrupled its per-barrel prices in late 1973. The 1974
recession that followed was the most severe since World War II. No
economists had forecast it because, since the development of Keynesian
and monetarist policy tools, such recessions were not supposed to
happen—or at least hadn't happened yet. In fact, most economists
did not even acknowledge that the recession had begun until it was
many months old. It stands as the single biggest mistake the modern
forecasting profession would make to that point, and is only one of
several examples of how little understood those times were. In 1975
unemployment would soar to 9 percent in the United States, at a
time when most economists believed 3 percent or 4 percent was
normal. In Europe, unemployment rates eventually rose to record
levels, and in a society that seldom tolerated more than 1 percent or
2 percent unemployment. Industrial production, which measures
the factory output of the nation, fell almost 9 percent. The U.S.
standard of living stagnated between 1973 and 1976.

For all that, the recession would put only a temporary dent in the rising inflation rate. In 1974, consumer prices were rising at what quickly became known as a double-digit pace, up 12 percent for the year. That was the fastest rate since the unusual economic period that followed World War II, when a tidal wave of pent-up demand was unleashed. The consumer inflation rate fell to 5 percent in 1976. But by 1977, it was already rising again. By 1977, consumer prices would rise at a 7 percent annual rate. By the end of the '70s, inflation would again be rising at double-digit rates, hitting a rate of 13 percent in 1979.

The oil price hikes can best be understood as a tax imposed by the Arab nations on the rest of the world. Any tax increase, without a compensating increase in spending, will result in a recession. In retrospect, the 1974 recession then looks inevitable. But when the proceeds of that tax are held by a relative few, in this case the Arab cartel nations, that also fundamentally changes the nature of the world economy. The Arab countries could not spend their new profits on goods and services. Instead, they invested them in short-term securities and put them in banks. The cash holdings of banks, in turn, swelled. In another time, perhaps, governments themselves might have united to redistribute this enormous cash flow. In the '70s, this task was left to the world's major banks. Their coffers swollen with money, they had to lend it out—and would make a handsome profit doing so. The Third World would get those loans. So would oil drilling companies, because oil prices were so high; and farmers, because food and farmland prices were rising. But so also would eager raiding companies looking for a fast takeover.

In the mid-1970s two conditions prevailed that could hardly be understood but which would provide corporations with ready access to cash. First, inflation was not beaten, even by the severe recession, and second, inflation was making the country cash rich, although it did not necessarily reflect healthy business. Because rising prices for products sold, and for inventory bought in the past, combined to put cash in the coffers, the inflation of 1973 and 1974 left corporations cash heavy by the time the economy was turning back up in late 1975 and 1976. Simply because prices continued to rise, corporations would book profits even if volume of sales shrank, or did not rise as fast. Moreover, just by buying inventories six months ahead of time, a corporation earned money, because the price of those inventories was rising so rapidly. While the price of the final product rose, the cost of the inventory of raw materials did not rise commensurately, because such materials were typically bought months earlier.

In light of cash flows recorded by the Federal Reserve over this period, American corporations looked very prosperous. Even a cursory glance at the balance sheets of *Fortune*'s list of the 500 largest companies was instructive. IBM had $5.4 billion in cash (which includes investments in short-term liquid securities like Treasury bills and bank certificates of deposit). General Electric had $2.3 billion in cash. Exxon had $4.7 billion. Smaller companies had equivalently large cash positions. American Express had nearly $700 million in its coffers. The raw materials and metals companies were especially cash heavy. They enjoyed huge cash flows in the early '70s, when inflation was just beginning to rise virulently and shortages of materials during the economic boom in 1973 allowed them to raise prices even more. Inco was an example of that. So were most of the major copper and other metals companies. And Wall Street analysts who specialized in seeking such companies could turn up literally dozens whose cash positions plus assets, such as accounts receivable and inventories, were worth as much as their stock at its publicly traded value.

Second, even if the corporations did not have cash, the banks did, and they were eager to lend. In 1975 and 1976, several corporations would call on their banks to finance hostile tenders. But in the early stages of this movement, with corporations so cash rich, the availability of loans at banks was not critical.

The key point was this: A business community still dwelling in the memories of the '60s believed that cash was real money compared to stock. They deceived themselves. With cash on hand, they were very willing to spend it. And with inflation so high, cash lost its value quickly. In fact, a company with cash, especially a public company, is virtually required to spend its cash. Distributing it to shareholders as dividends is penalized by the tax laws, which tax corporate profits and then tax shareholders on the dividends they receive as well.

In the '70s, cash was the real funny money, not stock. In the 1970s, cash became the cheapest financial asset of all, the least valuable. It was very available, and it was losing its value fast. This would dawn only gradually on businessmen, though just like the average consumer, they would spend it because they had it. Because they had it, they would spend it. But believing in the value of cash, they could tell themselves they were parting with something very dear when they bought a company only with greenbacks. And so the mythology of the new takeover movement was aided by a fundamental misunderstanding. The raiders could tell themselves this movement was different; Wall Street could tell itself this movement was different. It provided them distance from the shame of the '60s, and it warded off their critics. The takeover movement could build its foundation without any serious attacks because this time it was different, more serious. It turned out that cash is paper like everything else. Business was willing to part with it only because they had so much of it, just as in the 1960s business was willing to pay for acquisitions with their stock. That availability—whether of cash or stock—would lead to precisely the same excesses.

Felix Rohatyn was one of those who believed this takeover movement was different. He was not above the common myths of his time, either. Stock prices began to rise again in 1975, but they were still well below the highs of the early 1970s and the late 1960s. Compared to book value, they were especially low. And though you had to pay with valuable cash, the values were there this time around. "It was much more careful than in the sixties," says Rohatyn. If 1974 was Greenhill's year in terms of historical precedents, 1975 would prove Rohatyn's. He says that he really saw no difference between his role in the '60s and in the '70s. Rohatyn did not have to overcome the strict demeanor of Morgan Stanley. His firm, Lazard, had been doing hostile tenders all along, and of course had helped ITT develop into the most successful conglomerate of its time. "Greed would outweigh good manners," Rohatyn reflects, a touch of irony he enjoys now that even Morgan Stanley has to play in what was always the real world to Rohatyn. As noted earlier, ITT's chairman, Harold Geneen, remembers Rohatyn as an eager young man always bringing him deals. In the '70s, Rohatyn was less young,

more confident, but still bringing deals to chief executives. Early in
1975, Rohatyn brought Otis Elevator to Harry Gray and Ed Hennessy.
It would be the biggest hostile takeover to that point, and one of
the most successful United Technologies would ever make. It was
Rohatyn's first big deal in the takeover movement to come.

In the summer of 1975, Otis Elevator was selling for $32 a
share. Its earnings came to $43.5 million on $1.1 billion in sales.
United Technologies, which had recently changed its name from
United Aircraft to reflect its new diversification, was about three
times Otis's size. Otis's book value was recorded at $38 a share. The
well-known elevator manufacturer was one of the dominant companies in its business. In 1973, Otis had stood as high as $48 a share.

But to Gray and Hennessy, Otis had several other attributes
that they liked. Foremost, more than one third of the business came
from service contracts to maintain elevators. Perhaps the elevator
manufacturing business was slowing, but servicing elevators was
more like an ongoing income stream, an annuity. There might be
less need for new elevators, but there would always be need to
service those in existence. And by and large, such a business is
recession-proof; it didn't turn down when the economy did.

Gray also was attracted by the size of Otis's international
business, which made up about 60 percent of the firm's revenues.
Gray had long been seeking more presence overseas. Finally, both
Gray and Hennessy thought Otis was well managed. But they would
be more than pleasantly surprised. "They had an amazing depth of
management," says Edward Large, United's general counsel. One
manager, Hubert Fauve, was put in charge of all United Technology's international operations within a few years.

But for Gray, Otis would mark another kind of milestone. It
was the first hostile tender bid that he undertook at United. In
1974, after he lost in the bidding contest for ESB, Gray paid more
than $300 million for Essex International, a maker of metal wire.
But that deal was friendly. This time, Gray first tried a friendly offer
and then turned hostile when he was turned down. Rohatyn says

Gray did not really like a fight, and Large says the United management did not really expect one. Once a battle was joined, however,
Gray was tenacious. "It's a quality he and Harold Geneen have in
common," says Rohatyn.

What had fooled Gray into thinking he had a basically friendly
deal was a lunch arranged between himself and Ralph Weller, the
chairman of Otis Elevator. Rohatyn had been friends of both. Gray
told *Business Week* magazine that Weller said the time was not
appropriate for the offer. But Rohatyn says Weller's demurrer was
not very strong—as do other United insiders. Gray and Hennessy
apparently thought that once the bid was on the table, Weller would
relent. Hennessy still maintains the battle was never very bitter. On
October 15, 1975, United bid $42 a share for a little more than half
of Otis's stock. Weller surprised Gray and his management team by
soon countering with several suits. He also aggressively sought out a
white knight, Dana Corp.

But Gray was now in the middle of the fray and not about to
give up. He revised his bid and made it for all Otis shares. Weller
continued to seek a white knight. Gray upped his bid by $2 a share,
which brought it a full $6 per share above Otis's stated book value.
Dana dropped out, and Otis management at last gave in.

Gray had used most of his excess cash, but he arranged a
short-term bank loan for some $160 million. "The banks had a lot
of liquidity," reminds Rohatyn, though some feared that Gray was
spreading United Technologies too thin. In total, the acquisition
cost close to $360 million for about $44 million in pre-tax profits,
some eight times earnings. From Gray's point of view, Otis added
another 40 percent to United Technologies' earnings, and sales were
a third again as high. United was a $4 billion company. In retro-
spect, many say it was probably the best deal Gray would make, Otis
ultimately pulling in far more money, especially in Europe, than
anyone had anticipated. And the success in battle would groom
Gray for a bidding contest two years later that would change the
nature of the takeover movement forever. But even in success, there
was a disturbing truth in the Otis takeover. The payoff from Otis
was partly a surprise to Gray and Hennessy, especially the depth of
management they discovered. They talk of it a little as if they had
spun the roulette wheel and it came up on their number.

*   *   *

In 1975, takeovers had not yet captured the attention of the public and were only just beginning to capture the imagination of the press. In late 1975, that would change. And one other theme of the movement to come would be established: the flowering of a warlike argot that would shape the nature of takeovers in the public's mind. That language would be mostly combative and violent, full of machismo and bravado, always conveying the sense of a fight. The public relations men and bankers and lawyers who would invent the terminology said it was designed to appeal to the press, but it was also clearly a confirmation of their own propensity for derring-do and bellicosity, or at least their desire to see it that way.

In 1975, Colt Industries was a very successful industrial conglomerate with more than $1 billion in sales. Its best-known operation was the Colt Firearms Division. But it had come a long way since then, through acquisitions and new products, and its largest subsidiary was the Crucible Stainless Steel Company. Colt was built by two former employees of Harold Geneen at ITT who were steeped in the thinking of conglomerate management that characterized the '60s. George Strichman took the reins at Colt in 1962, after serving as president of ITT Kellogg. He brought David Margolis in soon after as financial vice-president. The company was then known as Fairbanks Whitney, and it lost nearly $5 million in 1962. They made a series of acquisitions, including Crucible, and turned the company profitable in two years. In 1964 they changed the name to Colt, after the famous gun company acquired by Fairbanks nine years earlier.

But in the early '70s, Strichman and Margolis, by then chairman and president respectively, decided they wanted to disengage from most of their few remaining consumer businesses and own industrial operations. It was the sort of thinking that was typical of conglomerators, the portfolio approach to running a corporation, much like a pension fund's buying stocks. What dominated their thinking were the shortages of raw materials and industrial capacity during the 1972 and 1973 boom. The boom convinced many that basic industrial America was making a comeback. In one report to shareholders, Strichman wrote, "We positioned [ourselves] for a serious shortage of productive capacity in American industry. . . ."

Felix Rohatyn and Margolis were friends. Margolis served on New York City's Emergency Financial Control Board while Rohatyn was managing the city's fiscal crisis. Ironically, Marty Lipton, too, was involved in the financial crisis as a lawyer for the city. Rohatyn says that he and Margolis had been separately eyeing Garlock Inc., a maker of gaskets and other industrial products. Margolis says Rohatyn brought up the possibility of acquiring the company.

Garlock made a host of packing and sealing products, which comprised about 95 percent of its business. Sales reached $159 million in 1974. Garlock had a record of rising earnings, and in 1974, earnings per share reached $2.70. By the fall of 1975 it looked as though Garlock would earn about $3.30 for the year, despite the recession. But its stock was selling for only about $20. Its book value was just above $21 a share. Rohatyn and Margolis liked what they saw.

The battle to come would be a classic. Colt retained Joe Flom as well as Rohatyn. Garlock, once Colt made its bid, hired Marty Lipton and Steve Friedman of Goldman Sachs. Once Flom was hired, he recommended that Colt strike quickly. At that time, the Williams Act allowed a company to make a tender that would expire within seven calendar days, giving a target little time to react or find a friendlier suitor. If Strichman and Margolis had any doubts, Rohatyn relieved them. "Surprise was the advantage," he says. "If you talked to the other guys, you just gave them time."

Ironically, Garlock, like ESB, had prepared for a possible takeover. They changed the company bylaws to stagger the election of directors, a strategy designed to thwart a proxy contest. They acquired companies to reduce their excess cash. They had a file of potential white knights to seek out. They even had organized a tender defense committee. Nothing would work.

On Tuesday, November 18, 1975, Colt took out ads in *The New York Times* and *The Wall Street Journal* to announce its tender for all the shares of Garlock at $32 a share. With 2.4 million shares outstanding, the total cash purchase price came to about $77 million. The day before, Garlock's stock had closed at just under $22. The offer would expire only a week later, on Wednesday, November 26, the day before Thanksgiving. Garlock hired Lipton and

Goldman Sachs that day, the day the offer appeared, and the next day they had filed suit in a New York federal court to enjoin the tender. Garlock charged that the takeover would violate antitrust laws as well as the securities laws—a charge that became an automatic response to virtually every hostile tender. Garlock claimed that it and Colt both sold products to the same customers, and that there was actual or potential competition in several lines of business. Garlock also claimed that Colt did not disclose all the information required by the Williams Act, a legal tactic first successfully used by Flom and again, successfully, by Lipton in defending CNA.

But what would stick in the minds and imaginations of the men involved in this takeover was a phrase written by Richard Cheney of the public relations firm Hill & Knowlton. Over the signature of Garlock's chairman, A. J. McMullen, Cheney wrote a letter to Colt, published in the *Times* and *Journal*, which questioned Colt's motives. "Why the rush?" McMullen asked. "Why didn't you contact Garlock's management about your offer? Were you afraid of a competitive bid at a higher price than you are offering?" The letter went on to urge shareholders not to accept Colt's bid. Then came Cheney's famous phrase. He would take advantage of Colt's household name as a gun company. The letter said:

I'm one of the largest stockholders of Garlock stock, and neither I nor any other director will accept your offer. We don't think your rush "Saturday Night Special" tender offer is a credit to American business and we don't think it's in the best interest of our shareholders.

Steve Friedman did not believe in using public relations to stop a bidding contest. The stock by now would be in the hands of arbitrageurs and sophisticated investors who wanted to make the fastest dollar, not loyalists who might support Garlock management. He aggressively sought a white knight, just as he had for ESB. Nevertheless, the epithet *Saturday Night Special* would stick, and would be used to describe every lightning-fast tender offer that followed. The letter did not do the intended job, which was to embarrass Colt. In fact, it unwittingly added glamour to the takeover movement. An appetite for the violent metaphor had been fed.

It would be followed by equally bellicose names to describe other takeover strategies, and it became effective shorthand for the press. In the public's eye, the takeover movement was probably born that day, November 19, 1975, when Cheney struck a nerve with language.

It would take Steve Friedman until the next week to find a white knight, though Morgan Stanley would get the public credit. The knight appeared in the form of Rodney Gott, head of AMF Inc. Gott could not top Colt's offer in cash. Instead, he wanted to exchange stock. The investment bankers worked up a formula that they believed would appeal to the arbitrageurs. Essentially, it guaranteed shareholders a value in AMF shares of $40 a share, significantly higher than the Colt offer. On November 24, Strichman, who probably had gotten wind of another offer in the works, raised Colt's cash bid to $35 a share and extended the offer another week, to December 3. That same day, even while negotiations with Gott were still under way, Garlock's board suddenly agreed to accept the Colt offer. One source close to the negotiations said it was beginning to look to Garlock as if Gott might be turning into a black knight, more unfriendly, in fact, than Colt. Gott kept his offer open and the Garlock board announced it was still considering it. But on November 26, Gott dropped out, and Garlock announced that it had accepted the Colt offer.

Colt had won handily. It now owned Garlock for about $85 million. It only had to raise its bid by $3 a share, about $7 million. The Saturday Night Special was indeed very effective. What members of Garlock's defense team would later acknowledge was that the defense could have been better. It should have been able to push the bid higher. "Too many people were making decisions for Garlock," says Steve Friedman. "We learned that it is better to have a very small defense team with few decision makers." For the future, however, the defenders had learned their lesson. They would soon win much higher competitive bids for their target clients. But in the meantime, the hostile tender offer only gained in stature. The Saturday Night Special was an explosive weapon.

The Garlock acquisition worked out well for Colt over the next few years. Colt went on to make another major acquisition in 1977, of Menasco, which made landing gear assemblies for aircraft. But in the late '70s, Strichman and Margolis found the acquisition game too rich even for their blood. The stakes had escalated out of proportion, the prices now too high to be justified, and they stopped making acquisitions. Eventually they would find that they themselves had become takeover targets. At one point in the early '80s, they were willing to rush into the arms of Penn Central rather than be bought out by a potential hostile bidder. Ultimately, Colt was not acquired, but over the longer run its vision of an industrial resurgence would not turn out to have been prophetic. The recessions of the 1980s would take a toll on Colt as America's manufacturing industries started to decline.

Felix Rohatyn earned Lazard Freres a fee of $750,000 on the Garlock acquisition. In those days, these sums were very high, and they have to be kept in proportion. An investment banking firm commits only a handful of personnel, travel expenses, and computer time to any single merger, and typically no capital. The expenses are relatively minuscule. Against that, a fee of three quarters of a million dollars, virtually all gravy, was enormous. Yet by the late '70s, these fees would look inconsequential. In 1975, when Rohatyn was the undoubted master, Joe Perella was just making the inroads at his old Yankee investment house that would put him in the same league as Morgan Stanley and Goldman Sachs, and eventually leave Lazard and Salomon Brothers behind.

When George Shinn, the number two man at Merrill Lynch, had been hired to run First Boston, Perella had found his source of support, just as Greenhill had in Frank Petito. "We've got a lot of building to do," Perella says Shinn told him in 1975, "and, Joe, your department's going to get help." The year before, Perella's cause—to build a mergers and acquisitions team—had been helped by an acquisition made by one of First Boston's longstanding clients, International Paper. The paper giant hired First Boston to study an acquisition, and eventually General Crude Oil was settled on as the target. But International Paper also sought Morgan Stanley's help because the First Boston oil team had no merger experience. "No one called me," says Perella. Morgan Stanley was First Boston's chief rival for old-line, establishment business, and now First Boston had to share its fee on the $500 million merger with Morgan. If bad manners were okay at Morgan—that is, hostile deals—First Boston could not afford to be left behind.

In 1976, Perella would complete his first big merger. Valley Camp, the coal company, was raided by Bethlehem Copper Corp., represented by Morgan Stanley. Valley Camp hired Perella on the defense, more respectable for the still-timid First Boston than to take the offense. Perella found a white knight for his client in Quaker State Oil Refining. First Boston earned a $500,000 fee. "In those days," says Perella, "that was a lot of money." For Perella, it represented several firsts. It was the first time he brought in new business: Valley Camp became a client. It was his first takeover defense. And it was the first time he hired Joe Flom, whom he credits for his education in the business.

Before the end of 1976, Perella would have his second deal. Marathon Oil Co. bid for by Pan Ocean Oil. Perella, with Flom's help, was now on the offense, for Marathon Oil, a client of First Boston. He won his firm a $750,000 fee. First Boston now acknowledged his mergers and acquisitions department. They had made $4 million in fees in 1976, and Perella was convinced it was only the beginning. He wanted the leeway to hire more bankers for his department, and he got the go-ahead. He would soon build a profit center for the struggling old-line investment firm that it had never dreamed possible.

Another of the new breed would also get his feet firmly planted in those years. Marty Siegel of Kidder Peabody would start out on the offense. He would successfully represent Babcock & Wilcox in its Saturday Night Special takeover of American Chain and Cable. He also represented Gould International when it took over I-T-E Imperial. But it was his defense of Pargas against a bid by Empire Gas that whetted Siegel's ambition. Siegel won, and the advantages of specializing in defense for Kidder became clear. Like almost every other investment banker in the business, Siegel attributes his start to Joe Flom. During his first lunch with the takeover lawyer, Flom suggested that Siegel try to set up a retainer program, much like those used by law firms. In fact, both Flom's and Lipton's firms put corporations on a retainer in case of a takeover. Kidder did not have anything like the sort of client list that Morgan, Goldman, or

First Boston enjoyed. Siegel knew he had to build one, and this might be the way. Within a few years Siegel had signed up eighty corporations who each paid $75,000 a year to tap his defensive expertise.

If the public was slow to catch on to the new takeover movement, state governments would act quickly. Responding to pleas from target companies, several states adopted tough anti-takeover statutes that made a raider's task far more difficult. While the raider had an enormous advantage because of the speed of the hostile tender offer, those corporations located in states with anti-takeover statutes had a special weapon to help them. The state statutes were mostly made ineffective when the U.S. Supreme Court held in 1982 that the federal law had jurisdiction. Lower federal courts began to rule against them in the late '70s. But until then they were a potent defensive weapon that had to be cleverly circumvented. Essentially, the state statutes could create delays in a bidding contest that could usually win a target company time to find a white knight. By 1977, thirty states had adopted such anti-takeover regulations.

In a classic early example, a vicious fight for control of Microdot, a maker of electronics equipment, broke out between General Cable Corporation and Northwest Industries. Microdot, domiciled in Ohio, made excellent use of the Ohio state law to keep the General Cable bid from being effective. The Ohio state law kept General Cable at bay for two full months. In the meantime, Goldman Sachs, Microdot's advisers, found a white knight in Northwest Industries. Soon, if a company's state did not have a takeover statute, a corporation would relocate in a new state. And states kept adding laws all the time.

7

In 1932, Adolf Berle and Gardiner Means wrote the well-known book *The Modern Corporation and Private Property,* which defined a revolutionary shift in the way business was run. Berle and Means held that owners no longer controlled their businesses; professional managers did. The owners of major corporations, for the most part, were now the hundreds or thousands of shareholders. This shift had to have consequences, they argued, because owners and managers had to have different objectives. And if many criticized their thesis, Berle and Means did succeed in focusing the issue. No one would again lose sight of the fact that a distance did separate owners and their businesses. It was not an issue that would go away.

Since then, there has been another major shift in the managerial nature of major corporations, but its focus has never been as sharply defined. Its by-product, diversification, has been criticized roundly, but never stopped. Peter Drucker, the respected management theorist, long ago criticized business managers for thinking they could transfer skills learned in one kind of business to another. But diversification has continued unabated, despite continual evidence that it rarely works.

However, diversification is only the symptom of a broad change in business perspective. Where once a business was established to make a product or perform a service, now an individual business was run by a mammoth organization. If the professional manager of the 1930s was divorced from the needs and objectives of the owner, he was not separated from the nature of his particular kind of business. In the 1950s and 1960s, managers began to see their corporations differently. They were entities distinct from the nature of their business. Managers inevitably began to assume that they had obligations to employees and to themselves that had little to do with whether they sold aluminum or made toasters. After World War II, the needs of the organization to prosper and grow, to provide new jobs and opportunities for advancement, higher salaries for current workers, and to fulfill the natural greed for power by the business managers, changed the nature of the modern corporation as surely as the advent of the public company with its thousands of shareholders did. Harold Geneen of ITT, the foremost implementor of this point of view, speaks frankly about it. "A company has a momentum of its own," he says, years after having relinquished the reins of his conglomerate. "When you have an organization, you need room for people to expand, to grow into new jobs. I always say there is one word for happiness in a business organization: growth."

If the survival of the organization took precedence over the survival of the individual business, diversification became the inevitable answer. Buy new businesses and prune away the tired ones. Never mind that it was hard to understand another business, that they could seldom be bought cheap, that so few diversifications worked out. There was a new law of nature in the modern corporation, and that was to grow at any cost. It's also important to note that this did not necessarily benefit the shareholder. An investor can diversify into any business he desires by buying and selling shares. He does not need his management to do it. The tax laws also promoted this way of thinking, as previously noted, by twice taxing the dividends passed along to shareholders. The 1986 tax reform reduces this incentive somewhat. Technical revisions in the new tax law also reduce the tax advantages of takeovers.

Of course, professional managers would argue that diversification was in the best interests of the shareholder, that it could keep earnings per share rising fast. And in the 1960s, it was this argument that was bought whole. The rising economy and stock market seemed to give their blessing to diversification, as corporations bolstered earnings merely by acquiring others with their high-priced stock.

The failure of that movement, and of so many conglomerates, should have humbled the diversifiers. But managers in the 1970s were well groomed in the ways of thinking of the '60s. More to the point, diversification was for most the easiest, surest way to expand. Rationalization followed exigency. The dependence on diversification was inevitable once the organization took precedence over the business, even over profits. The failure of the 1960s could not change this inexorable process. And all the rationalizations of businessmen would in retrospect sound like so much silly hyperbole years later. The impulse to expand, to acquire, was not a business or economic one; it was an organizational one. In the '70s and '80s, just as in the '60s, it was the organization that would dominate business, not the other way around. And so a takeover movement of giant proportions once again became inevitable.

In the early 1970s, General Electric Company was probably considered the best-managed large company in the country. Its chief executive officer, Reginald Jones, was seldom missing from the lists of best managers in the nation. General Electric's record was extraordinary. In 1973 it was the fifth largest U.S. industrial company, according to *Fortune,* with sales of $12 billion and profits of more than $500 million. Its growth rate was solid for so large a corporation.

By some standards, it could also be argued that it was the most diversified company in the world. GE made a variety of electrical products, and was in several service businesses. It was able to manage well both stodgy businesses, such as its line of electric light bulbs, as well as products on the frontier of technology, such as the B-1 bomber. *Fortune* magazine figured that GE was involved in 100 different businesses which made 500 products at more than 240 plants. It employed nearly 400,000 people.

There was a common bond to GE's businesses, though. They were essentially products or services with clearly defined customer bases. The products were typically electrical products, and no one business dominated the company. Diversified, yes, but all in businesses that GE's careful planning staff, one of the largest of any company's in the nation, could fully understand.

In 1975, however, Reginald Jones would make a decision that would deviate from many of GE's carefully honed practices. Citing the need to protect GE from inflation, he would acquire Utah International in a mutually agreeable merger for more than 2 billion dollars' worth of stock. GE had never owned a natural resources company, and certainly not one of Utah's size, one of the largest coal and copper producers in the world. By taking that one step, GE would raise its profits by more than 20 percent, expand itself internationally, and complete easily the most dramatic diversification of its long history. By some measures, it was the most radical diversification in modern corporate history.

For the takeover movement, the GE decision would inevitably be momentous. For one thing, the acquiring company was highly respected General Electric, now making even more plausible the case for diversification. The acquired company was in natural resources, an inflation hedge according to Jones, and if GE thought it needed an inflation hedge, why shouldn't just about everybody else? Finally, it was the largest merger of all time to that point. If it passed the Justice Department's antitrust scrutiny, it could help open the floodgates to more billion-dollar combinations.

The merger eventually accomplished all these things. What it did not do was earn GE a sufficient return on its investment. GE sold Utah International. It reported a profit on its books, but that did not take into account the true cost to the company of the low investment return of the Utah purchase.

On the face of it, anyone would have expected the Utah decision to come out of GE's highly respected planning department. But the decision was almost entirely Jones's own, and some would later argue that he was very much taken by the achievements and persuasive power of Edmund Littlefield, the chairman of Utah. Indeed, Littlefield had an extraordinary record at Utah. A relative of one of the original owners, Littlefield took over Utah International in the 1950s, when it was still a heavy construction company. He shaped up that business, sold it off, and put all Utah's capital into mining. The result in the decade that preceded his ultimate sale to GE was an annual growth rate in earnings of 24 percent. In the fiscal year ended October 1975, Utah earned $135 million on nearly $700 million in sales. Its earnings per share were $4.29. Finally,

Littlefield served on the board of GE, and Jones had grown to know him and trust his advice.

By comparison, even GE's record looked mediocre. Its annual growth rate was 5 percent—very respectable for a giant company, but nothing like Littlefield's. More to the point, inflation would turn GE's head, as it would turn the heads of most of corporate America. The rapid escalation of prices caught GE flat-footed in the early '70s, locked as it was into long-term contracts with inadequate price escalators for many of its major products. GE had also decided to get out of the computer business, which Jones had successfully sold off to Honeywell when he was the company's financial vice-president. Finally, the recession of 1974 and 1975 was costing GE. Profits would be down in 1975, which would surprise Wall Street analysts who were generally accustomed to a rising curve of profits at the old-line giant.

Littlefield proposed the merger to Jones in the spring of 1975, only a couple of months after GE reported its first drop in quarterly earnings since the 1950s. Jones, who had taken over as chairman in 1972, and inherited both double-digit inflation and the most severe recession since World War II, was receptive to a new approach at GE. Jones had worked for GE since graduating from Wharton in 1939. He started as an auditor and worked his way up the financial side of the company. Tall, laconic, in a certain way Lincolnesque, he seemed in every way the slow, deliberate decision maker, and he was all GE. It was not a company that let individual egos get in the way of good management. Or so everyone assumed.

Littlefield also was looking for a solution that repeatedly eluded him. He believed that Utah International was too narrowly focused. He wanted to diversify out of coal. For an individual family, diversification would make sense. His immediate family had $50 million in stock. Utah also needed capital to expand mines and explore for new ones. Jones had his chief financial officer, and no one else, examine Utah's books. He himself visited Australia to see Utah's coal holdings there. By December, Littlefield and Jones had agreed. They would announce a merger, an exchange of stock worth about $61 a share to Utah, about fourteen times their earnings.

The announcement was made on December 16, 1975, and Wall Street analysts were shocked. The purchase was hailed by *The New*

York Times as "the first effort toward diversification in GE's 83-year history," a serious oversimplification for this already diversified company, but essentially correct in that GE had never gone this far afield. If surprised, the analysts generally approved. Wall Street analysts typically reflect the conventional wisdom, in any case, especially concerning a decision made by a company as respected as General Electric. And the decision seemed well thought out. In the circumspect language of a GE executive, Jones put it this way: "The natural resource reserves of Utah will serve as a stabilizing factor against inflation." Jones also argued that it would give GE much more international scope, which he said the company seriously lacked. Only about 5 percent of the many GE product lines were sold overseas. Almost all of Utah was international. Jones boasted that now one third, rather than one fifth, of all GE's earnings would come from overseas, and that in an increasingly global marketplace, GE would now have a much more important presence. Even then, however, some critics thought the internationalization argument sounded too much like the wishful thinking of the '60s conglomerates.

GE would issue to each Utah shareholder 1.3 of its own shares for every Utah share held. But even though Utah's shares would be worth $61 based on GE's closing price of about $47 that day, Utah's shares closed at only $49. The problem, of course, was the specter of the Justice Department. Would the antitrust authorities actually allow this largest of all mergers, made by one of the largest of all companies, to go through? Investors in general doubted it, and Utah therefore traded far below the value of GE's offer.

The Justice Department took only two weeks to decide it would review the case. On December 29 it announced that it would indeed investigate whether the merger violated the antitrust laws. To many observers, including the most respected antitrust theorists, the GE case presented serious obstacles. GE was a major manufacturer of power plants that used coal and uranium, which Utah International also mined. An antitrust case could be made that GE was buying a supplier. There was also an issue back then over conglomerate mergers of any kind. Some argued that mergers should be disallowed simply because the corporations they created were too large, and would therefore reduce competition. It did not matter that a merger involved entirely different products or markets. Conglomerate mergers were most seriously challenged in the late 1960s—especially a series of acquisitions by ITT. ITT's proposed acquisition of Hartford Fire Insurance, Canteen Corp., and Grinnel Corp. were all challenged on these grounds, though the courts did not uphold any of the challenges. Similarly, Northwest Industries was kept from purchasing B.F. Goodrich until the courts cleared it. But the Supreme Court had never ruled on the issue, and a strong body of opinion still supported the idea that conglomerate mergers should be stopped.

Now, with the GE-Utah merger, President Gerald Ford's administration had a significant opportunity to establish policy in this area. Jones and Littlefield had hoped the deal could be closed by the spring, but the Justice Department decided to take a longer look. In the end, the issue of conglomerate mergers would not be brought to bear. And it would not be raised again. The door instead would open wide to giant mergers.

The only grounds on which Justice ultimately found the merger anticompetitive was Utah International's uranium reserves. The Justice Department believed that if GE controlled a uranium supply, it could gain a major advantage over competitors in the sale of nuclear reactors. In late July, Justice announced that it did indeed oppose the merger. But even the December before, Jones, in making the merger announcement, had stated that GE had no interest in Utah's uranium, which comprised a small portion of its assets. It took only two months for GE to work out a compromise with the Justice Department. GE and Utah would spin off the uranium mines into a separate subsidiary controlled by independent trustees. They would have no access to the uranium until the year 2000. On December 20, 1976, one year after it was announced, GE and Utah International were merged. General Electric stock traded for nearly $53 a share, which made Utah's conversion value worth nearly $69. Littlefield, his family, and all other Utah shareholders could rejoice. Littlefield and his family enjoyed a paper profit of nearly $19 million.

No doubt Jones thought he had prepared himself for the new world. Inflation had been virulent and was apparently here to stay; the great scarce resource would surely be energy; the demand for coal would only rise; and finally, the world was growing increasingly interdependent. Utah International was in very good operating shape. Littlefield had run operations at a very low cost. But the demand for coal would never meet expectations, even after OPEC nearly tripled prices in 1979. And the world would adjust far more rapidly than anticipated to more expensive energy.

Utah International remained very profitable, though many other mineral and copper companies in the coming years would not, but that in itself did not make it an investment that would pay off for GE. This irony highlights how difficult it is to make an acquisition succeed. In 1982, GE sold Utah for $2.4 billion.

Between 1977 and 1981, Utah's profits grew handsomely, to $284 million. Overall, total profits added up to more than $1 billion in the years GE owned Utah. But GE also returned $900 million of that as new investment in Utah's businesses. In other words, Utah's assets, which came to $1 billion in 1976, were now built up to a value of about $2 billion, but GE was able to fetch only a few hundred million dollars more for the company than the $2 billion it paid for it.

According to an analysis by a Harvard Business School researcher, there was an implicit but nevertheless very real additional cost to GE's shareholders. GE's stock rose substantially in the period, because its other businesses grew rapidly, and the 41 million shares now owned by Utah International shareholders were worth more than $4 billion, twice their original value. Yet GE could fetch a price of only $2.4 billion for Utah when it sold it. The difference of $1.6 billion was value lost to the original GE shareholders. In other words, had GE not bought Utah, the 4-billion-dollar value of those shares would have accrued to existing shareholders, and they were getting back only $2.4 billion on its sale. Utah shareholders did very well indeed, at the expense of GE's shareholders.

If an acquired company was able to produce an earnings increase of 50 percent in five years, as did Utah, how far wrong could GE have gone? GE's purchase of Utah was not a catastrophically incorrect decision. Many other acquisitions would collapse entirely, just as ESB did. Nor was it a business GE completely misunderstood, as Inco had misunderstood ESB. Nor was it seriously mishandled. Moreover, inflation rose very fast in the late 1970s, especially after OPEC again raised the oil prices several fold, just as Jones anticipated. But still this natural-resource investment did not pay off. In the end, an acquisition that may have looked like a bargain compared to past growth rates, book value, and historical stock prices, that did not by any means fall to pieces, and that even showed a small book profit, was indeed no bargain at all if analyzed properly.

In this same period, Mobil Oil Co. and Atlantic Richfield undertook far-reaching acquisitions that underscored the difficulty of diversification as well. Mobil Oil's purchase of Marcor, the large retailer, for approximately $1 billion was completed in 1976. It could never turn the retailer into a sufficient moneymaker and at last sold it in 1985. Atlantic Richfield bought the copper company, Anaconda Co., in 1976 as well, seeking an inflation hedge in the metals company. The weak copper market over the succeeding years turned Anaconda into a money loser, which it later sold.

Both acquisitions stand as among the most clearcut examples of diversification gone wrong, far more wrong in fact than GE's purchase of Utah. But GE's acquisition, by sheer virtue of the company's high reputation for good management, would leave an early mark on this takeover movement, give it a special seal of approval and confirm the truth of several very tenuous assumptions about the business future. In truth, all three diversification efforts were classic examples of organizations trying to preserve themselves first, rather than their businesses.

8

Ivan Boesky had always wanted it all. To describe his career as Wall Street's leading arbitrageur, and his later transgressions, as the result of simple material greed is to misread the man. A high-school classmate from Detroit says he was determined to make the school's wrestling team. He had little natural ability. But, says his classmate, who was himself a high-school wrestling star, Boesky as a boy worked relentlessly at improving what skill he had. "He worked out every afternoon for a couple of hours," the classmate says. And Boesky eventually made the team, though never to star.

He once got a part in an Off-Broadway play produced by a friend. At night, say the producers, Boesky's limousine would pull up in front of the Van Dam Theater in New York's SoHo, where Boesky would perform. He was even mentioned favorably in a review. He once told a journalist that if he could write a novel, he would certainly not be doing what he was now doing. He taught English in Iran, and spoke French reasonably well. After his astonishing financial success, he talked to producers about doing his own television talk show with business guests. He considered backing movies and plays, and joined the board of the American Ballet Theater.

But Boesky rarely attended the ballet or the theater. He would search out the best restaurants in New York and, most affectionately, Paris—not merely the poshest ones. But he would only sample the food, rarely eat with gusto. He talked about buying a Paris apartment on the Left Bank or the Ile Saint-Louis but wound up in a very establishment part of the Right Bank.

And there lay his contradiction. Boesky continually impressed one with what he knew about himself; he knew what he should not do, but he did it anyway. At bottom clearly lay a deep insecurity. Perhaps it stemmed from his father's restaurants' going out of business. William Boesky, who died in 1964, long before his son's extraordinary financial success, ran several thriving restaurants in Detroit for years. But when the neighborhood changed, William Boesky's business declined. Ivan Boesky paid many of his bills the very day he received them, as if business failure haunted him too. He was part of one of his father's operations, a Detroit nightclub, when it went bankrupt. He carefully checked even his firm's smallest expense. Some would conjecture that the anxiety of success would be too much for him and that he would wish his ultimate destruction on himself. That, if too simple, may have been true.

His obsession with his place in society seemed unnatural in a man who talked as if he prided himself on being a maverick, who indeed liked mavericks. He turned down investments because he did not want to be publicly associated with certain kinds of people, even some fellow takeover professionals. One relative says that he always insisted on such perquisites as limousines, even before he made much money. The fact that he was not a Harvard graduate never deterred him from enjoying his well-publicized membership in the Harvard Club. He became a prominent contributor to Jewish philanthropies—an interest in his religion developed as his four children got older. He apparently needed these trappings badly, so badly it altered his judgment about them entirely. People had him figured out, but he didn't change anyway, even after he read their criticism in articles. He didn't seem to understand, or care.

Perhaps there were other insecurities. Boesky did not have an underprivileged background, by any means. His father sent him to a private school, though he graduated from a public high school. Boesky always exhibited a hyperactivity. He had a short attention span, slept for only a few hours at a time, and would eat very little. As he got older, this restless nature would drive him from college to college. Eventually Boesky graduated from Detroit College of Law, but there is no record of an undergraduate degree. In the early '60s he married Seema Silberstein, an attractive daughter of Ben Silberstein, the owner of the Beverly Hills Hotel—

and a man apparently about as competitive as one could ever be bequeathed as a father-in-law. Silberstein, who separated from Seema's mother, went to California and bought the Beverly Hills Hotel from Hernando Courtright, the man who had built it into the legend it still is. Then he proceeded to marry Courtright's wife. Courtright built another success in the Beverly Wilshire Hotel, but Silberstein, now the doyen of the Beverly Hills, had surely arrived in Hollywood. He later divorced Courtright's wife, who returned to her home in Arkansas.

Boesky's peripatetic nature carried over to his search for a job. An accountant and lawyer by now, he was naturally attracted by the fast profits of Wall Street. He tried his hand as a securities analyst, but found it too nebulous an occupation. The relationship between the rightness of your analysis and the price of the stock was tenuous at best, he would later say. Friends introduced him to arbitrage and he thought he had found what he wanted to do. Arbitrage made sense; it was an analyzable craft, not like stock picking, which was so subject to unpredictable changes. It fit his active nature and need for quick results. And Steve Sherman, one of Wall Street's most highly regarded arbitrageurs and a Boesky friend, was willing to take him under his wing. Boesky found a job as an arbitrageur with Edwards & Hanley, a brokerage firm that went out of business in 1975. But he would not be defeated. By 1975 he had raised enough family money—about $700,000—to open his own arbitrage firm, one of the few independent operators in the business. One of his first investment deals, Copper Range, looked for a time as if it would be a bust. And one can only imagine the frown on the tough old father-in-law's face. But Boesky searched for more capital, and found his first outside injection from the European Lambert family, later to be associated with Drexel Burnham. In 1975, Boesky's luck would change radically. He ran head-on into the takeover wave that would prove more lucrative to the arbitrage community than any other. Even Copper Range turned out to be a good investment.

Boesky was in some but not all ways a born arbitrageur. He is not patient enough to be analytical; he is a glutton for taking risks. But he was a born arbitrageur for the period he was about to enter, one where betting hard usually paid off, and being careful did not. Less well known, Boesky's real success came from the deal he would cut with his investors, not in being right about his arbitrage investments. Almost incredibly, he demanded—and received—more than 50 percent of any profits he would earn on investors' capital, and gave up only a few percentage points if he lost. A typical hedge fund, by comparison, which invests in stocks and bonds, might give 20 percent of the profits to its managers. Other arbitrage partnerships that followed more or less adopted Boesky's structure, a bonanza for them as well.

One other point about Boesky, then, often went misunderstood. It made sense for him to take bigger risks than most. If you get paid when you make money, and don't get penalized when you lose it, you should take risks for the big payoff.

Many who knew Boesky agree he was neither heartless nor ruthless. It is hard to find malice in the man, they say, and he rarely had a bad word to say about anyone but a few enemies, and no large number of them for a man who had risen as far and fast as Boesky did. Boesky's gift was that he knew what he wanted and he was tireless in going after it. He did deal well with defeat, which he would face a few more times in the succeeding years. He was never to be fully accepted by Wall Street—too brash and aggressive for some, too ambitious for others—even before the scandal. That, too, he seemed able to bear. One arbitrageur said that Boesky could bear more pain than anyone he had ever known. It was the talent of a classic gambler, not to let one day's losses affect the way you make the next bet. At that at least, Boesky may have been the best.

Boesky loved competition. He professed to believe in competition. He religiously kept his appointments to play squash, usually at the Harvard Club, and before that at the City Athletic Club. He had a squash court at home in Bedford, New York, and a tennis court as well. But it is unlikely he would be able to compete in club tournaments. He occasionally foot-faulted in tennis, by up to twelve inches. It may have been a telling clue to his personality. Some men are so involved with themselves that they believe they live by other rules than the rest. One prominent corporate raider simply calls it Boesky's arrogance. Boesky was not a victim of a system that provided too many enticing opportunities. He would have always made those opportunities, and probably he always would have looked for the edge. He didn't hide that fact. You can't hide a foot-fault. He was a foot-faulter, and a man who kept his own objectives foremost in mind. Even when he bought control of the Beverly Hills Hotel after his father-in-law's death, he used the holding company's credit to finance more risk arbitrage. If there was any sympathy for Boesky when his insider trading was uncovered, it was gone when it was reported that he had taped and trapped his business friends. Boesky would not have gone out of his way to hurt others, but when he himself was threatened, he apparently did what he could to save himself.

Through 1976, the investment profits available by investing in takeover targets had not yet dawned on the still-unsuspecting investment community at large. Through the mid-1970s, the field was left almost entirely to professional arbitrageurs. Arbitrage itself was an ancient practice. But since the 1960s, the term *arbitrage* was an anachronistic description of what these professional investors and traders did.

Arbitrage, in its original meaning, had to do with equating values in different markets. The most common early practice of arbitrage was in the currency markets. The French franc, selling in the London market against pounds sterling, might fetch a slightly higher price than in Paris. The arbitrageur would therefore buy francs in Paris and sell them in London. He would do this until he had supplied enough francs in London to bring the price down to the level in Paris. Typically, an arbitrageur took no risk at all. He made it up in volume, so to speak. And in the early days, the best arbitrageurs were those who were the quickest, had the best systems of communication, and the ability to trade in markets all over the world. The benefit provided to the marketplace by the arbitrageur was that he would help equalize prices throughout the world. The franc in Paris should trade at the same level as the franc in London if markets are to work properly.

Currency arbitrage spread to stocks as well. Big internationally known corporations such as Royal Dutch Shell and Exxon were traded in cities throughout the world. Arbitrageurs spotted the opportunity. Royal Dutch would sell at a slightly different price in London or Amsterdam than it did in New York City. If it was selling low in Amsterdam, the arbitrageur would buy it for immediate sale in New York at a higher price. The difference might be only an eighth of a point, 12.5 cents a share, which arbitrageurs call the spread. But if an arbitrageur could deal in enough volume, he would make substantial profits. Moreover, there was virtually no risk.

Eventually, arbitrageurs would see fit to take on some small amount of risk. The arbitrageur would know his marketplace in New York, for example. He might realize there was a healthy demand for Royal Dutch, or at least be willing to take the risk that he could sell, say, ten thousand shares at a given price. He might sell those shares in New York City in the afternoon with the idea of not buying the shares he had to deliver until the next morning in Amsterdam, where he knew or sensed the price would be lower. If he was wrong, he would take a loss. So now there was some risk. Arbitrage moved one step away from its classical riskless nature. One commentator called this *tendency arbitrage,* the attempt to feel out the tendency of the market to be moving in one direction or another. Still, the risks were carefully limited.

The rise of instant communications and high-volume marketplaces throughout the world in currencies and stocks would reduce significantly the profits of classic arbitrage. As arbitrageurs searched for new opportunities, several major financial shifts in industries in the United States provided a new avenue for these professionals. Both the railroads and the utilities were being reorganized in the 1930s. Bankrupt railroads in the Depression would issue new securities as they would be reorganized. These securities would be exchangeable for the old securities, but typically there would be a difference in value—a spread—which the knowledgeable professional could assess far better than the average investor. The arbitrageur would buy up the old securities if the price was right and wait to exchange them when the new securities were to be released. There was risk: it might take longer for those securities to be issued than the arbitrageur had anticipated, and time is money. The arbitrageur would lock up his capital, usually borrowed, and be paying interest on it. Second, the terms under which the securities were to be exchanged could always be changed. In fact, the financial reorganization might not go through at all. The arbitrageur was now taking on significantly more risk than classic arbitrage ever did. And a new term evolved to describe the activity: *risk arbitrage.*

In the mid-1930s, the Public Utility Holding Company Act also forced utilities to divest themselves of many of their widespread subsidiaries. This was an added impetus for the development of risk arbitrage. Again, exchanges of securities were involved, spreads opened up, and arbitrageurs were able to exploit them.

In the 1950s, risk arbitrageurs applied these same techniques to mergers. An acquiring company would offer securities for a target company and a spread would frequently arise. The arbitrageur would essentially buy the securities of the company being taken over if he was reasonably certain the combination would go through. By the 1960s, an active risk-arbitrage community existed, and it was prepared to take advantage of the conglomerate wave of mergers.

Risk arbitrage, while essentially different in many respects from classic arbitrage, does retain some of the same risk-limiting principles. To simplify, if XYZ Company offers two shares of its own stock for every share of the ABC Company, and the arbitrageur thinks the deal will go through, he will complete a transaction that is very similar to classic arbitrage. Presumably, XYZ is paying a premium for ABC, offering a price higher than it is currently trading. The arbitrageur will buy the cheaper security, ABC, just as if it were the low-priced Franch franc selling in Paris. Now, he will sell two shares of XYZ, just as if it were the higher-priced French franc selling in London. He has locked in his spread. But unlike the currency trades, which are completed immediately, the investment in the merger will have to wait until the merger is completed before it is paid off. The principal risk is that it won't be completed.

Let us say that the ABC Company was selling for $6 on the day XYZ Company made its offer. XYZ was selling for $5 a share. Two shares of XYZ would be worth $10 a share to ABC shareholders on the day the merger is completed. ABC rises to $8 a share in anticipation of that. The arbitrageur buys ABC at $8 and simultaneously sells two shares of XYZ at $5 a share for total revenues of $10.* The arbitrageur has a $2 profit now, no matter whether XYZ

---

*You can sell securities you don't own—known as selling short—as long as you promise to deliver those securities eventually. Typically, you must borrow those securities from someone who already owns them.

shares fluctuate in price. When the merger is completed, he will collect his two shares of XYZ for every one he owns of ABC. He then returns the XYZ shares, which he previously sold short, to the party from whom he borrowed them. Even if XYZ's shares fall to $3 apiece, and the value of the offer is only $6 for every ABC share, the arbitrageur already has locked in his $2 profit. The risk then is limited to whether or not the merger will go through, and almost as important, whether it goes through in a reasonable time. The longer it takes, the less the arbitrageur's profit margin, because his capital is tied up. Some mergers indeed take so long that the profitability is negligible, once the cost of capital is deducted, and this risk must be assessed from the outset. But by putting the simultaneous buy-and-sell transaction into effect, the arbitrageur eliminates the risk that the share price will fluctuate over time. His potential profit is guaranteed at $2 a share.

In the 1960s, when all kinds of securities were being exchanged in mergers, risk arbitrage thrived. In the 1970s, risk arbitrage would take one more large step away from its classic origins. Cash became almost as plentiful in the '70s as paper was in the '60s. And the cash tender offer did not provide opportunities for any arbitraging of risk. There were no securities to sell short in order to lock in a spread. For the most part, all the arbitrageur could do was buy a target company and await the outcome. If the company was taken over at a premium, the arbitrageur made money. Now it was all risk, and no arbitrage. But the arbitrage community had learned better than any other group of Wall Street professionals how to assess the likelihood that a takeover could be completed. It was only natural that they would dominate this investment activity. Through most of the 1970s, they'd have the extraordinarily lucrative field almost to themselves.

Arbitrageurs are essentially different from the other groups of professionals who took part in takeovers throughout this period. They are decidedly not organization people. Salesmanship and old school ties, which play such important roles in investment banking and stockbroking, count for little in arbitrage. These men by and large survived only if they were right. Few came up through the Ivy League, and generally they were not organization men. To some degree, they were all iconoclasts, and all were very clear about their objectives. Most of them talked tough, and acted tough.

Several firms had long-established arbitrage traditions. Goldman Sachs, in particular, had cultivated an active successful arbitrage department since the 1930s. In the 1940s, Gus Levy, who started as a stock trader, was the firm's arbitrageur. He rose to become the flamboyant head of Goldman, and probably to have more influence than anyone in making the banking firm the most respected on Wall Street. L. Jay Tenenbaum followed Levy in the position in the late 1950s, again developing a reputation that, by Wall Street terms, became legendary. Tenenbaum emphasized analysis and research to support the arbitrage decisions. In 1975, Robert Rubin, a low-key Yale Law School graduate, formally took over from Tenenbaum, who had originally hired him. Rubin himself would eventually become a leading candidate to take over the reins of Goldman. A man with cultural and political interests, Rubin deepened the analytical tradition of Goldman. The size of their investment positions would remain among the largest in the business during the '70s, but Goldman's public face was also very quiet, reflecting Rubin's diffident personality.

Bear Stearns also maintained a long arbitrage tradition. Its guiding light, Salem Lewis, was the firm's arbitrageur. Lewis was a product of City College of New York. And his successor, Alan Greenberg, an alumnus of the University of Missouri, kept Bear Stearns's arbitrage department very profitable. In 1978, Greenberg succeeded Lewis as head of the firm.

At Salomon Brothers, a trading firm that would come into its own in the 1970s, there was no arbitrage tradition. Richard Rosenthal, a high-school dropout from Brooklyn, joined Salomon as a trader when he was twenty-three. By twenty-seven he was a partner and running the arbitrage department, which in fact he had built up virtually single-handed in the 1960s. By the '70s he was a veteran of the previous decade's takeover wars.

Guy Wyser-Pratte describes himself as a second-generation abitrageur. His father traded shares on the Paris exchange, and then set up a firm on Wall Street. Guy, who studied history at the

University of Rochester, took over the business, which soon was bought by Bache Securities.

Through 1976, Ivan Boesky was not classified among such heavy hitters of arbitrage as Rosenthal, Rubin, and Wyser-Pratte. Only one other arbitrageur then raised substantial money independently of the major brokerage firms. In fact, in the mid-1970s, Leonard Sheriff may have had more money invested in arbitrage than anyone else.

To raise money, Boesky assiduously cultivated the press. With the help of a public relations counsel, he made the rounds of key business journalists, offering himself as a source of information about takeover deals. Nothing about Boesky bothered his colleagues more, or would bother them more in the future, than his bringing the limelight to risk arbitrage. Until Boesky came along, arbitrage was a closed business, intensely secret, and arbitrageurs succeeded in conveying an esoteric image to outsiders. But by getting his name in the papers, Boesky could attract potential investors. Yes, he was a bona fide arbitrageur. Look at this quote in *The New York Times,* or this picture in *Business Week.* The strategy worked, and Boesky continued to raise money.

There were several good reasons why arbitrageurs who already had access to capital would want to keep the business out of the newspapers. For one thing, why let others in on a good thing? Arbitrage had been enormously profitable over the years. But, too, there was the question of inside information. An arbitrageur who knew for a fact that a merger was going through had a distinct advantage. The securities laws disallowed use of inside information, but no one had yet come up with a satisfactory definition of what the illegal practice precisely entailed. Public attention to risk arbitrage, however, might attract more government scrutiny.

The arbitrage community had one other interesting secret, however, that hardly ever received public attention. There were enormous tax benefits in the basic arbitrage transaction when securities are the form of exchange. (It is not true for cash tender offers.) When an arbitrageur sold XYZ Company short, for example, and then delivered shares against it to close out the transaction, he typically could take a short-term loss against ordinary income. Any income taxed at ordinary rates could be offset to the extent of that loss. The gain on the purchase of ABC shares, however, if held long enough, was taxed only at capital gains rates, typically about half of ordinary rates—advantages that have since been nullified by the Tax Reform Act of 1986, which treats ordinary and capital gains equally.

If arbitrage was very lucrative, its consequence for takeovers was to make them more straightforward: The highest bid would usually win. Once the "arbs," as they were called, bought the stock of a target, there could be no pleas for loyalty to management, or to keep the foreigners out, or to help the labor unions. The arbs bought out the traditional investors in anticipation of a short-term return. The raiding company would win if it provided them with the best return, the best bid. In these years, an active arbitrage community forced the takeover specialists to grow up quickly. There was nothing but money involved in these transactions. Takeovers were not for the sentimental.

In fact, the arbitrage community would enjoy its least competitive days through 1976. In total, arbitrageurs could muster only maybe $100 million in any one deal. A few years later, the game became so popular that the capital available to arbitrage had grown to several billions of dollars.

What the relatively few arbitrageurs could enjoy in the mid-1970s were very handsome spreads. GE's bid for Utah International is a case in point. The day it was announced, Utah would have been worth $61 a share if the merger went through immediately. The stock rose only slightly, to $49. Part of the reason was concern about the antitrust investigation to come. But also, Wall Street had not yet tuned in to the potential profits of investing in takeover targets. Years later, such a spread would have disappeared quickly.

Even as the GE–Utah International merger got closer to consummating in 1976, the spread remained very wide. Boesky was actively seeking more capital from investors. The GE merger was a gift, he argued. In May 1976, GE and Utah signed an agreement to merge. Utah could soon be worth $65, based on GE's price of about $50 at the time, but the stock traded for only $55. Although there was still no word from the Justice Department, both GE and Utah made a public statement in July, saying the merger was continuing. The arbitrageurs were certain an agreement with Justice could be worked out, but they didn't have enough capital to send the stock higher. It traded for $57 when it was worth about $74 in terms of GE's price. The merger was finally completed in December at a price for Utah shares of nearly $69 a share. Until October, Utah was selling at around $60.

But what really started to make the arbitrage game exciting in 1976 were the number of hostile bidding contests. The returns were earned fast, and the bidding often pushed the premium way up, just as it had in Inco's battle for ESB. The rest of Wall Street had not yet caught on. Hostile deals were still relatively small in size, nothing like GE's friendly $2 billion takeover of Utah. But for the arb, the spreads were quick to be realized, and often very high.

In 1975 there were fifty-eight tender offers for corporations. In 1976 there would be seventy. But the premiums for hostile deals were growing quickly, and far beyond what the arbs could ever have hoped for. Valley Camp Coal was eventually bought by a white knight, Quaker State Oil Refining, for nearly $67 a share. The initial bid was made by Bethlehem Copper for $55. And Valley Camp's market price before the bid was only $35. Bristol-Myers upped a bid from AIRCO for Unitek Corp. by almost twice. Bristol-Myers offered stock when too few investors tendered their shares to AIRCO's low-ball bid of $30. Unitek was selling for $23 before the bidding began. Here, the arbs played a critical role, waiting for the higher bid, and ultimately being rewarded very well.

Harcourt Brace Jovanovich took Sea World from the clutches of MCA with a bid of $28.75, nearly $7 higher than MCA's. Combustion Engineering outbid Petrolane for Gray Tool, $38 to $35. H.K. Porter had to top its own $17 bid for Fansteel in order to chase away a counterbid by Lear Siegler. Porter took Fansteel for $23.50 a share.

To the arbs, the higher bids were almost pure profit. They would enter the fray perhaps a dollar below the original bid, and see

$5, $6, or $7 tagged on to their $20 investment in a matter of weeks. A $5 profit on an investment of $20 came to 25 percent, often received within a month. On an annual return basis, it was 300 percent. In one sense, the arbitage business was now ideal: little competition, plenty of opportunity. The aggressive world of Wall Street does not let such opportunities pass for long. In 1976, risk arbitrage was still relatively unknown. By 1977, however, the secret would be out. Still, the arbitrageurs would make more money than they thought possible, because the size of hostile acquisitions would rise.

At the end of March 1977, Harry Gray's United Technologies made a bid that would ultimately set the takeover movement on a course that would change corporate history. And it would make a relative handful of Wall Street professionals more money than they ever dreamed of. Boesky alone would make $7.5 million. And if that spun Wall Street's head, Boesky took it in stride. Before this movement was over, he and his partners earned five and six times that on one hostile bid.

By 1986, Ivan Boesky had long played arbitrage as hard as, and probably harder than, anyone. Few would be surprised that he might stretch the boundaries of the law regarding inside information. Ed Hennessy says that when he was United Technology's chief financial officer, Boesky would call him at ten at night to find out how a deal was coming along, and then wake him with another phone call the next morning. "No one was as persistent," Hennessy says. In the heat of one major bidding contest, one insider said Boesky was among the first to call, while some arbs did not call at all.

But even the most cynical arbitrageurs had doubts that inside information could be too useful to an investor as large as Boesky. It would be impossible to hide trades in such big size. And smaller trades did not matter to the bottom line. Few if any could believe how openly Boesky flouted the law. Several who worked as his employees and had since left were shocked that he would pay for the information, then blatantly use it to trade on. It not only showed no respect for the law, some would say it was just unintelligent.

But Boesky had shown before—in his philanthropies, in his

obsession with the Harvard Club, in his everpresent smile—an
extraordinary lack of judgment and control in some matters. There
was no natural braking mechanism in him. He sought the extra
edge, rewrote the rules for himself. He did not mean to harm
others, many agreed. But the consequences of what he did would be
vast, for many individuals and for Wall Street in general.

What was good for the arbitrageur—a bidding contest—was
not good for the raiding corporation. Defensive tactics were honed
in 1976 by investment bankers and takeover lawyers. Companies
were no longer left with as few options as the bankers claimed ESB
had had. In fact, one defensive specialist said that only one year
later Garlock would have gotten a much higher price from Colt, or
found a white knight at a higher price. In 1976, as the arbitrageurs
well knew, the final winning bid was 25 percent to as much as 50
percent higher than the original bid. And some companies would
eventually be bought at 65 percent to 100 percent higher than their
market price before the bidding began.

But what had changed was that *the first bidder was losing.*
While Inco and Colt were clear winners, now the white knight was
taking the company away. The bankers and lawyers on the defense
could often tie an offer up in the courts—the antitrust laws still
provided a barrier in the mid-1970s—until the target company
found a more friendly white knight to make a higher offer. The state
takeover laws helped enormously. They often called for more time
before an offer would expire, demanded demonstration that a merger
would not hurt a company or the state economy, and imposed other
requirements for disclosure of information that could be onerous.
More important, the local courts were very willing to grant injunctions against a bidding company if a merger was challenged according to those laws. Over time, state and federal courts would be less
willing to support the management of target companies. The right
of a shareholder to receive a fair price for his investment began to
dominate the judicial decisions, and in turn would provide more
fuel for takeovers. The state laws would virtually be nullified by
1982. But while they were operative, they could effectively delay the

tender. They did not necessarily stop a bidder, but gained time for a target to find a white knight.

When Herald Co. wanted to take over the Booth Newspapers in 1976, Herald hired Marty Lipton as its lawyer. Lipton, of course, knew well how easily Herald could lose if Herald bid first. He proposed a stark version of a technique that was beginning to be adopted. Herald simply sent a letter to Booth's management that it was going to make a bid and reminding the management that it had a responsibility to shareholders to accept a premium price for the shares. The procedure became known as a "bear hug"—management squeezed into submission. With the state takeover laws providing so much time to look for a white knight, it no longer made as much sense to initiate a Saturday Night Special raid.

Herald did take over Booth. In the next few years the bear hug became very popular. The best-known bear hug was Exxon's controversial diversification, accomplished by the purchase of Reliance Electric in 1979. Only when the courts began to rule that management had more discretion in choosing offers than many feared, was the effectiveness of the bear hug diminished.

The bidding contest, however, could also provide opportunity to profit, even for the losing bidder. What a couple of the wilier corporate chieftains discovered was that an unfriendly bid could, as the Wall Street community would eventually term it, put a company "in play." No one was more adept at that in the mid-1970s than Thomas Mellon Evans, nearly a septuagenarian then and a man who controlled two companies, Crane Co. and H.K. Porter. Evans learned that he could make a profit even if he lost the bid. For him, a public company was first and foremost a vehicle to make acquisitions, pure and simple. A cranky man, generally disliked, he bought the likes of Missouri Portland and Fansteel. But he also bought a minority stake in Anaconda, only to be acquired at a higher price by Arco, the white knight.

Had Evans been younger, perhaps he would have continued on this path. He made Crane tens of millions of dollars this way. But those profits would pale by comparison to what T. Boone Pickens would earn in the 1980s for his Mesa Petroleum in much the same way. Pickens initiated several tender offers for major oil companies after acquiring stock in the company, only to have them bought away at a much higher price, and profits of tens of millions of dollars to his company. Pickens's first such potential gambit, however, took place in 1976, and he did not realize it.

Pickens is quick to admit that he has always been an outsider among the giant oil companies. He is comfortable in the role of maverick and industry goad. In the '50s, Pickens, then a young geologist, quit Phillips Petroleum to scout for oil on his own. He was good enough, or lucky enough, to find several gushers. He formed Mesa Petroleum in 1964, and his properties continued to come up winners. The oil price rise in 1973 and 1974, plus a big strike in the North Sea, gave Pickens the wherewithal to start searching for more oil reserves, only this time on Wall Street. In early 1976 he made a $22 per-share offer for oil-rich Aztec Oil & Gas, which was then selling for $15. The irony was that he did not buy any shares before he bid.

It was a bold move for Mesa, which was not that much larger than Aztec but coveted its oil and gas reserves. Aztec hired Goldman Sachs to search for a white knight. Both Houston Natural Gas and Southland Royalty had had previous discussions about a merger with Aztec. Oil and gas reserves had become popular acquisition targets with the price of oil so high, yet the companies' stock prices were still relatively low. Both Southland and Houston made offers. Goldman recommended Southland's $32 bid. In a tender, Southland got almost all of the stock. And Pickens was left in the cold because Mesa hadn't bought any. "It was one of my dumbest moves," he says, and it was a mistake he would not make again.

9

In 1977 the takeover movement itself, as a financial phenomenon with a life all its own—a life separate from any single acquisition deal—was stamped on Wall Street's way of thinking by one massive merger. In itself, the acquisition of Babcock & Wilcox by J. Ray McDermott changed the nature of the way takeovers would be viewed. They would now be acknowledged by many to be here to stay. If one deal failed, others would arrive to take its place. By virtue of this one deal, the takeover assuredly became the most-discussed business strategy of the time. No doubt that would have happened anyway over time, but probably without the sort of finality that this takeover contest established. Ever since Inco took over ESB, the series of takeovers that followed were seeds that may or may not have grown to fruition. With this one acquisition, it became obvious that the seeds had taken hold and the takeover movement would not wither.

By 1976, the number and size of acquisitions, many of them hostile, had expanded sharply. In both 1974 and 1975, there were about 12 billion dollars' worth of mergers transacted. That figure jumped to more than $20 billion in 1976. Bidding contests, especially, had blossomed. But no one deal had as yet caught Wall Street's imagination. One of the largest contested offers so far had been United Technologies' acquisition of Otis Elevator for $400 million; the largest friendly merger, GE's acquisition of Utah International.

The hostile acquisition of Babcock & Wilcox would eventually cost about twice as much money as did Otis Elevator, as the most frenzied bidding contest Wall Street had ever seen unfolded. Eleven separate bids were made by United Technologies and J. Ray McDermott for Babcock & Wilcox before McDermott finally won. The winning bid, a total of $750 million, was 50 percent higher than the opening bid, and almost twice as high as Babcock's closing stock price before the bidding began. The contest involved an array of defenses exploiting the state takeover laws that existed then, as well as proceedings before federal regulatory commissions. The bidding tactics were intricate, and ultimately helped the financially weaker party to win. Bad feelings among the contesting parties were very high. The contest took more than six months to complete. It made arbitrageurs more money than they had ever before made on a single deal, and would attract much more investment money to their business. It demonstrated clearly that it was very difficult for a target company to stay independent, and that its only recourse was typically to find a white knight at a higher price. No set of circumstances was more conducive to big arbitrage profits than that. Those Wall Street professionals involved still speak warmly of the fight for Babcock.

The winner, J. Ray McDermott, would eventually have the Three Mile Island nuclear accident to contend with, a catastrophe that the Wall Street pros, once they made their money, could comfortably read about at a distance. A little less than a year and a half after McDermott officially acquired Babcock, an alarm went off at a nuclear electricity plant a few miles from Harrisburg, Pennsylvania, on Three Mile Island, the small, damp stretch of land in the Susquehanna River. Radiation had leaked from the plant, and in the next few days the governor of the state would advise evacuation of all children and pregnant women within a five-mile radius. Before it was over, it would prove to be the worst nuclear accident in the United States. The plant was built by Babcock & Wilcox.

No one could accuse McDermott of a bad business decision simply because it did not foresee catastrophe. In fact, in the next few years coal-powered generating plants produced a surprisingly healthy cash flow for McDermott, though the company quickly wrote off the nuclear business. Later, the electric business would also slow dramatically, and Babcock's contribution was reduced to strong showings by its control and tubing divisions. What was not reported publicly was that McDermott also discovered about $100 million in cash that they had not known about when they made the acquisition. In short, the Babcock purchase more than paid for itself. But to Wall Street, this deal is not remembered in terms of whether or not it was a good business decision. It was simply the hottest takeover contest yet, and stands as a watershed in the movement's history.

Not every Wall Street banker who got involved in mergers early in this takeover movement would come up a winner. Paul Hallingby broods over his bad luck in the 1970s. Then, he was chairman of White, Weld & Co., an elite investment banking firm. But he never landed the giant takeovers for clients that would eventually earn several other firms many millions of dollars in fees. What he did do, however, was get Harry Gray interested in Babcock & Wilcox.

Hallingby probably had a more romantic view of Wall Street banking than many of his colleagues in the takeover business. Having grown up in the San Francisco area, he earned a bachelor's degree from Stanford in 1941. He then entered Harvard Business School, but was called away to Washington to serve as a naval engineer during World War II. He always remembers wanting to be an investment banker, and traces the ambition to a book an uncle sent him that he read during the war. Hallingby recalls that *Lords of Creation,* by Frederick Lewis Allen, was a glorifying history of the great investment bankers of the period. Hallingby's imagination, he says, was sparked by the seeming heroics of these men. He joined First Boston in 1946 as a trainee. His uncle told him that finance was the business end of business and urged him to reread *Lords of Creation* every five years.

Hallingby spent a couple of years at First Boston, several more at E.F. Hutton, and then joined Middle South Utilities in Illinois, where he rose to financial vice-president. It was at Middle South that Hallingby became acquainted with Babcock & Wilcox. The big electric utility had bought many boilers from Babcock, as well as a pipeline. Hallingby left Middle South to join White Weld in 1958, where he rose through the ranks to the presidency in 1973. In 1975, he was named chairman. But in the wave of mergers that followed the unfixing of stock brokerage commissions in the 1970s, White Weld was a victim. It was acquired by Merrill Lynch, the largest brokerage house, and Hallingby was given the post of vice-chairman.

Hallingby had worked with Harry Gray during his acquisition of Otis Elevator in 1975, and he knew Gray was very interested in acquiring a company in the energy business. In fact, Gray had given a speech to analysts in which he listed his criteria for acquisitions. Energy was very much on his mind, just as inflation was on the mind of General Electric. Says Hallingby: "Babcock was the most attractive of the lot. It was in an industry they liked. It was the size they liked. It had little debt. The price was reasonable. It had only one negative. Nuclear energy."

In 1977, Babcock had just come off several years of fast-growing profits. The company was founded just after the Civil War to sell industrial boilers. Babcock was now the largest producer of coal-burning boilers. It was the third-largest company in the manufacture of nuclear reactors for electricity. It also produced steel tubing and several other products.

To a world that had its doubts that oil would long be the principal fuel, Babcock was very tempting. While Babcock had earned only $10 million in 1970, and the nuclear power business remained soft, Babcock's profits began to rise sharply in 1974 with demand for coal boilers. It hit $34 million that year, about the same as its level in 1967. By 1976 it would rise to $53 million, or $4.37 a share. In the meantime, its stock was still selling in the low $30 range, a price-earnings multiple of only seven or eight.

In short, Babcock looked by the standards of the conventional wisdom of that time like a company with a strong future. More to the point, it was a company with a strong immediate past, and that would prove a criterion of great importance to acquiring companies, despite all the rhetoric that takeovers were healthy because they got rid of bad managers. It was good companies that corporations wanted to acquire. There was no reason to believe demand for the coal-powered boilers would do anything but rise, according to conventional thinking, because the price of oil was so high. And while orders for nuclear plants were way down—from fifty-two in

1975 for the entire United States to only twelve in 1978—theoretically, nuclear energy would probably make a comeback. On paper, few companies looked better able to exploit the energy crisis than Babcock in 1977. To the portfolio-minded Harry Gray, Babcock was a natural. And Paul Hallingby was smart enough to realize that.

Acquiring Babcock would do one other thing for Gray. It would raise United Technologies from its rank as the nation's thirty-fifth largest company, according to *Fortune*'s list of the 500 largest industrial companies, to nineteenth. Babcock's $1.7 billion in sales in 1976 would look very handsome alongside United Technologies $5.2 billion. Only three years before, United had been the nation's fifty-ninth largest company with $2 billion in sales. Through acquisitions of Essex and Otis, Gray had pushed his way much higher, tripling profits to $157 million in the process.

That the hostile acquisition of a billion-dollar company was unheard-of would not deter Gray. First, he tried to make a friendly offer. But that was the way Gray always started.

In 1977 the first choice among acquisition candidates for both Harry Gray and Ed Hennessy, his financial vice-president, was Combustion Engineering. In a meeting with Hennessy, Hallingby presented the case for Babcock. He then offered to have White Weld do a study. For $20,000, a small sum Hallingby giggles about with some embarrassment in retrospect, White Weld analyzed the financial condition of Babcock. At a meeting in early February in Hartford, White Weld presented a formal case to Gray and Hennessy for taking over Babcock.

White Weld proposed that Gray bid $45 a share for Babcock, whose stock was selling at about $35 at that time. Gray thought the proposed number was outrageously high and ended the meeting. Gray entertained no bid higher than $42 a share. And according to many observers, Gray would lose Babcock because of his initial low bid. Some bankers say Gray's hesitation would serve as a lesson for many, but not all, future bidders not to low-ball if they really wanted a company.

Gray ultimately bought Hallingby's idea and geared up to bid, and Joe Flom was hired to run the legal side of the effort. All had agreed that Gray should first approach Babcock with a friendly offer. Hallingby, in fact, was confident that Gray and George Zipf, the tough-minded chairman of Babcock, would get along. "If you put them all in one room," he says, "you couldn't tell the United people from the Babcock people." The pretense for the meeting was a joint project with Babcock on better ways to burn coal. Gray telephoned Zipf, explained his proposal, and according to later court testimony, claimed United was willing to put up between $30 million and $50 million in research funds for joint projects. Zipf agreed to meet.

On the last Friday in February, Zipf and Gray got together in Babcock's Manhattan headquarters. After a couple of hours of discussion, Gray brought up the possibility of Babcock and United's combining forces. Gray had approached ESB in the same seemingly gentle way.

George Zipf realized that United Technologies would probably make a hostile bid for Babcock. Babcock's longtime investment bankers, with whom he consulted, were Morgan Stanley, by now very experienced in the most aggressive defensive strategies. Zipf also hired Marty Lipton, who was previously approached by Hallingby. However, Lipton had adopted a business strategy that, where possible, he would enter a contest in opposition to Joe Flom, and United had already hired Flom for the offense. Lipton told Hallingby, whose idea was to tie up the two best takeover lawyers on one side—his own—that he would wait to see whether Babcock was interested in hiring him.*

Nor was there any strong reason at this date to presume that Babcock would inevitably fall to even a rich and aggressive United Technologies. In 1977 there were fresh hopes that a target company could defend itself. In some cases, the state anti-takeover statutes, now adopted by more than thirty states, were working to a degree.

*Lipton does not recall this conversation.

Essentially, they served to delay a tender offer long enough to find a white knight.

Lipton, for example, successfully tied up a bid by Congoleum for Universal Leaf for eight months in the Virginia courts. Similarly, Copperweld was able to put off a bid by the Rothschild company, Société Imetal of France. It first challenged Imetal's bid in federal court for violating the Williams Act. It next brought action in Ohio, which agreed to restrain the bid until the issues were settled in state court. In all, the bid was delayed nearly three months, until Imetal dropped out when Copperweld got its unions to object to the takeover.

In a furious battle the next year, Microdot, under the collective wing of Goldman Sachs and Joe Flom, challenged a bid by General Cable. Microdot even sued its own lead bank, Irving Trust, for lending part of the takeover funds to General. It charged that Irving Trust had a conflict of interest as a result and not only filed suit in New York State, but took the matter to the U.S. Congress, where it got Congress to hold hearings. Irving Trust and General Cable argued, as expected, that General Cable was not aware of Irving's relationship with Microdot. As noted earlier, Microdot challenged General Cable before the then very active Ohio Securities Commission, in the state where both Microdot and General Cable were domiciled. In these very proceedings, Microdot learned of Irving's General Cable relationship. The Ohio Commission delayed the tender long enough for Northwest Industries to make a higher bid, and Microdot accepted it. Northwest bought Microdot for $21 per share, compared to General Cable's initial $17 bid. Microdot and Irving settled their suit out of court.

Later in 1977, Gerber Products would fend off an unwanted bid from Anderson Clayton in one of the most dramatically aggressive defensive campaigns of the period. Gerber took to the Michigan courts to sue Anderson Clayton, and the courts delayed the bid long enough to frustrate Anderson, who eventually dropped out.

But for all the fighting, by the end of 1977 only a relative handful of companies that were targets of hostile tenders would actually remain completely independent. Most would eventually fall to a third party—the white knight—although at a much higher price. The target company's management could at least argue that it got its shareholders more money, and usually much more money.

The investment bankers would earn very handsome fees, usually computed as a percentage of the increase in the final bid price over the initial bid. And the arbitrageurs would bring home extraordinary profits.

In any case, that it was inevitable that a target company would succumb was not yet clear in early 1977. And it is possible that George Zipf pursued his defensive strategies with the sincere hope of remaining independent. It turned out that United Technologies would give him almost a month to prepare. White Weld prepared a presentation for the United board and delivered it on March 21. The board approved any bid up to $42 a share. Two days later, Gray again met with Zipf, trying to induce a friendly surrender. Zipf would hear none of it. According to Hallingby, Gray picked up his board's papers authorizing him to make a hostile bid, and waved them in Zipf's face. Zipf told Gray that he was ready to fight, and in court testimony he said, "We had the guns ready and the guns pointed; if he wanted to pull the trigger, go ahead; he was asking for it." Hallingby says Zipf never had a calm moment after that second meeting with Gray.

On Tuesday, March 29, Harry Gray announced the bid for all Babcock's 12.2 million shares at $42 a share, a total of $512 million. The low bid was noted immediately by Wall Street analysts, who were widely quoted in the newspaper accounts. The implication was that higher bids were to come.

The United bid was delivered to Babcock with an unusual letter. The letter gave Zipf until Friday of that week to accept or reject the offer. It also urged him not to use the state takeover laws as cover. Harry Gray had already had a bad experience fending off these laws in his takeover of Otis. When United had made its partial offer for Otis shares in the fall of 1975, Otis brought several separate lawsuits. United was temporarily prevented from undertaking its tender by the Indiana securities commissioner. Otis also sued in the Indiana Superior Court, where it won a restraining order against United, as well as in federal court. The upshot was that United refiled and made a new bid—and raised the price. Otis ultimately relented, but Gray did not want to go through the layers of legal battles again.

In a letter to Zipf, Gray wrote: "Certain tender offer statutes, which might be applicable to transactions of this nature, severely complicate the cash tender offer process and can result in such inordinate time delays as to frustrate the offer." The hint of a bear hug followed. The letter reminded Zipf that he had an obligation to let shareholders determine whether or not to accept the bid.

> *Such statutes, [wrote Gray] as you are no doubt aware, grant you the right and impose on you the duty of determining in good faith whether to facilitate the offer. Our offer, therefore, is subject to your advising us that you will cooperate in permitting your stockholders to have an opportunity to determine for themselves whether or not to accept the offer either by recommending its acceptance or by agreeing to take steps to assure full and fair disclosure to your stockholders so as to make a hearing under such statutes unnecessary in your opinion.*

But Zipf was not about to give in to such demands, and he had Marty Lipton at his side to help. Lipton was prepared to launch as aggressive a defense as he could muster. Zipf had decided he would plunge forward as vigorously as anyone else in the defense of his company. He immediately responded to Gray's letter with a strongly worded one of his own, implying that he was prepared to take court action despite the warnings:

> *The proposals contained in your letter of March 28 raise very substantial and difficult financial and business and antitrust and other legal issues. We will study these issues and the other questions raised by your letter with our investment bankers and legal counsel and we will consult with the various federal and state agencies as required.*

On the Monday following Gray's proposal, Zipf and his board formally rejected the takeover bid by United Technologies as inadequate. It also filed an antitrust suit in an Ohio federal court purporting that the merger would violate the antitrust laws because United and Babcock both manufactured steam-generating equipment. The next step in the "total-litigation defense," as Marty

Lipton terms it, was to sue under the state anti-takeover statutes. The Justice Department filed an antitrust suit in Hartford. Courts in both states issued temporary injunctions against United's bid, effectively tabling the any-and-all offer until the courts issued their final rulings.

If Gray was rocked by the tenaciousness of the Babcock defense, he was not about to pull out of the contest. He had Flom and his investment bankers pursue the suits. Flom believed that United would eventually prevail in court. Lipton's goal was to frustrate Gray at every turn. He and his advisers would now come up with more ways to block the bid, if only temporarily, if only to buy time and maybe cause Gray finally to throw up his hands and give up.

When Gray made his bid, Babcock's stock had been trading in the mid-thirty-dollar range. After the bid, once trading resumed, it traded in the low forties.

To one investment banker, John Morgan, who ran the mergers and acquisitions department of Smith Barney & Co., a medium-sized investment banking house, Babcock & Wilcox looked like a good buy at these prices. If his corporate client quietly accumulated shares on the open market, at the least he thought they would turn a handsome profit if the bidding went higher. He sent some public financial information to his client company about Babcock, and they agreed to start buying. Within a couple of months, they would spark the most dramatic bidding contest in Wall Street's modern history.

John Morgan was the great-grandson of J. Pierpont Morgan; the grandson of J. P. Morgan, Jr.; the son of Henry Morgan, the founder of Morgan Stanley; and an investment banker who wanted to prove he could do it on his own. In appearance, he is reminiscent of the eldest Morgan, the great patriarch of modern finance. His features are less exaggerated, but he has the ruddy complexion, and a slightly bulbous nose.

In 1977, J. Ray McDermott earned $192 million on $1.3 billion in sales. Along with the number two company in its industry, it enjoyed a nearly monopolistic hold over its market, offshore oil-drilling rigs. McDermott had about 40 percent of all sales; Brown & Root, about 38 percent. McDermott was headquartered in New Orleans; Brown & Root in Houston. Most such oil-rigging equipment was used for exploration in the Gulf of Mexico.

The market for oil rigs proved lucrative for McDermott and Brown & Root. A year later, the companies were both sued for price fixing. They pleaded guilty. In addition, McDermott would be found guilty of making bribes to government officials. Both McDermott and Brown & Root had been in business for more than fifty years.

In 1977, McDermott had accumulated nearly $500 million in cash. Fully aware that takeovers were becoming a way of corporate life, the company's management was concerned that it was a likely takeover target. Most important, its stock was selling for only about four times earnings. At that price, plus its cash, it looked to be a handsome catch.

On the other hand, there was a reason McDermott sold at so low a price-earnings multiple. According to analysts at the time, the fast growth in the oil rig markets was probably over. In 1977, despite higher than expected earnings at McDermott, most analysts were forecasting a drop in earnings by 1978. If history was a good guide, John Morgan says that the oil drilling could go into a seven-year drought. McDermott believed its growth prospects for the foreseeable future were limited.

Given the takeover atmosphere of the time, then, it was small wonder that McDermott believed it should diversify. Like so many other companies of the time, it wanted to smooth out its cycles. The ups and downs of the electric utility business could help do just that. The two cycles historically had little in common and would tend to move in opposite directions. When one business was up, the other would be down.

It was John Morgan, long a member of McDermott's board, who would assure McDermott that it could take on United Technologies in combat. Doubts were common. After all, McDermott was only about one-quarter United Technologies' size in sales, and less than half in profits. It was even a bit smaller in sales and profits than Babcock itself. And finally, Harry Gray was a towering business figure of his time. McDermott's Charles Graves was a major figure in the Southwest, but still suffered by comparison to Gray's stature in the Northeast and on Wall Street.

In Morgan, however, McDermott had an investment banker with unusual confidence, and maybe a man out to prove something. John Morgan, of course, was born with stature. But he was as decided a maverick as any figure in the takeover movement. A Yale graduate, he did briefly work for Morgan Stanley, but it was his father's firm. His older brother, Charles, was already there. After three years in the Air Force, he returned to Wall Street to join Dominick & Dominick, a comparatively small brokerage firm, where he eventually ran their corporate finance department. Morgan then joined Smith Barney in 1968. J. Ray McDermott & Co. had been a Dominick client, and when Dominick went out of business in the early sixties, Morgan brought McDermott with him to Smith Barney. Morgan rose to run the corporate finance department at Smith Barney, and eventually was named co-chairman of the firm. He was also a longstanding member of the board of McDermott.

John Morgan had reviewed a number of possible takeover targets with the McDermott management. Babcock had already been on the list. Morgan says the criteria for seeking a company were three. The first was that it be of sufficient size. The second was that it manufacture engineered products, which is what McDermott understood. Finally, like so many others over the period, its third criterion was that it should be an energy-related company.

When United made its public bid, Morgan was also savvy enough to see that he would at least cover expenses. A good reader of the likely events, Morgan assumed Babcock would be bought one way or the other, a notion it turned out that George Zipf, the Babcock chief executive, would take a long time to concede. Morgan called McDermott management and suggested they take a close look at Babcock. He also suggested they simply buy some shares and wait and see. "It was pretty obvious," says Morgan, "that we'd probably make some money on the investment."

The reply from Graves, the chairman, and James Cunningham, McDermott's executive vice president, was that it looked good to them. Also at Morgan's suggestion, McDermott hired takeover lawyer Edmund Kelly, of White & Case. Kelly was a veteran of several major takeover battles in the 1960s and '70s, including the successful defense of B.F. Goodrich in 1969 against Northwest Industries. Kelly would quickly retire from the law after the Babcock battle and enter investment banking himself, depriving this movement of perhaps a competitor to the budding and dominating careers of Lipton and Flom.

McDermott started buying shares on the open market on April 6, just after Babcock filed its several suits against United. The purchases, even in relatively small blocks, were difficult to hide—no activity attracts arbitrageurs' attention as quickly as block purchases of a company that has already been bid for. The one piece of information the arbs had was that the trading was being handled by Smith Barney. While Smith Barney had its own arbitrageur, Arnold Amster, who would play a vital role in the takeover, his department was still small. Smith Barney never allocated the capital to Amster's operation that would allow him to buy shares in such size. Amster's limit was only between 25,000 and 35,000 shares, a commitment of no more than $1.25 million. Amster says he was barraged with phone calls asking who was buying the shares. He was not able to reply.

By this stage, the hostile bidding contest was well-understood, and most believed the contest for Babcock & Wilcox would escalate. Hardly an arbitrageur on Wall Street was not as heavily committed to this deal as his capital would allow. By the end, the arbs controlled more than 25 percent of the outstanding shares, 10 percent of which were already in McDermott's hands. They knew Gray was a committed fighter. They had strong doubts that even with the state takeover laws then in existence, and given a few successful defenses in the recent past, Babcock could keep itself independent. The real issues for arbitrageurs were these:

• When would United clear all the defensive legal hurdles thrown at it? Timing is critical to the arbitrageur, who pays high interest on the capital he invests. Even a week, when investments and borrowing are so large, makes a big difference in the rate of return. But here, the arbitrageurs knew the matter could be tied up for months.

• Would all the legal obstacles eventually convince Gray he should give up? Here the arbs were pretty certain they understood their man. Gray was a fighter, even if he bid low-ball.

• Most important, would there be another bidder? The arbs had by now grown accustomed to bidding contests, and this one had all the makings of a potential winner. The efforts to find out whether a second bid is coming are traditionally intense, whatever the purported insider-trading restrictions.

Whatever the arbitrageurs' certainty that a bidding contest would get under way, they could have in no way anticipated the intensity of it.

As J. Ray McDermott accrued the stock, its management became increasingly convinced that Babcock was the candidate for a bid from them. Morgan could not assure McDermott they would win, but he was certain of what would become a key factor in future contests: *McDermott probably could not lose.* If Harry Gray bid too high for them, they would drop out and sell the stock they had bought at a very substantial profit. In fact, Morgan pointed out, buying more stock would in effect kill two birds with one stone. The more stock they owned, the easier it would be to fight United, especially if Zipf did not agree to support United's bid. The more stock they owned, the more profit they would make if they lost to United.

Morgan also knew one other thing. He recognized that the recalcitrant Zipf, who had joined Babcock in 1942, might not be open to an approach by McDermott as a white knight. He did not want to take any chances. He wanted a foothold well before he approached Zipf with a counteroffer. Once McDermott owned 5 percent of Babcock, it would have to make a public announcement of its purchases. After having accumulated just under 5 percent, Morgan had one of his Smith Barney colleagues call Zipf to tell him McDermott was interested in making a bid for the company. In Morgan's words, Zipf "stonewalled" Smith Barney. "He wouldn't talk," says Morgan. "I think Marty Lipton had him convinced he could keep him independent. George Zipf would not believe anyone could touch him." Later, Zipf claimed he was only seeking the highest price for his shareholders. In fact, however, he would not allow his investment bankers, Morgan Stanley, to negotiate with McDermott.

McDermott continued to buy up stock, and soon announced, on a Schedule 13D, that it owned more than 5 percent of Babcock. It also stated that at the moment, the purpose of its stock purchases was only for investment. The schedule requires such a statement of purpose, and the courts have seldom challenged the traditionally innocuous claim even after the most hostile tender offers ensued. Within days, the litigation-happy Babcock now sued McDermott. Again, it was a common ploy to buy time and delay any further purchases. McDermott continued to buy, however, before court action could stop it. Babcock sued on May 4. On May 12, McDermott announced that it owned just under 10 percent of the company.

During this period, Babcock's shares continued to climb. The big purchases of shares had now convinced the arbitrageurs that another bidder was waiting in the wings. And McDermott's purchases themselves bid up the stock. When they had stopped buying, McDermott had paid an average price of $42.75 for each share of Babcock, a total of just over $51.5 million. McDermott was clearly playing for keeps. The arbs were convinced a bid for control of the company was coming.

In the meantime, however, United, under the direction of Joe Flom, was fighting the Babcock litigation defense on all fronts. With several suits as a shield, Zipf thought he could feel confident in disdaining McDermott's advances. But by the time the weather was turning warm, the curtain started to fall on Zipf's zealous defense.

The suit to stop McDermott's purchases never had a chance, but McDermott was not to buy more stock anyway. The first star that dimmed for Zipf in what was to be a constellation was a ruling by the Ohio State Securities Commission. After about two months of deliberation, the commission ruled on June 3 that the United offer did not violate the Ohio State takeover statutes. Lipton immediately appealed to the Ohio Common Pleas court. In the meantime, the federal court was hearing Babcock's claim to stop the suit on antitrust grounds. But the court refused to issue an injunction to delay the tender offer, so, if it cleared other hurdles, the tender offer could go through. On July 15, the Ohio federal court refused to grant Lipton's appeal. Aside from a government antitrust suit, only one legal barrier remained for United. Babcock had requested that the merger be stopped by the Nuclear Regulatory Commission, the federal agency that had to grant approval if nuclear energy was involved. In early August, the NRC gave United the clearance. Says Lipton: "They won everyplace."

The most important legacy of the most important deal of the twelve-year takeover movement was to be found in this round of legal battles. The advantage of a "total litigation" defense was its sheer aggressiveness. But when the best defense fails, it suggests that anyone is now ready prey for the aggressive bidder. That was the lesson of Babcock's failure. To the arbitrageurs, it was the most pleasant one they could imagine. No matter how hard a target company tried to defeat a bidder, it probably could not. The courts continued to rule in favor of the right of shareholders to get the highest bid. The antitrust authorities were getting progressively more lenient, challenging fewer mergers. Even where state takeover laws did work, they would almost certainly eventually be overturned by the U.S. Supreme Court, which would indeed eventually rule that federal law superseded state law. Ironically, in the second half of 1977, several bids would not succeed, and overenthusiastic arbitrageurs would take severe losses. But longer term, the lesson would hold. Once a company was bid for, it was almost certain to lose its independence. Fewer than one out of five target companies remained independent in this period. Arbitrageurs had discovered a money machine, and the Babcock & Wilcox battle would teach that lesson to a broad, eager audience of new investors.

Harry Gray and his aides were fully prepared to issue his tender offer, once he had received the green light from the Nuclear Regulatory Commission. But in a surprise to the Wall Street community, now accustomed to Gray's cautious bids, he upped the ante considerably. His first bid had been for $42 a share. Now, with the prospect of another bidder in the wings, Gray would bid $48 a share. On August 5, United made the announcement. It issued a new tender offer for all 12.2 million Babcock shares at the new price, the total cash bid equal to $584 million. Speculation was raised in the press about whether Gray's original bid was well informed. And again the wisdom of bidding on the basis only of publicly available documents was questioned. Of course, competitive tactics played a large part in the raised bid. Ed Large, United's general counsel and a close adviser to Gray, says that they thought they could win if they bid higher.

McDermott's team had been working feverishly before the new bid from United was made. John Morgan, with Ed Kelly's help, had devised a financial package to take over Babcock that McDermott could live with. The general guideline was to outbid United for part of the company, and then buy the remaining shares with a later offer, ideally for securities—stock, bonds, or other "paper." The objective was to lock in enough shares in the first partial bid, typically called the first step, to chase Harry Gray away.

Just a few days before United's new bid, John Morgan visited Zipf and told him the McDermott board had approved an offer of $55 a share in cash for up to 4.3 million shares, or 35 percent of the company. With McDermott's previous purchases, that would give it about 45 percent of Babcock. Morgan presented the offer formally in a letter. But Morgan says Zipf still would not talk. Nor would he let his bankers, Morgan Stanley, discuss any further bids with McDermott.

Losing in the Ohio courts would finally change Zipf's mind about the attractiveness of McDermott's offer. On August 12, he announced publicly that McDermott had presented Babcock with a counteroffer. He neglected to mention the price. McDermott wasted no time. It issued a press release announcing that it had just bid $55 a share for the third of Babcock's shares and that it would purchase the remainder with securities.

It was now time for Zipf to throw in the towel. To Zipf, the friendlier McDermott was much more appealing as an acquirer than Harry Gray and United. Reluctantly, on August 14, and with the advice of Lipton and Morgan Stanley, he accepted McDermott's advances, and recommended that shareholders take McDermott's offer, not United's.

Because of Zipf's delay, time was critical. Again, a rush to file the appropriate tender offer documents with the Securities and Exchange Commission was under way. Morgan says they filed on the weekend, allowing them to have their offer expire the day before United's.

The nature of the bidding battle that followed would be among the most intriguing of any deal over the period. Zipf had Morgan Stanley's team of Bob Greenhill, Yerger Johnstone, and Joe Fogg, hired recently from Lehman Brothers, together with Morgan and Kelly for McDermott. Lipton, who was also an integral part of the team, says the most difficult part of the proceedings was to get Morgan Stanley and Smith Barney to communicate. United's team consisted of Gray, Hennessy, and Large, working with White Weld's Hallingby and Felix Rohatyn, whom Gray had brought in for additional advice. Rohatyn had been Gray's chief adviser in his acquisition of Otis Elevator.

What dominated the tactics on each side, however, was one key perception. McDermott saw itself as the underdog, who had to fight diligently and aggressively if it had a chance to win. And it would do just that. Gray and United saw themselves as top dogs, several times McDermott's size. United was offering cash for all Babcock's outstanding shares. McDermott was only paying cash for one third of the shares, securities to come at some undetermined time in the future.

Hallingby says that it was harder for United to line up the arbs than he originally thought. Arnie Amster of Smith Barney says, by contrast, that United was much better at getting the arbs to tender than his side was. What United was counting on was that cash today was far more valuable to an arb than securities at some future date. The time value of money would reduce profits as interest costs ate into the investment. Furthermore, the arbs wanted their profits so they could invest in new deals. The rule of thumb suggested that the second step in McDermott's offer would not be completed for three or four months. Securities would be more valuable to conventional shareholders, because a simple exchange of securities was tax-free, as long as the shareholder retained the shares of the acquiring entity, but such advantages seldom appealed to arbitrageurs, who would in turn sell those shares anyway, and incur a tax liability.

With these considerations in mind, United's team did not try to deliver a killing blow against McDermott. On August 18, six days after the McDermott offer, United raised its bid for all shares to $55, some $670 million in all, only matching McDermott's price.

Morgan Stanley's Johnstone is given credit for the next step in the bidding contest. Morgan had already built up its reputation for bidding hard when it wanted something. Now it was representing the target and it made the same case to its white knight. Morgan Stanley urged McDermott to raise the bid by a substantial amount in order to show its determination, and perhaps to scare Gray off. Moreover, every increment in the bidding was cheaper for McDermott than it was for United in terms of cash outlay. McDermott was only buying 35 percent of the shares.* And it already owned 1.2 million shares at a far lower average cost—under $43 a share. Of course, the total purchase price to McDermott would always be less than it would be to United, because of those original stock purchases. This was precisely John Morgan's tactic all along.

McDermott agreed to raise its bid on the very next day to $60 a share. Large of United admits they were surprised by McDermott's temerity. Four days later United came back with a bid that looked limp. It raised its offer to only $58.50 a share. If Paul Hallingby can justly be accused of any fault, it was that he was' not persuasive enough to get Gray to bid higher. On the ability to wield such influence are investment bankers' careers made. Quick to react, McDermott immediately raised its bid to $62.50 a share. Again, United was probably surprised by McDermott's decisiveness, a very deliberate tactic on the part of McDermott, which was now consulting closely with Babcock & Wilcox's team.

By an arbitrageur's calculation, the bids were fairly close. Assuming that McDermott would offer a package of securities worth $62.50 in a few months, and then deducting interest costs on the borrowed capital, the offers were within pennies of each other, depending on one's assumptions. The expiration date of United's offer was the following day, August 25. And in that twenty-four-hour period one of the most unusual stories of financial one-upmanship, and hard work, would unfold. It would make the weaker party the winner.

Morgan Stanley conceived the idea on August 24 of having Babcock & Wilcox issue a dividend of $2.50 to be paid to current

---

*The cost of the second step did have to be weighed, and would not be slight to McDermott if it paid in stock. In fact, it could dilute earnings considerably.

shareholders. Babcock made the announcement at three P.M., only a night before United's offer was to expire and shareholders would have to tender their shares. The purpose of the dividend was to induce arbitrageurs to tender to McDermott because it assured them that they would receive that extra $2.50 in cash for the shares they still held after McDermott's partial tender. The $2.50 would defray some of the interest cost on the investment funds tied up until McDermott came up with the package of securities. With United's all-cash bid, the arbs would not get the $2.50 dividend; United would when it bought the shares.

Worried that the special dividend would persuade arbs to tender to McDermott, United announced at about five P.M. that it would pass half of Babcock's special dividend to shareholders of record that day if it succeeded in acquiring the company. But by that time, events were under way that would make McDermott the winner. It is not entirely clear how McDermott got enough shareholders and arbitrageurs to tender to it. Those on the McDermott and Babcock team, including Marty Lipton and Arnie Amster, made the rounds through the night. That same night, McDermott, apparently caught off guard by Babcock's proposal for the dividend, decided that it would pass along not half but all of the dividends to stockholders. McDermott's team figured that with that extra, they topped United's offer by about 85 cents a share. In addition, they would point out that some corporations would pay an effective tax rate of only 7.5 percent on the dividend, because such income was largely excluded from taxes for corporations. Finally, McDermott also decided to raise the number of shares it would accept from 4.3 million to 4.8 million shares. Amster thought the last step was unnecessary. The McDermott team had enough ammunition to persuade the arbitrageurs to tender to it.

Early the next morning, McDermott counted its shares and was mildly surprised, as well as overjoyed, that it had received its minimum number of shares: about 20 percent. The tender was therefore consummated, and McDermott made a public announcement. Soon after that announcement appeared on the news wires, McDermott also first made public its decision to pass on all the dividends to shareholders of record, and that it was raising its offer to 4.8 million shares.

Less than thirty minutes later, the Dow Jones news wire ran a story that would subsequently be controversial. The story stated that McDermott had more than 30 percent of the shares; 30 percent was the threshold that would probably keep Gray away. United announced that it would extend its deadline two hours, to twelve noon, after McDermott reported the new terms of its offer. But once word was out that McDermott had 30 percent of the vote, McDermott was confident Gray would drop out. A little before noon, United folded its hand and announced its withdrawal from the contest. The poorer, smaller, and more determined side had won. Technically, McDermott's tender offer was open until September 3. As of that date, more than 9.3 million of Babcock's 12.2 million shares were tendered to McDermott.

John Morgan says the clue that McDermott was going to win, and that United had lost some of its determination, was the bid by Gray of $58.50, actually below McDermott's $60 offer. He says at that point, McDermott decided to show how determined it was and bid still higher right away. Morgan Stanley, says John Morgan, was always urging McDermott to bid still higher. But John Morgan maintains that McDermott was not prepared to bid any higher than $62.50. In fact, Smith Barney had already had a press release in preparation announcing McDermott's withdrawal from the bidding.

Whether or not McDermott would have dropped out remains conjecture. It is intriguing that Harry Gray, who had already raised his bid from $42 a share to $58.50, more than $200 million in total, would not raise the ante another 25 or 30 million dollars. On the other hand, that kind of logic can carry bidding endlessly higher. Inco's Charles Baird probably wished he had adopted such a discipline in his runaway bidding for ESB three long years before.

But Gray did not lose interest in Babcock. Several months later, while McDermott and Morgan Stanley were still trying to work out a package of securities to buy the remaining shares of Babcock, Paul Hallingby and Felix Rohatyn held an unusual meeting with John Morgan in Hallingby's Park Avenue apartment. Hallingby and Rohatyn represented Gray, and they told John Morgan, who was representing McDermott at the meeting, that Harry Gray, claims Morgan, might consider a bid for J. Ray McDermott.

Morgan was furious and went right to the press. He issued a press release for McDermott the next day announcing that United was considering a bid for McDermott. The release also stated that United said it might consider hostile action.

Morgan's going public with the meeting infuriated Hallingby, who did not speak to him for years afterward. In newspaper accounts, Harry Gray denied that United had studied McDermott or was prepared to make an offer. He claimed that at most, the discussions were exploratory. McDermott and Babcock were having trouble coming up with a package of securities for the rest of Babcock's shares. Gray wanted to see whether, according to one newspaper account, "there is something we can do." Gray did not pursue the matter any further.

The two winning investment banking firms profited handsomely from the merger of McDermott and Babcock & Wilcox. Smith Barney earned in total about $2.5 million. Morgan Stanley, whose fee was partly computed as a percentage of the increase in the bids over the initial bid, earned nearly $2.7 million. The incentives for bankers to find more deals, and to push bidding contests higher, were clearly growing.

But the most significant result of the contest for Babcock & Wilcox was that it put the major arbitrageurs on the map. The magic of this deal for them was that once the bidding between McDermott and United was under way, there was almost no losing. The arbs had bought into the deal almost immediately on the bid by Harry Gray. According to *Fortune* magazine, Ivan Boesky was one of the first, but once the courts cleared United's tender, and Gray raised the bid to $48 a share, the arbs bought with a vengeance. Some bought right up to the closing bell. The biggest positions were held by Richard Rosenthal at Salomon, Guy Wyser-Pratte at Bache, Robert Rubin at Goldman Sachs, and Boesky. These four alone had investments of $100 million, much of that, of course, borrowed. Over the course of the deal, they would earn $30 million. Boesky himself earned about $7.5 million of profit on the deal for himself and his partners.

In all, it was the biggest killing the arbitrageurs had ever made, and it would attract more publicity to them than arbitrage had ever received before. Even *Time* magazine featured an article on "Wall Street's highest rollers." What it would do as well was to attract more investment money to takeover speculation. Until Babcock & Wilcox, takeover fever was at a comparatively low pitch. Within a couple of years, the prices of target companies would exceed the opening bid within minutes, in anticipation of higher bids to come. Even after United's original $42 bid for Babcock, the stock only moved up to about $40 a share.

Yet by the early 1980s even a $7.5 million take from one deal would look relatively small. At the peak of the bidding contest, arbitrageurs would earn up to $40 million on one deal, and more. And fees to individual investment banking houses would reach $20 million for one deal, and more. But the contest for Babcock & Wilcox was really only the beginning.

Ironically, the arbitrageurs would have done better had they tendered to United Technologies. Most major arbs, including Boesky and Rubin, did initially tender to United. When McDermott looked like the winner, they had to scramble to retrieve their stock and tender to McDermott. What they did not anticipate was that fashioning the package of securities that was to be paid for the remaining shares—the so-called back end—would prove far harder and take longer than anyone had anticipated. The first source of controversy was over the actual amount McDermott had paid for the first half of Babcock's stock. When the tender expired on September 3, McDermott had collected 39 percent of the outstanding shares of Babcock. Together with its original holdings, it had just under 50 percent of all the Babcock shares. It was now required to devise a package of securities that would be equal to the cash offer for the shares.

But what was the cash offer? *The Wall Street Journal* reported, and ran on the Dow Jones news wire, that McDermott had effectively paid $65 a share. That combined the $62.50 actual bid with the special dividend of $2.50. Morgan Stanley latched on to this story as evidence that the second step of the purchase should also equal $65 a share. Though bedfellows in their fight to ward off United Technologies, Morgan Stanley and Smith Barney again squared off on this matter. McDermott refused to pay the $65 price, and Babcock took them to court.

In addition, according to John Morgan, the books of Babcock were a mess. McDermott demanded complete audits and it took months for the accountants to go through the ledgers and for the two sides to agree on just what added up to what.

In November, negotiations between Smith Barney and Morgan Stanley on what the package of securities would consist of were at last under way. The original suggestion was to come up with a combination of bonds and common stock. The idea was to balance the package with part debt and part equity. That would provide a certain amount of stability, because the two had different character-istics that would offset each other under varying circumstances.

The final package was still more complex. Morgan eventually agreed to accept $62.50 a share for the remaining Babcock shares, and the two sides chose a combination of preferred shares. Each shareholder would receive one share of a preferred stock that was convertible into common stock and one share that was not. The dividends paid on the preferred would determine the value of the issues, because they would basically trade as debt. Morgan says the last disagreement was on the level of the dividend to be paid on the nonconvertible preferred stock.

Just a couple of days after the flare-up with United Technolo-gies over its purported bid for McDermott, the terms of the merger were announced. To testify to the precision with which the terms were calculated, the combined preferred shares sold in the market-place on its first day of trading for $62.625, one eighth of a point higher than the target price. For the entire quarter of the calendar year ended June 30, the average price of the package was $62.41.

The arbitrageurs, however, as well as other shareholders, real-ized less money than they anticipated because of the long delay. Most computed they would receive their money for the second step of the McDermott offer within three to four months. That would have made it sometime in December. In fact, the new package of securities did not start trading until late the following February. The arbs had clearly lost a couple of months of interest, a meaningful amount given the size of their borrowings.

McDermott had paid about $750 million for Babcock & Wilcox. The bidding had been escalated by $240 million since United's initial bid. A handful of arbitrageurs alone had earned $30 million of that as pure profit for their speculation. The winning investment bankers earned $5 million between them. The final price represented a market value nearly twice the value that the stock market itself had placed on Babcock & Wilcox in the spring of 1977. In short, Wall Street had never seen anything like this. And the profits of the bankers and the arbs had opened their eyes to the prospect for more deals.

Moreover, this time around, the press had caught on. *The New York Times* and *The Wall Street Journal* covered the proceedings closely. Follow-up stories continued for weeks. *Fortune* magazine had discovered arbitrage. *Time* magazine led its arbitrage article this way: "Arbitrage until a few weeks ago was only a somewhat mysterious word to the average investor."

Babcock & Wilcox had changed all that. Now the centerpiece of the takeover movement was firmly established. It was the bidding contest. As long as an investment banker could find a stock selling below its book value, you had a fighting chance to sell it as a takeover target to a hungry corporation eager to join the pack of acquisition makers. In 1977, the year Babcock & Wilcox was taken over, $22 billion of deals was consummated. In 1978, the dollar level would rise to $34 billion.

10

To many participants in mergers back in the 1970s, the change in the environment after the Babcock & Wilcox battle was fought and finished was clearcut. The profits and publicity of the contest made takeovers the hottest game on Wall Street to the speculators. But more important, the willingness of two giants to cross swords with such determination at last took the shame out of the hostile bid, at least in the eyes of once-hesitant chief executives. Now, said many investment bankers and lawyers, it was no longer as difficult to sell a CEO on whether or not he should make a hostile bid. It had risen to become an acceptable management tool for expanding and reorienting a company. In the next few years the hostile bid would become not merely another tool, but the predominant one, and a threat that literally every management in the nation would have to deal with.

Once the CEOs acknowledged the practicality of a hostile bid, another turn in the nature of the merger movement would also occur. Where once a takeover decision had been dominated by whether or not to undertake a tender offer, now takeovers would be dominated by which tactics to adopt. And the tactics became more clever, more hostile, and more bold. The tactical experts—the investment bankers and lawyers—won even more influence with their clients. After all, of the many ironies that the business community drew from the Babcock & Wilcox tender contest, one of the most telling was that the smaller company had won. And while some still claimed Harry Gray had lost only because he was unwilling to bid any higher, at the time McDermott's win looked like a consummate tactical victory. The late 1970s would be characterized by this emphasis on tactics, which would give the takeover movement a body of concerns apart from its original purpose. As in every war, dealing with the tactics would often muddle the original intention as well as the ultimate objectives. As the frenzy of the contest began to outweigh the purpose of that contest, the stakes seemed poignantly out of perspective. At stake in this takeover movement were hundreds of thousands of jobs, reinvestment in industry, and the ability of America to compete with a fast-growing industrial revolution across the globe. But what would supersede all that was the drive to win, encouraged by the investment bankers, and often at a very heavy price.

In 1976 the total dollar value of mergers rose substantially, to $20 billion from only $12 billion in 1975. Now, the takeover contagion would spread even more quickly. In 1978, there would be announcements of mergers worth $34 billion. In 1979, that would rise again to $43.5 billion. As another way of measuring it, the takeover staffs of major Wall Street firms would and were double in those few years. In all, one investment banker figures that about two hundred Wall Street professionals were out seeking to engineer mergers and takeovers by 1980, compared to perhaps twenty in 1974.

For the individual deals themselves, these should be called the tactical years. Several acquisitions, and attempted acquisitions, that would take place in the next few years reflected best the new emphasis on tactics. In 1977, Eaton Corp., based in Cleveland, had 120 plants with 46,000 employees making transmissions, truck parts, and materials-handling equipment. In 1976, it earned $90 million on $1.8 billion in sales. In 1977, a year of economic expansion in the United States, its sales increased to $2.1 billion and profits rose to $106 million.

Eaton was strong, well entrenched in America's manufacturing bedrock. But it must have looked with envy at the smaller Carborundum Company, based in Niagara Falls, New York. In 1976, Carborundum had just come off five consecutive years of record profits. Sales had risen from $340 million in 1972 to $614 million. Profits had risen in the same period from $17 million to $33 million.

Carborundum was also a company with substantial promise. It produced abrasives for industrial use and made insulating material and pollution-control products. But Carborundum had also established a record for successful research and development. Its management, widely respected, was well known for pouring money into R&D. In 1976, that amount came to $40 million, a substantial investment for a company its size.

Carborundum was working on a new method for removing pollutants. It had also developed a promising new pilot light. But what tantalized Eaton, and many others, was Carborundum's development of ceramic parts for engines. Engines manufactured out of ceramics could be used at very high temperatures. In turn, at high temperatures, an engine could be run very efficiently, requiring far less fuel than under more normal temperatures. No surprise then that in this age of soaring oil prices, Eaton, too, saw energy conservation as the stuff of business dreams. And in this age of takeovers, why build your own dream when it was so much cheaper to buy it?

Eaton management, under the tutelage of Lehman Brothers, first approached Carborundum with a merger proposal. When Carborundum turned Eaton down, the Cleveland firm filed a tender offer for $47 a share. The price was immediately deemed cheap by the Wall Street pros. It came to only about twelve times earnings, and it was less than Carborundum's stated book value of nearly $49 a share. Carborundum filed an antitrust suit and started to look for a white knight. Kennecott, the copper and metals company, came forward within a week with a competing bid.

Once again, a bidding contest was under way, each bid closely weighed for its tactical logic. When the bidding ended, Kennecott had agreed to pay $66 a share, or a total of $565 million. That was about 40 percent again as high as Eaton's first bid. The bidding contest had driven the price to about double the market's original valuation of the company, just as Babcock's price was driven to nearly double its stock market valuation. The speed and size of this contest was again eye-popping. And it followed close on the heels of the Babcock & Wilcox epic.

Eaton, the loser, would not be satisfied to sit back and lick its wounds. It had made the decision to search for acquisitions, and it would stick with it. Many other corporations were making the same choice. As the net of such acquisition-hungry corporations widened, the potential for takeover fireworks grew with it. In early 1978, Eaton would become involved in a round of takeover attempts that would foreshadow what almost everyone agrees would be the lowpoint in the movement four years later, the Martin Marietta–Bendix bidding contest, which would also involve Allied Corp. and United Technologies.

In the coming battle, the number of companies involved would total six, but the stakes would be far smaller than in the Bendix-Marietta struggle. Several of the same advisers would cut their teeth on this many-sided battle, and corporations once friends would turn on one another like family members who were now fighting for an inheritance. The events could almost certainly not have occurred only a couple of years earlier. By 1978, the takeover contagion was fast spreading and those corporations susceptible to its temptations were now reaching a threshold. Enough were now involved that any tender offer could breed a competing bid, and sometimes bids from several corporations.

The potential in this new network of likely acquirers was not lost on Kidder Peabody's Martin Siegel, who was then adviser to Joseph Gaziano of Tyco Laboratories Inc. in Exeter, New Hampshire. Early in 1977, Tyco began to buy up shares on the open market of the Leeds & Northrup Co., a Pennsylvania manufacturer of electronic equipment. Tyco was well aware that if it did not win Leeds itself, the smaller company could benefit by buying up the shares and selling out to the higher bidder. The tactic J. Ray McDermott had used as a sort of backstop was alluring to other corporate managers. Wall Street advisers assured the CEOs that it was eminently practical. Thomas Mellon Evans had shown that it was profitable.

When Tyco's stock purchases were publicly announced, Leeds tried to protect itself by quickly selling 10 percent of itself to Milwaukee-based Cutler-Hammer Inc., a manufacturer of electronics. Siegel says proudly it was probably the first time so much smaller a company was able to put a larger company "in play." But actually Tyco took the contest a bold step further. When Leeds sold shares to Cutler-Hammer, Tyco in turn sold its 19 percent of Leeds to Cutler-Hammer. Tyco turned around, helped by the funds Cutler paid it for Leeds, and Tyco bought up 32 percent of Cutler-Hammer itself over several months.

Cutler immediately sought a white knight, and thought it had found one in Koppers Co., Inc., a construction, manufacturing, and engineering firm based in Pittsburgh. Koppers eventually bought 21 percent of Cutler, and Tyco started to look for a bigger buyer for its block who might be able to fight off Koppers. Eaton, still hungry for a major acquisition after its loss to Kennecott, was an obvious possibility. It had since completed a couple of smaller acquisitions. Tyco sold its 32 percent of Cutler to Eaton, with the provision that if Eaton eventually took over Cutler-Hammer, it would sell Tyco back its shares in Leeds & Northrup, Tyco's original target. And Tyco made several million dollars on the sale, anyway. Cutler would ultimately thwart Tyco by selling its Leeds shares to General Signal, the electronic systems and controls company based in Stamford, Connecticut.

When it was all over, General Signal had taken over Leeds & Northrup, Eaton had won Cutler-Hammer, and Tyco had a tidy profit. It also had the distinction of setting in motion one of the earliest of round-robin takeover festivals. The tactical takeover movement was well under way.

The new hostile takeover ethic was not lost on David Mahoney, a businessman who liked the limelight and was known to be quick off the mark. He had taken over the vast food conglomerate built by Norton Simon. Based in New York, Mahoney had been at the top of the city's social ladder, one of those rare powerful businessmen interested and active in cultural events as well as politics. He was clearly a man who relished a role as a leader.

In May 1977, Babcock & Wilcox was still bottled up in the courts, but Mahoney's willingness to launch a quick strike for Avis, the giant auto rental company, reflected the new aggressive attitude. Avis had been in the hands of a court-appointed trustee since 1975. In 1971 the Justice Department ordered ITT to divest itself of the car rental company because, they argued, its ownership violated the antitrust laws. ITT searched for a buyer, with no success, and in 1975 placed its 47 percent of Avis shares with a trustee chosen by a Hartford court.

In the spring of 1977, Fuqua Industries, Inc., a conglomerate under the control of its founder, J. B. Fuqua, bid $15.50 per share for all Avis shares. Just before the Memorial Day weekend, the court trustee, Richard Joyce Smith, resisted the Fuqua offer. Ira Harris, the Salomon Brothers investment banker, saw this as an opportunity. On Memorial Day weekend he contacted Mahoney, who had already expressed an interest in Avis, and told him he thought the time was right for a bid. By the end of the weekend, Mahoney had made a decision to go. It was fast thinking by any standards, but over the years fast decisions would become commonplace in the takeover movement. Mahoney's quick decision stands as one of the first of its kind.

Mahoney, with Marty Lipton as adviser, met with Richard Joyce Smith on June 1. The trustee indicated he had already turned down another offer for $20 a share. They knew they would have to bid higher. What would rile the Avis board, and other corporate bidders for Avis, was that the trustee would agree to a bid from Mahoney two days later of only $20.25. Moreover, the trustee had apparently been prepared to accept a bid even before it was made, a press release without a dollar figure already having been typed up for distribution before the Norton Simon team made its bid.

The Norton Simon team was also able to get a fast decision from a Justice Department that had long been very careful about the antitrust considerations of an Avis purchase. Within two weeks the Justice Department cleared the Norton Simon takeover. The Avis board of directors was not about to sit by idly, however. They had hired Marty Siegel of Kidder, and sought out a white knight. Takeover contests were falling into an established pattern.

The Avis board rejected the Mahoney bid at $20.25. But at the court hearing to consider the bid, the fast-moving Mahoney suddenly surprised the opposition with a higher bid. He offered $22 a share and he kept the offer open only until six that evening. Richard Joyce Smith accepted the bid in the courtroom. The Avis board immediately tried to appeal the ruling, but soon relented and accepted the Mahoney victory. Late in June, Norton Simon bid for the remaining publicly held shares of Avis and had control of the company. To Wall Street it would be a lesson in decisiveness. Mahoney won because he was willing to bid higher, and to bid quickly. For the defense, it was a lesson in the high price of being unprepared.

As for the economic stakes—the real world of profits and jobs and investment—the muddled pattern was also becoming set. Even Wall Street agreed that Kennecott paid an extravagant price for Carborundum. "That was a whopper," said one arbitrageur. Says a former executive for Carborundum: "I don't know how their advisers got to that price except by assuming a very low discount rate." In other words, the future growth of Carborundum could justify the price only under very optimistic assumptions.

The executive went on to say more. He had been involved in searching for acquisitions for Carborundum, as well as fulfilling several other financial and marketing capacities at the firm. "These executives treat their takeovers like toys that you move around. They discovered that it was easier to buy than to build. But they never realized how hard it was to manage once you did buy. Kennecott spent so much to take us over that they had no money left to help us expand. The R&D budget was cut, though some of that was going on before the merger. Within a couple of years, the R&D department was reduced from about three hundred people to only one hundred." R&D, of course, is what Carborundum had been known for.

And of the promise of ceramic motor parts and superefficient engines, the executive said that even back then, there was little genuine optimism that the research could pay off any time in the near future. "It's one thing to be at the forefront of technology, but none of the engineering had been done yet."

Countless mergers would take place, and had taken place, on the strength of a technological promise. Many during this period were linked to the search for low-cost energy. Babcock & Wilcox's promise was linked to the high price of energy. There was talk of electric cars and the rise of diesel power. Carborundum reeked with technological mythology. And time and again, astute businessmen accepted these promises, no doubt with the aid of their pencil-sharp investment bankers. "They treated these companies like toys," the former Carborundum executive repeated. "Of course, they did take much of our management into Kennecott." But when asked whether an old-line metals company really needed such high-powered management, he shrugged: "Probably not. It's one thing to be a good manager in one business. It's another to come in right away and make smart decisions about another." There is very little of the old Carborundum left in the mid-1980s. No one argues that it was a sensible acquisition. Kennecott itself was bought by Standard Oil of Ohio in 1981 for $2 billion.

The evolution of Harry Gray, from a chief executive who was hesitant to launch hostile takeovers to one who did not hesitate to move swiftly and decisively, sums up the changing attitude of America's major corporate chiefs. They probably learned from Gray. And the lesson was that hostile takeovers were no shame, and that they could produce a rising stock price for shareholders in a time when conventional economic and business growth did not. No doubt they also came to believe they could manage these disparate companies well. And probably that presumption met the least resistance. The temptation to take on and manage "better" a new company must have been akin to the romantic yearning to produce a movie or write a book. Anyone can "write," of course, if he can afford a typewriter. Anyone can produce a movie if he can afford the several millions to do it. Anyone can run just about any company if he cares to buy it.

To hear business executives tell it, the talk at the country club began to change. Every company executive would decry unfriendly takeovers in the earlier years—everyone was vulnerable; every job was on the line. But soon after Babcock & Wilcox, the waging of a hostile takeover contest began to confer prestige on corporate executives. It mattered less how you got there, just that you got bigger. And a hostile tender got your name in the newspapers as well.

There was machismo to it all, too. As tactics got more bold, the CEO as warrior was a far more potent image than simply the CEO as the powerful head of an organization with tens of thousands of employees. The Wall Street advisers were his superb technicians, and if there was a hint of Iago in them, to the CEOs' Othello, it is likely the CEOs were about as unaware as the Moor was of how their advisers may have been victimizing them.

If those on the offense got bolder, those on the defense were also armed with new tactics and deft defensive specialists. At the least, a target could win delays long enough to find a white knight or simply discourage a bidder who would have his money tied up too long. Judges, too, had not yet altogether thrown their weight on the side of the shareholder, as they would do by the 1980s. Some of them still looked at a hostile bid as an incursion on the rights of managers and did not give precedence to the right of the shareholders, the owners, to receive the highest available price for their shares. Marty Siegel of Kidder Peabody would make a standard speech in those days that the odds were good that you could remain independent, or at least be taken over by a white knight to your liking, if you had the right defense. Siegel was trying to sell defensive programs in order to gain clients for Kidder, but during that period, targets would have more defensive tactics than they would ever enjoy again until the advent of the poison pill.

The need for good defense would be driven home, however, by an extraordinary battle between Harry Gray of United Technologies and Melvin Holme of Carrier Corporation. Carrier, the highly regarded manufacturer of air conditioners, was based in Syracuse. In the nine months of its fiscal year ended July 1978, sales rose more than 60 percent, to nearly $1.6 billion over the year before, and profits rose still faster, to $72 million. Gray, who already had Otis Elevator, had been thinking about acquiring Carrier for a long time. The alternative for Gray at the time was Trane Corp. A takeover by Gray of Carrier would make United Technologies the twenty-second-largest industrial company in the Fortune 500. In mid-September, Gray bid $28 a share for Carrier's common shares. Carrier also had an issue of preferred stock that was convertible into common. That had to be bought as well, and was included in the bid. It would take six months, but Gray would win the furious contest without having to raise his offer.

If there was any more clearcut example of a management's short-sightedness than that of Carrier, the story had not yet been told. The lesson in general for corporate America was that if you are going to fight a takeover bid, you'd better be very smart about it. The lesson in particular was that you could no longer count on judges to stop mergers on antitrust grounds—at least not very easily.

As usual, Harry Gray met with the Carrier management before he made his hostile bid. He proposed to pay cash for 49 percent of the shares, and consummate a merger for the rest later. If not, United would go ahead with the tender. Carrier's chairman, Melvin Holme, turned him down immediately, eventually calling the United offer blackmail. With lawyers from Davis Polk in attendance, Carrier filed an antitrust suit. Few outside lawyers thought it was a very strong one. United went ahead with the tender, which would expire in early December.

Carrier would call on other defensive tactics as well. It raised its quarterly dividend to shareholders by 25 percent in order to attract support. In early October it agreed to acquire Jenn-Air Corp., which made kitchen equipment, including ranges. The defensive objective was to use up some of the cash on hand and make Carrier less attractive.

If the principal idea was to delay the offer long enough to deter Harry Gray, Carrier underestimated its opponent. Never once did Gray raise the bid in order to woo Carrier harder. Holme of Carrier nevertheless tried to pull out all the stops except the one that could have worked—finding a white knight. The irony was that he himself had served as a white knight when he bought Inmont for $244 million while it was under the attack of a hostile bid from Esmark, the food conglomerate.

Moreover, Carrier had a powerful ally in one of its unions. The United Auto Workers asked the New York State attorney general to block the takeover on grounds that United did not disclose its antiunion activities in its tender filings. The UAW had a longstanding complaint against a United plant in Indiana. The attorney general did impose a temporary ban on the tender. The UAW also warned its own banks that it would be unwise to lend money to United to make this acquisition.

In mid-November, the attorney general lifted his ban. But a
few days later, the Justice Department sued United to stop the
merger, claiming that it sold control devices and electric motor
parts to Carrier, and that that was anticompetitive.

But on November 30, it looked as if United had won the
victory it was seeking. A federal district judge in Syracuse refused to
grant a temporary restraining order to the Justice Department or
Carrier over violation of antitrust laws. It appeared to be the victory
United was waiting for. On December 7, Carrier won a temporary delay in the federal appeals court. It was lifted a little more
than a week later, however. The judge denied the appeal. Again it
looked like a United victory. But again there would be a court-
imposed delay in January 1979. To defense specialists, such delays
were exactly what a target needed in order to find a friendly white
knight. But Holme apparently thought, or was advised, that he
could win outright. At the end of January, United finally got the
go-ahead to acquire Carrier, though it had to keep the company
separate until the Justice Department finished its antitrust investigation. In early April the two companies announced an agreement to
merge had finally been reached. In July the merger was completed—at
$28 a share.

There is little doubt that Carrier's loss to United on the first
bid jarred other corporate chiefs who were not already aware just
how vulnerable they were. It made tactics all the more important.
"You had to know what the chances of winning were," says Marty
Lipton. "That antitrust defense would not wash."

The Justice Department did not complete its work on the
United-Carrier merger until September 1980. It demanded that
United share any air-conditioning or heating trade secrets with its
competitors. Under those circumstances, United could fold Carrier
completely into its tent. For United, it was obviously a small price
to pay. Lipton figures that Carrier's intransigence cost shareholders
a minimum of another $2 a share for their stock. If he had chosen
to bargain with Gray, he almost certainly could have gotten him to
raise the bid. By fighting to the end, it would be generally per-
ceived, he and his advisers did his shareholders an injustice.

*   *   *

There is no easy way for Wall Street investment bankers to escape the charge that the size of the fees they would eventually earn would shape the nature of their offensive and defensive tactics. The simple fact was that if a merger was consummated, Wall Street earned fees that were far more than merely handsome. They would literally become the main profit centers of several investment banks, keep one or two others independent, and make dozens of individual bankers very rich. The lawyers, who rightfully saw themselves as equal if not greater contributors to takeovers, would eventually bristle with jealousy over the huge investment banking fees. The reason is that the lawyers still charged by the hour, even if that charge was very high. The bankers charged as a percentage of the size of a merger, and as mergers got bigger, fees rose astronomically. By the mid-1980s, lawyers, too, were gearing their fee schedules to the size of deals.

The fee explosion also began in the late 1970s. While $1 million fees were not unheard-of, the defensive work of Goldman Sachs in staving off the advances of MCA Inc. for Coca-Cola Bottling Co. of Los Angeles was among the first deals that would set a new high standard for fees for investment bankers.

The network of Coca-Cola Bottling companies was a unique and immensely profitable group of franchises. For the lucky early franchiser, they would provide a monopoly for distribution of the planet's most popular soda. The value of such monopolies would not be lost on the takeover community, and several Coke bottling companies became targets of takeovers in these years. MCA, the respected entertainment company, which owned Universal Pictures, had long sought to diversify out of the unpredictable movie business. Los Angeles had by the mid-1970s been one of the fastest growing areas in the nation, and Coke of L.A. participated proportionally. Between 1974 and 1977, profits of $7 million about doubled.

With Lazard Freres as advisers, MCA's highly regarded chairman, Lew Wasserman, bid $30 per share for all of Coke L.A.'s shares in early October 1977. Coke's earnings per share in 1976 were $2.27. Coke also had a convertible preferred issue outstanding, which MCA bid $58.50 a share for. The all-cash offer came to $140 million. MCA had already bought 3 percent of the common shares and 5 percent of the preferred.

Coke L.A. wanted no part of the offer. It hired Goldman Sachs for the defense and sued MCA in federal court. It charged that MCA had bought stock illegally before the offer, and had announced the offer before filing the proper papers. The objective was to throw up every barrier possible, and was later dropped. Coke management also sent a letter to shareholders urging rejection.

But Goldman was worried MCA would prevail unless it found a white knight. In a matter of days, Goldman had an interested party, Ben Heineman, who ran Northwest Industries. Northwest had completed the acquisition of Microdot with Goldman's help only the year before. Goldman hurriedly arranged for the two managements to meet.

On October 17, Northwest announced a bid of $40 a share for Coke L.A.'s common stock and $78 a share for the convertible preferred, a substantial hike in the stakes of about 30 percent. Coke L.A. endorsed the Northwest bid and embraced its white knight in a letter to shareholders. "Although our initial preference," wrote Arthur MacDonald, Coke L.A.'s chairman, "was to remain an independent company, your Board has concluded that in light of all the circumstances, acceptance of the NIW Inc. offer is in the best interests of the Shareholders, employees and suppliers of the company." All this was decided, of course, within a matter of days, because of the quick expiration dates of the tender offers. Coke L.A. really had no choice but to make the momentous decision in very little time.

The unmistakable winner, however, was Goldman Sachs. They collected 5 percent of the raised bid for their troubles, or about $3 million. What they also did was directly tie the size of the fee to finding a white knight. If they could keep the target company entirely independent, the fee paid to them was at the discretion of the management. But a fee tied to a rising bid was a sure thing.

It is all too facile to accuse investment banks of bias in their search for white knights because of this fee procedure. Some bankers assuredly were more concerned for their clients' welfare than others. But the bias was unambiguous and tantalizing. The fee schedule rewarded very well the finding of white knights with higher bids. And certainly it rewarded well the ability to persuade managements to undertake acquisitions as often as possible.

The question of investment bankers' objectivity came to ironic focus in the proposal to acquire the minority interest of Shell Oil Co. that Royal Dutch still did not own in 1984. Morgan Stanley, employed by Royal Dutch, provided an analysis demonstrating that Shell Oil was worth $53 a share. Goldman Sachs, employed by Shell Oil, gave its opinion that the shares were worth between $80 and $85 each. Goldman would be compensated according to how high a price Shell would receive. Morgan's client, of course, wanted to pay as little as possible. In later litigation, the judge was very explicit about the inadequacy of both opinions. The Morgan opinion, he noted, was based on limited information. "It would defy reason to find that an oil exploration company such as Shell could be valued without any in depth inquiry into the estimated value of the probable reserves," he wrote. As for the valuation made by Goldman Sachs, he concluded that Shell shareholders, "with some justification, must discount the opinion of Goldman Sachs which has a stake in the outcome and is most certainly not impartial."

By the late 1970s, a general fee schedule was more or less set. A banker would get 2 percent for a merger valued at up to $50 million, 1.25 percent up to $125 million, and 1 percent up to $300 million. As mergers reached $1 billion in size, the fees scaled below 1 percent. Eventually, fees of $3 million would no longer be unusual, and indeed would be small compared to the compensation produced by some future deals. It is fair to say that Wall Street had never seen a money machine like the takeover movement before. The prize was great for those who could prove themselves the best takeover tacticians in the business. Within a handful of years, many of these men were running the entire investment banking departments of Wall Street's biggest firms.

Marty Lipton's penchant for bold experimentation would never be riper than it was in those days of the late 1970s when the movement was still testing its tactics and seeking new ones. He called his strategy to take over Becton Dickinson for Sun Oil Co. the "dawn raid." It was probably his boldest step yet, maybe the boldest he would ever take. From this man who would probably be more adventurous in giving advice than anyone else, and in this period of tactical cunning, it was probably the most extreme. And it helped define just how far the takeover practitioners could go, because it would fail.

Becton Dickinson, the health care company located in New Jersey, was as likely a takeover candidate as there was in 1977 and '78. Fairleigh Dickinson, Jr., the son of the founder, had run Becton since the late 1940s. Dickinson moved aside in 1973 to let a new president run the firm while he took the title of chairman, but Dickinson apparently could not let go the reins and friction developed. It came into the open when Dickinson finally disapproved of a proposed acquisition of National Medical Care by Becton. The board removed Dickinson after the deal fell through. Stung, Dickinson, with 5 percent of Becton's stock, suggested to Salomon Brothers that he might be interested in an outright acquisition of the firm his father had founded.

At the time—late 1977—Sun Oil Company, based in Philadelphia, had been a client of Salomon's. The company was considering a recapitalization with Salomon's help, and it had already made open its desire to diversify. Sun, like many giant oil companies, was looking to lessen its dependence on energy. It was also heavy with cash it could not adequately use. Salomon naturally proposed an acquisition of Becton.

Sun's management, headed by Robert Sharbaugh, was quick to say yes to Salomon's suggestion. Salomon had warned them that other buyers were interested in Becton and they had best move fast to find a friendly buyer—a convenient fact for Salomon, eager to make a big score. But probably most alluring, Marty Lipton had conceived of a way to buy up enough Becton shares to assure a victory, without the public relations and legal retaliation that Becton was sure to try to engineer. Becton had loudly rejected a merger offer from American Home Products just recently.

Lipton's plan must have seemed straightforward to the Sun executives, but it was legally daring. Sun could have tried to buy up shares on the open market, but that would have signaled other bidders of its intent, and would have alerted Becton, who could have launched a defense. So would a traditional tender offer, of course.

Lipton, prodded by having in Dickinson, Jr., a 5 percent owner already eager to sell, suggested that Salomon could round up enough big investors in Becton Dickinson to account for 20 percent of the company, maybe more, and could offer them a substantial premium over the current market. Salomon corroborated that there were very big holders of Becton stock and they could contact them all. Sun bought the strategy. On a mid-January afternoon, just after the market closed, Salomon Brothers launched a selling blitz to a targeted list of financial institutions. They would offer them $45 a share for all their Becton shares, pure and simple. That afternoon, trading on Becton closed at $33 a share.

Dickinson's 5 percent was already aboard, and not all institutions chose to sell. But by five-thirty that afternoon, Salomon had commitments for more than 20 percent of Becton's shares. In all, Salomon had bought shares from thirty-three financial institutions, such as the Bank of America and IDS mutual funds, and six individuals. By the end of the evening it had lined up 34 percent of the shares of Becton Dickinson. No seller received more than $45 a share for his stock. What was bold about the tactic was that not all shareholders were given the opportunity to participate. This was a bid to a select few, and in spirit, at least, that violated the idea of public tenders.

That night, and the next day, Sun and Lipton's law firm sent emissaries throughout the nation to collect stock certificates from the sellers. It would take time, and that could be a hurdle. Salomon also got the New York Stock Exchange to halt trading in Becton without telling the Exchange who the bidder was. The first news to Becton, then, was the cancellation of trading in its stock. Only by late Wednesday did Sun contact Becton about the pending purchase of stock, after Sun had rounded up most of their shares. Becton's reaction was to fight it everywhere they could. Unlike their colleagues at Carrier Corp., however, Becton also agreed to talk with potential white knights.

Becton was surprised to find that Sun was not making a tender offer but rather filing a 13D form with the Securities and Exchange Commission that they already had bought a block of one third of the stock from financial institutions and other shareholders. Joe Flom had been hired by Becton some time before, because Becton had known Wall Street was shopping it around as a takeover target. Flom's first defensive response was to try to show that the 13D should have been filed long before it was.

But there was a deeper issue involved. When does an offer to buy shares from a relative handful of shareholders constitute a tender offer? And if it is a tender offer, it must abide by the various rules under the Williams Act. Most important, it must be made available to all shareholders, not a select group of big investors. In the end, the SEC would claim that it was a tender offer. Sun was also able to pick up support from Congress. The SEC sued, as did Becton of course, and several shareholders. The suits were combined and went to trial in November.

The judge would rule against Sun Oil Co., but not before Sharbaugh left his job, some claim over the publicity and personal divisions the action had engendered. The judge ruled that the stock purchases were indeed the equivalent of a public tender offer for the company and that Sun therefore should have abided by the Williams Act. He went on to say that the purchases were designed to get around the safeguards the Williams Act was established to assure.

Sun's immediate reaction was to appeal. But that, too, came to a halt when Sun's new CEO turned his attention to another takeover. Sun bought Texas Pacific Oil from Seagram in a bidding contest for more than $2 billion. Apparently, the giant oil company had decided to stick to its knitting and buy more of what it understood best: oil and gas assets.

What had led to the Becton Dickinson raid in the first place was the lack of an unambiguous definition of just what a tender offer is. The Williams Act is the government's attempt to protect all shareholders. The court found that private purchases, in the manner of Becton Dickinson's, did in effect keep other shareholders out. Those thirty-three institutions and six individuals got a higher price than anyone else. The outcome of the fight for Becton Dickinson was that the lightning move—Marty Lipton's dawn raid—was disallowed. That at least went too far. Tactics had their limits, though by 1986 an approach very similar to Lipton's dawn raid would be allowed by the courts.

*   *   *

If the offense was upbraided in 1978 for going too far, the defense would also lose an important battle. State takeover laws had temporarily turned the balance of power, not so much in favor of targets, but at least to keep them from being top-heavy for acquirers. Legal opinion, however, was growing that the state takeover laws were unconstitutional because they were superseded by federal laws. Should that be found to be true, the state laws would be almost useless. Cases were filed to test the constitutionality in the courts. But in late 1978, acquirers had found a way temporarily to paralyze the laws.

Dart Co., the large consumer products company based in Los Angeles, wanted to acquire Mallory, the makers of Duracell batteries, in late 1978. After approaching Mallory, and being turned away, Dart issued a tender offer at a substantial premium. In mid-November, Dart offered $46 a share in cash for a stock that had closed the day before at under $30. The total price was $215 million.

Again under the tutelage of Marty Lipton, Dart also filed a suit in federal court in Indianapolis. In that suit, Dart asked for a temporary restraining order against the states of Indiana and Delaware that would keep the state anti-takeover statutes from being applied. On the grounds that the law may have been unconstitutional, the courts granted the temporary restraining order. The state laws could not be used. On November 14, Dart's tender was under way. Mallory rejected it the next day. Dart sweetened its offer to $51 a share two days later. On November 20, Mallory, only about one-fifth Dart's size, endorsed the bid.

Dart had won. But so had all other potential acquirers. After Dart-Mallory, many takeovers were accompanied by a suit asking that use of the anti-takeover statutes be blocked. For the most part, they were. It was not until 1982 that the Supreme Court ruled that one of the state laws was unconstitutional. But long before that, those laws had begun to be neutralized. After a few years of legal resistance, raiders had by 1979 the clearest sailing they would enjoy in the takeover movement. They would not get every target they sought, but a drawn-out defense was far harder to put together. The even harder-edge tactics used in the deals that followed were now to be aimed at competing bidders. The targets, with a few notable exceptions, were truly maidens in distress waiting to be rescued by their white knights.

11

In the urban and suburban architecture that houses America's corporate giants today, one can seldom discern the size or community that these corporations represent. A big tower in Hartford does not suggest the breadth of United Technologies, or the sheer number of its people. Allied, on an expansive campus in New Jersey, does not tangibly reflect the corporation as community. AT&T's "post-modern" edifice in New York gives no sense of the long tradition of the thousands of workers at the company, nor does Exxon's sleek but nondescript office on the Avenue of the Americas or Mobil's art deco building near Grand Central Station. Visit MCA in Burbank, California, and you see movie executives housed in a tall glass building that seems more appropriate for Manhattan than Southern California. Occidental's most visible representative is a tower in Westwood, California, near UCLA. Houston Natural Gas is a modern glass and cement building in downtown Houston.

As examples of alienation from what businesses actually do, these buildings are perfect sterile specimens. They do not reflect the dozens of huge department stores the management may control. They do not reflect the acres of oil rigs, or the scores of individual plants scattered throughout the world, of so many of these corporations. At first glance, they do not reflect the movie stars who occasionally walk through their halls, or the size and drama of the technological aircraft they manufacture. They do not reflect the hopes of thousands of employees to advance and find some kind of meaning in their work. They in very few ways convey the scope of any business organization they house, and certainly not its struggles and history.

Inevitably, this is the view of corporate America to a visiting investment banker or lawyer, and to an acquiring corporate management. The view of a corporation as a stock certificate in one's portfolio is by and large not contradicted by a visit to the corporate office. And it is hard to escape the conclusion that some of that distancing eventually did seep into the corporations themselves. Where once the "organization man" was feared and criticized for his willingness to conform, and to stay loyal to his employer, the pendulum may have swung very far the other way during the 1970s and '80s. Money and position were as important then as in the '50s, but organizations were too transitory to trust, and opportunities were usually best found by jumping from job to job. The flight of jobs to the Sunbelt was only the starkest consequence of a shifting economy and of rising opportunism. If such an environment did in fact help foster the takeover movement, the takeovers in turn assuredly promoted mobility, a lack of loyalty, and probably some serious disintegration of the spirit of community. Only a few years later, after the oil price had collapsed, the Sunbelt was in recession while Boston and the Northeast were again ascending.

But there would be exceptions to all the rules in the takeover movement. In retrospect, the size and hostility of the wave of takeovers appears inevitable. Most would, probably correctly, scoff at the notion that a few men could have changed or shaped the movement in a different way. But some men would stand up and defy the odds. They would keep their companies independent, despite all the arguments that they could not. Philip Hawley did just that with Carter Hawley Hale Stores Inc., despite the fact that he once launched a hostile bid for Marshall Field & Co. Houston Natural Gas did it as well. They retained the independence of their companies, and their success did influence others. Occasionally, there were such setbacks in the ineluctable march of the takeover movement. But history's proof is that the movement grew, anyway. Economic conditions were right for it. The ethic of making money, the decline of corporate loyalty, the economics of high interest rates and low stock prices, of inflation and slow growth, outweighed consistently the efforts of a few individual men. But for that reason, the efforts of those men are an important part of the history. And they are based in old-fashioned values, the corporation as a community of workers dedicated to producing a certain kind of product. These men were not necessarily noble. Their actions were harsh. But they did not believe, or act as if they subscribed to, the notion that their company was just another stock in America's great investment portfolio.

To visit Grumman Corp., the large defense contractor, in Bethpage, Long Island, is to get an immediate sense of a corporate community. It is almost an anachronism in the sophisticated world of corporate skyscrapers. The grounds of Grumman's home base spread for hundreds of acres. They are covered with airplane hangars and low office buildings that house fifteen thousand employees. You see the product of their efforts in high-performance jets and radar planes. Nor can you escape their ultimate purpose as machines of war. The company planes land on an airstrip in the middle of the grounds. Later in the afternoon, softball games are in progress on several of the eighteen separate playing fields. Fathers and their sons work, or have worked, at Grumman. They live in two- and three-bedroom split-level homes in the immediate middle-class environs that surround the Grumman facilities. They are not above griping, but there are no unions. Their livelihoods—and, one might argue, their lives—depend on the well-being of Grumman Aircraft.

The argument that would dominate the takeover movement and win over the federal courts eventually, as well as the reigning administrations in Washington, was that the rights of shareholders more or less prevailed over anyone else's. Managers were not independent once their companies had raised money from the public. The price of that needed capital, if the system of capital-raising was to thrive, was that the management now worked for the public shareholders. If, in spirit and tradition, the CEO's first duty was to the long life of his company and the jobs of his employees, in reality his master was the public shareholder. Increasingly, the public shareholders were sophisticated giant pension funds which would learn that they, too, were obligated to go after the highest bid for their stock.

The intriguing controversy, much less well answered by Wall Street, was that target companies were much more the victim of shareholder scrutiny than were the acquirers. Studies would show that most acquiring companies did not profit their shareholders by their acquisitions. But the shareholders of targets, of course, profit immediately when the share price rises as bids get raised. In fact, the allegiance of a corporate acquirer was to much more traditional big-business. Acquisitions were made to help a company grow, to insure its survival, to create more jobs for managers. No one had yet convincingly demonstrated that shareholders on average benefited from acquisitions made by companies they owned. Because the consequences were more subtle and longer-term than for shareholders of target companies, they did not apply pressure for change. It makes good sense that some of the most aggressive acquirers were also the most aggressive defenders of their own companies. These men, like Philip Hawley, were dedicated to survival. Take over another firm because we strengthen our business, keep our jobs. That's not necessarily to the direct benefit of shareholders. Don't allow anyone else to take you over even if shareholders are deprived of more money for their shares. For all the lofty talk, the motivations of this movement were contradictory and often flagrantly hypocritical. In the end, the system sided with the rights of the shareholders to decide, not employees or management, certainly not a local community. It is an extraordinarily ideological choice that was made, and few ever realized just how radical it was.

John Bierwirth, chairman of Grumman, was more consistent than many others. He did not believe in making hostile bids, and he believed in defending his company against them. He was something of a hero at Grumman. In the early 1970s, Grumman was on the verge of bankruptcy. Bierwirth, a chemicals executive, was brought in to save the company. The tall former history student accomplished his task, though the going was seldom easy. By the mid-1980s, his company had developed several high-technology weapons systems that were leaders of their kind. It took a dozen years, but Bierwirth was eventually acknowledged by his colleagues and Wall Street to have done a fine job.

In 1981, Bierwirth would fight off a takeover attempt by LTV Corp., with every weapon at his disposal. What he had most was the backing of his community, the employees. Deep down, he said to himself, he did not save this company to have it taken over by someone else. For those who do the building, it is not so easy to accept the argument that it is cheaper to buy than to build. They know that already, and don't like it.

LTV, a defense contractor itself, knew at the least that it had a fight over antitrust issues if it merged with Grumman, even though the Justice Department had become more lenient in its enforcement. But Bierwirth would not rest his defense on an antitrust case, even a strong one. Grumman management had its own corporate pension funds buy up a large chunk of Grumman stock, in probable defiance of a law that restricted pension investments. The courts eventually enjoined the purchases of Grumman stock by the pension funds. But the antitrust issue went against LTV. "I believe the employees should own a large piece of the company," says Bierwirth. And what of the shareholders? "The employees are the shareholders," he answers. It is one answer to a tide of ideology that was running very much the other way.

No fight for independence fired Wall Street up more than Gerber Products Co.'s successful defense in warding off a bid from Anderson Clayton & Co., also a food company. If it angered Wall Street, however, it also concentrated their philosophy in one direction. The 1977 contest made clear that the profit-makers on Wall Street had a fundamental philosophical issue to support. Corporations could not be allowed to keep shareholders from getting fair value for their shares; they could not deprive shareholders of a choice over whether to accept a higher bid. The courts would eventually agree. If economic ideology was on Wall Street's side, it was no small coincidence that their own bottom lines would also best be served by the proliferation of such notions.

By 1977, Anderson Clayton had been in the market for a major acquisition for some time. The Houston-based company was not well known on Wall Street, but it was very successful. It specialized in processing soybeans. It also had operations in other commodities, including coffee, and owned a life insurance company. Several months before, Anderson had made a friendly overture to acquire Stokely Van Camp, a major food processor. Stokely turned it down.

This time around, Anderson was apparently more determined. Gerber Products, with its famous line of baby foods, would look handsome lying beside Anderson's other food businesses. Apparently with some hope that Gerber would agree to a friendly acquisition, Anderson's chairman, T. J. Barlow, presented his proposal to Gerber's chairman, John Suerth. Anderson offered $40 a share for Gerber, a cash package worth more than $300 million. That afternoon, Gerber had closed at just above $33 a share, and only a couple of weeks before it had been selling for about $25 a share. Gerber told him they would consider the offer.

But Gerber, too, was a company that commanded great loyalty from its hometown of Fremont, Michigan, near Grand Rapids, as well as from its employees. Its management was old-fashioned, almost countryfolk, by the standards of the Wall Street pros. Gerber management rejected the offer the next Wednesday and prepared a staunch defense that would capitalize on state anti-takeover laws. Anderson Clayton immediately announced that it would go ahead with its takeover anyway. Arbitrageurs remained optimistic and bid Anderson's stock well up into the high $30 range.

What gave the arbs confidence was that the $40 bid for Gerber was by most accounts quite generous. Gerber stock had hit a high of more than $53 a share in 1971, but the slowing birth rate would take much of the growth out of Gerber's market. They had about two thirds of all baby food sales. The general decline in the stock market did the rest. The $40 bid represented a price-earnings multiple of more than fourteen.

Moreover, Anderson Clayton, with Morgan Stanley as its adviser, looked very determined. Gerber would provide it with a well-known brand name that could open new consumer markets for its food products. And of course Gerber's huge market share, went the conventional wisdom, was a guarantee of sorts that its business would remain solid.

But Gerber management had a lot more fight in them than most on Wall Street would have anticipated. With Goldman Sachs to help them, they first filed a suit against Anderson Clayton in federal court in Grand Rapids. The suit was a stinging one. First,

Gerber cited potential antitrust conflicts. It relied on the once-potent idea that not only actual but potential competitors should not be allowed to merge. Anderson Clayton could develop a baby food business on its own, Gerber would contend, and a merger with Gerber would preclude that. And Gerber in turn was considering entering the salad oil market, where Anderson Clayton had a sizable hold.

But Gerber's hard hit would be filings made by Anderson Clayton with the SEC concerning illegal or questionable payments overseas. It rehashed the issue in public. The $2.1 million in questionable payments raised a sore point with Anderson. Gerber claimed that the payments should have been disclosed in the tender papers.

Gerber had one other factor on its side. The anti-takeover law in Michigan would automatically delay any tender offer by Anderson for sixty days, giving Gerber plenty of time to fashion its defense, nasty if necessary, or find a white knight.

Anderson Clayton was determined, however. Its chairman, T. J. Barlow, wrote a letter to Gerber's board, dated the next day, that reiterated his plans to proceed with the offer. He insisted the tender was not unfriendly, and that Gerber's management would be retained by Anderson. Finally, he urged the board simply to allow the shareholders to decide whether to accept the offer and not try to hold the proceedings up in court. In one other show of determination, Anderson Clayton filed a countersuit against Gerber, charging disclosure violations, among others.

To meet the requirements of the Michigan Takeover Act, Anderson Clayton said it secured a credit agreement with several New York banks to borrow the necessary funds. Gerber had previously charged the company disclosed no such agreement. It also made other required technical amendments to its filing. But the antitrust hearing was still ahead.

The actions of Gerber's management sufficiently angered Guy Wyser-Pratte, the Bache arbitrageur, that he participated in a shareholder suit. Wyser-Pratte, one of the leading arbs at the time, took the fight as an ideological one. He attended Gerber's July annual meeting in Fremont, where he publicly questioned management for not accepting Anderson's offer, and not negotiating for a higher price from someone else. But the big surprise for Wyser-Pratte and others was a Gerber announcement that its earnings in the quarter ended June 30 had fallen nearly 33 percent. That made it the third quarter in a row that earnings had fallen. The speculation was that the lower earnings were a little too coincidental to be fully trusted. Gerber might have understated earnings to scare Anderson away.

But Anderson made an aggressive countermove of its own. After the announcement of Gerber's earnings drop, Anderson lowered its first bid for Gerber from $40 a share to $37. The move was designed to put pressure on Gerber's board. Because of the board's inaction, shareholders could claim, they had lost $3 a share. Two shareholder suits were eventually filed. But Gerber was not about to give up. For one thing, it was widely reported that it had lined up a white knight that it found more suitable than Anderson Clayton: Europe's Unilever. Second, it was winning rulings on its original suit, the first one filed in federal court in Grand Rapids. Judge Noel Fox ruled favorably on a request that Anderson Clayton hand over to Gerber papers concerning their $2.1 million of illegal or questionable payments. Legal bickering over the embarrassing payments had already won Gerber considerable delays in setting a court date. Anderson Clayton wanted to hand them over to Gerber only on the condition they be kept confidential. Judge Fox worked out an agreement that some documents would qualify for confidentiality. Anderson appealed that judgment, and eventually Gerber agreed to the request for confidentiality.

On announcing its decision to reduce its bid, Anderson hinted that it might withdraw from the contest altogether. The delays were costly. And it was becoming clear that Noel Fox was ruling all too often for the home team. The trial of the suit, first brought in April, was finally set for September. But in mid-September, Judge Fox would again make a ruling that would delay the proceedings. Essentially, he split the case in two. He also ruled that the antitrust issues would be considered only after a decision on whether there were securities-law violations. He was now making it very difficult for Anderson, and Anderson decided that enough was enough. They announced that the procedural delays would push back a tender offer until late 1978 or even 1979. With the probability that if Gerber lost the legal battle, Unilever would indeed enter the contest as a white knight, Anderson dropped out. And Gerber won its battle for independence. Even the shareholders' suits were eventually dismissed.

The lesson of the Gerber deal was that personalities would always play an important role in the outcome of a contest. While court rulings would move inexorably toward more protection of the shareholders' right to receive a bid, and therefore less protection for the target company, there would be many cases when the rule of thumb would not apply. And often these cases turned on the idiosyncrasies of judges, the personalities and determination of the corporate officers, the determination of the acquiring company, the control the officers had over their boards of directors. Directors, too, would eventually become more sensitive to their roles as independent guarantors of the rights of shareholders.

The success of a few corporate officers in staying independent demonstrated that individuals could make a difference, though it might mean fighting dirty. The arbitrageurs, who played according to the rule of thumb, were hurt badly when Anderson dropped its bid. Gerber shares fell in one day from $34.375 to $28.25. The shares had traded as high as $39.50, and reports circulated that the arbs owned as many as 1.5 million shares. Soon after their biggest score ever on Babcock & Wilcox, they took a good-sized loss of maybe as much as $10 million in total.

Even for those who believed the good fight during these years was to retain independence and keep the raiders away, a high level of hostility and the willingness to take extreme measures became the only strategy that worked. In 1974 the maverick and controversial chairman of Occidental Petroleum, Dr. Armand Hammer, was under hostile attack from giant Standard Oil of Indiana. The influential Hammer got senators to call a hearing, where he proclaimed, "If Standard succeeds . . . a message will reverberate through every competitive zone of American business. Free enterprise and independence are dead."

Four years later, in August 1978, despite that eloquence, Armand Hammer made a hostile bid himself. (In fact, he had made a hostile bid as far back as 1967.) Occidental, a large oil company on its own, made an unfriendly bid for Mead Corp., the forest products company based in Ohio. A successful takeover would have made Occidental the nineteenth-largest industrial company in the nation. Occidental already ranked number twenty-seven in size, with $6 billion in sales, if only $218 million in profits the year before. Mead earned nearly half as much—$98 million in profits, on sales of only $1.8 billion. And it had come off a year when paper companies were slowly recovering from a long, recession-induced slump. Profits would rise more than 27 percent in 1978 and another 20 percent in 1979. There can be little doubt, however, that by the end of this contest, Hammer had wished that he had stuck by his idealism so proudly proclaimed only a few years before. The contest would become perhaps the most viciously fought of the period.

Hammer's interest in Mead Corporation was no departure from the conventional investment wisdom of the time. At $23 a share, Mead was selling at less than six times its 1977 earnings of $4.10 per share, and its business was starting to perform well again. Considered a well-managed company, Mead had cut back on its poor operations in the late 1960s and early '70s. By the boom of 1972 and 1973, the paper business was back at full tilt, with prices for its products rising, and Mead was doing better than most. In the late '70s the rising economy helped boost profits again. Finally, there were Mead's modern plants and timberland holdings, which inflation had made far more valuable at current prices than the dollar amount at which they were carried on the books. Mead's book value alone was $23 a share. One analyst at the time estimated the timberland, if valued at current prices, would add $11 or $12 a share to that. Mead had all the characteristics of the classic takeover target of its time.

Armand Hammer, a medical doctor turned one of Los Angeles's most powerful businessmen, took control of Occidental in 1957 and, through a series of astute acquisitions and divestitures, built it into a mammoth organization, with operations in oil, coal, and chemicals. The deal-maker gained his biggest reputation with his overseas relationships, especially with Soviet leaders with whom he continually arranged exchanges of art and performing artists with U.S. artists.

Hammer was nothing if not audacious. But his company's growth made him vulnerable on two counts. Occidental was heavily indebted and bid for Mead using preferred stock. Preferred stock is not as desirable as a debt issue to shareholders.

Second, Hammer's deal-making would also come home to haunt him. He had made substantial cash payments to foreign governments that were not disclosed. In 1975, he had pleaded guilty to making illegal campaign contributions to Richard Nixon's reelection bid.

Mead and its advisers, Joe Flom and Goldman Sachs, would not stand above using all these points, and others, to defeat the Hammer bid. They had many factors on their side. The state anti-takeover laws were being widely challenged, but they were still in place in Ohio and could provide valuable delays for Mead in the tender process. A bid for securities as opposed to cash required additional filings with the Securities and Exchange Commission that would also delay bids. Moreover, Occidental was often raising money in the European capital markets, partly to circumvent the SEC red tape. And Mead would dig up any dirt it could find on Armand Hammer. That avenue of defense turned up far more than Mead could have hoped for. Gerber's flaunting of Anderson Clayton's illegal or questionable payments, embarrassing enough, would look like child's play compared to what Mead would do to Hammer. The no-holds-barred defense by Mead was winning a new name, taken again from the annals of war. It was called a scorched earth defense, which specifically described defenses that would cripple a target with its own debt, but now was loosely used for all very aggressive defenses.

According to court papers filed by Mead, Joseph Baird, Hammer's number two man, contacted James McSwiney, the head of Mead, in early August to arrange a meeting to discuss, according to Mead, "certain coal properties." McSwiney claimed he asked what the real purpose of the meeting was, and that Baird declined to provide any more information. The meeting was held on August 10.

The day before, Mead's stock had shot up more than four points to $27.375. At the meeting in the Mead Tower, in Dayton, Ohio, the next day, Hammer and Baird suggested to McSwiney and his president, Warren Batts, that another company might be preparing to bid for Mead. The Occidental executives urged Mead to merge with Occidental. They had produced a letter with an offer of preferred shares, but were quick to add that they weren't bound by it if Mead did not want to accept the terms. In other words, Occidental was leaving room to negotiate the price up.

Occidental made its offer public the next day. It would issue two kinds of preferred shares for all of Mead's 28.5 million shares. The financial experts figured the offer to be worth about $35 a share. That would make the total offer just under $1 billion, the largest hostile tender offer yet. Mead's public response was chilly. It said it had requested more information from Occidental and that it was calling a board meeting. That day, Mead shares closed on the New York Stock Exchange at $33.25, up more than $5 a share.

The scorched earth defense would begin one week later. The directors of Mead announced that they would recommend that shareholders reject the Occidental bid. They raised their quarterly dividend from 28 cents to 40 cents, about 40 percent. They announced that the Justice Department was undertaking an antitrust investigation. And Mead filed suit in the Ohio federal district court alleging violations of the securities laws. But that would be only the beginning.

Mead's district court suit was not the typical one that charged failure of proper disclosure. Mead charged outright that Occidental had manipulated Mead's stock price, leaking word that there was a secret takeover bid under way for it. Mead pointed out that Hammer and Baird had suggested to McSwiney and Batts, at their original August 10 meeting, that there was another bidder. Indeed, on the morning of August 10, the paper industry analyst for Blyth Eastman Dillon, where Armand Hammer had long been a client, told his brokers that the reason Mead had risen the day before was probably takeover rumors. He also indicated that an offer in the range of $35 a share would be reasonable. Later that day, that's exactly what Hammer offered Mead. How did the Blyth analyst know? Could he have been the unwitting carrier of a message that

Occidental wanted to plant, in order to produce rumors of another bidder? Occidental countersued, inevitably enough, charging Mead with making misleading statements. Both suits were eventually dropped.

Mead also prepared a long letter to shareholders which would leave few stones unturned. The letter called the $35-a-share offer inadequate. Mead also found plenty to criticize in Occidental's current financial picture. It pointed out that Occidental had reported a $36 million loss for the first half of 1978. Mead pointed out in the letter that 20 percent of Occidental's earnings came from politically unstable Libya, and that taxes were being raised on its important North Sea operations. Hammer was eighty years old, noted Mead, and its board was "unimpressed with Occidental's performance."

Mead would also remind shareholders of Occidental's brushes with the federal agencies. Mead pointed out that Hammer had pleaded guilty in 1975 to illegal campaign contributions. They also reported on three separate suits by the Securities and Exchange Commission against Occidental. On all three, Occidental consented to permanent injunctions without admitting any guilt. The suits involved false claims about oil and coal discoveries, questionable payments, and losses on tanker chartering.

Finally, the Mead letter stressed how strained Occidental's finances were. Occidental, noted Mead, already had $1.7 billion in long-term debt on its books. It was Mead's earnings that would in effect be used to pay off the preferred stock Occidental was issuing to take Mead over. In other words, the takeover was paying for itself. It also came out later, in Ohio State securities hearings, that Occidental wanted Mead's earnings in order to take advantage of investment tax credits it might otherwise not be able to use. And Mead found real gold in depositions of Occidental executives and directors during the discovery proceedings that preceded the hearings.

Mead would initially win just about every decision. In early September, the Ohio securities division began its hearings, and did not expect a final decision until mid-October, which effectively delayed Occidental's tender until then. One of the Ohio hearing officers would severely criticize Occidental, and demand more information before the tender offer could proceed.

In early October, the Carter administration's Justice Department was sufficiently disturbed by the merger that it brought an antitrust suit to block it. The Justice Department maintained that Occidental and Mead overlapped in three distinct products.

The most telling revelation from Mead's discovery process was a contention that Hammer had requested undated letters of resignation from his board of directors. The implication was that the board could not exercise its fiduciary responsibility to be independent of management: Hammer could fire them at any time. But there were other accusations, which included more questions about illegal overseas payments, including payments to the Soviet Union. There were contentions that Occidental overcharged for crude oil and that its accounting overstated earnings.

In November the SEC would undertake a new investigation of some of these matters. One new fact that came out during the takeover contest was that an interest-free loan had been made to the Peruvian government for $25 million. It was not disclosed to shareholders. There were also charges that Occidental understated its potential liability concerning the highly publicized chemical pollution by the Hooker Chemical and Plastic Corp., one of Occidental's subsidiaries. The Ohio securities division did finally approve Occidental's offer in November. And Occidental did agree to divest itself of the operations construed to be anticompetitive by the Justice Department, though the federal government continued to pursue the case. In 1980, Occidental signed a consent decree with the SEC involving some of these matters, including the resignation letters, which it agreed to disclose.

But in December, the federal district judge ruled to grant a temporary restraining order against Occidental's bid until the outcome of the antitrust case was decided. It was another major loss for Occidental, who had at least hoped to get the tender under way. This could delay it for months.

A few days before Christmas, Hammer pulled out of the contest. The arbitrageurs, having already lost confidence in the bid, were long out of Mead shares. And Mead's management was soon receiving phone calls from other CEOs asking how they did it. To some CEOs, Mead's defense represented hope that there was a way to stop a hostile takeover.

* * *

Cases like Mead's defeat of Occidental would turn out in the longer run merely to be conspicuous exceptions. In the heat of these battles, however, that was not so obvious. Another such fight would begin within a couple of weeks that would suggest to some observers that acquisition-seeking companies should be wary.

When Philip Morris successfully acquired Seven-Up in early 1978, another of the inhibitions against big acquisitions was torn asunder. Seven-Up had long been considered a family company on Wall Street, a large piece of the company still in the hands of several family members. But as the younger generations of these families received their inheritances, inevitable conflicts in interests and pursuits would develop. Sales of the family holdings were often the best way to settle the differences. Seven-Up was sold on a friendly basis. But the door had been opened to imaginative Wall Street bankers to a rich field of prospective takeover candidates.

McGraw-Hill was such a company. Family members still controlled about 20 percent of the company's stock. The large publisher was being run by Harold McGraw, the grandson of the firm's founder, James McGraw. McGraw was known as an easygoing man, one who didn't rock boats, and an unaggressive manager. McGraw-Hill had nearly thirty trade magazines in its stable, many of them the leaders in their particular fields. One of its magazines was the extremely profitable *Business Week*. The company's hold on educational publishing was also very firm. In addition, it owned Standard & Poor's, another leader in its field—credit ratings. It owned several TV stations. To an outsider, aggressive management applied to such assets would look as if they could produce exciting results. Maybe more to the point, dissension had developed in the family now that Harold McGraw was running the company, especially from two cousins who also were in line for the job.

By early 1979, American Express Co. had been a giant for years. Its extraordinary success in traveler's checks, credit cards, and a range of other businesses, even including international banking, had produced $4 billion in revenues in 1978 and more than $300 million in profits. American Express was rich in cash and looking for acquisitions. It was well known that it had been rebuffed by three targets, none of the businesses related to the others. Walt Disney Productions, Philadelphia Life Insurance, and the

Book-of-the-Month Club had all turned American Express down. At $26 a share, about ten times estimated earnings for 1978, McGraw-Hill looked very attractive to American Express.

James Robinson III, who had risen through the ranks after a stint on Wall Street, had been American Express's chairman for two years. A man bred of an Atlanta banking family, and conscious of patrician ways, he was not a likely candidate to start a hostile tender offer. He and his president, who, fatefully, was on McGraw-Hill's board, visited Harold McGraw on January 8 to present their merger proposal. They offered McGraw $34 a share, a deal valued at $830 million. Unlike Occidental's offer for Mead, it was all for cash. The low-key McGraw probably thought he was being noncommittal during the meeting. Robinson left thinking he might have a deal.

To Robinson's genuine surprise, McGraw would launch a vitriolic defense that apparently cut to the core of Robinson's self-image. In the end, what decided the contest was that McGraw wanted to keep his company more than Robinson wanted to buy it. But it also demonstrates that even in 1979, even in the wake of Mead's campaign against Occidental, the possibility that a target company would fight very hard, and pull every punch, was not yet obvious.

American Express was clever enough to hire one of the key architects of Mead's defense, Joe Flom, in part so that McGraw-Hill could not get him. McGraw, in turn, hired Marty Lipton and Morgan Stanley. Lipton says that McGraw waited in his reception room several hours for an appointment, in order to hire him. Lipton says his determination to beat American Express was surprising.

The two-page letter that Harold McGraw published in *The New York Times* and *The Wall Street Journal* stands as a classic of its kind. He cited a list of accusations and grievances that not merely angered but upset Jim Robinson. He called the takeover illegal and improper. He claimed that American Express lacked integrity. He cited a "secret plan" to acquire the company. He questioned whether the independence of *Business Week* and Standard & Poor's could be entrusted "to a company that pays virtually no federal income taxes on its hundreds of millions of dollars of annual income, operates in a manner that raises serious questions under the banking and securities laws, and pays no interest on the billions of dollars it derives from the issuance of traveler's checks to the public."

This was indeed fighting dirty by Jim Robinson's standards. McGraw would eventually get the House Banking Committee aroused over American Express's banking activities, raising the possibility that it would lose its needed exemption from the Bank Holding Act. It would get the Federal Trade Commission to investigate the merger. It got action from the Federal Communications Commission over the transfer of its TV stations, and the Securities and Exchange Commission on securities matters. It even got the New York State attorney general to take a look. Once Marty Lipton sensed that Harold McGraw was prepared to fight, he would seek every possible avenue of redress. Perhaps the suggestion that American Express made undue profits on its "float" from traveler's checks was the blow that hurt most.

The issue that raised the worst ruckus, however, concerned Roger Morley, who, until the offer, had been sitting on McGraw-Hill's board. Lipton, with his typical flair for labeling, called Morley a Trojan Horse. McGraw-Hill accused Morley of gathering confidential information in planning the corporate raid, and said it was a breach of his fiduciary responsibility. Robinson admitted that American Express had been considering going after McGraw-Hill for some time. American Express fought back, suing Harold McGraw for libel over the public accusations. But McGraw also sued, including taking state action against Robinson directly, and his board of directors.

American Express did not immediately give up. It pursued Harold McGraw's contentious cousins in hopes of winning shares to its side. It tried to provoke a proxy contest. Robinson said he would set up committees to maintain the independence of *Business Week* and Standard & Poor's.

In the end, American Express made one last strategic effort. It withdrew its $34 offer at the end of January and replaced it with an offer for $40. The idea was to ignite pressure by shareholders, including the warring cousins. Lipton insisted, however, that the board was not required to put the offer to a shareholder vote. And the board once again unanimously rejected the offer.

Now, it was up to the shareholders to challenge the board. The zealous Guy Wyser-Pratte was again involved. (There would be seven shareholder suits altogether.) A group of shareholders, with Wyser-Pratte among its leaders, considered polling shareholders and presenting their findings to management. A proxy contest was also considered, but eventually discarded.

On March 1, American Express's $40-a-share bid expired unaccepted. The worst that happened to Harold McGraw was that his slate of directors was voted against by holders of about 12 percent of the shares. The fight cost McGraw-Hill approximately $3.5 million in costs and fees, about $1.5 million of that going to Morgan Stanley. At McGraw-Hill, Harold won respect, however. He had shown spunk to his employees and the outside world. He probably came into his own with this battle. Wall Street, on the other hand, lost out on a handsome profit because Jim Robinson did not have the will to fight. All suits were dropped that month.

Armand Hammer of Occidental was clearly vulnerable. But Jim Robinson's story was a sharp lesson to CEOs who contemplated future takeover bids. He had all the chips and still lost. If you were going to undertake a battle, you had better have the tough skin needed to stick out a fight.

Some argued that the losses by American Express, Occidental, and Anderson Clayton would put a damper on acquisitions in 1979. But the total dollar value of mergers would rise to $43.5 billion, up more than 25 percent from the level in 1978. The takeover movement had by now spun a web of its own. Occidental would return, as a white knight, to take over Cities Service in 1982. This time, it hired as an adviser Goldman Sachs, the firm that had opposed it in the Mead fight. Mead would eventually offer itself as a white knight to Crown Zellerbach in its unsuccessful attempt to fight off James Goldsmith.

McGraw-Hill would make a friendly but expensive acquisition of Data Resources Inc. for $100 million. Anderson Clayton, which fought so hard and with such hostility for Gerber, would eventually fight off an unfriendly leveraged buyout, the family members closing ranks on the hostile pursuers. They had little hesitation in depriving other shareholders of a higher bid—just as they had accused Gerber of doing.

And most ironic, Philip Hawley, chairman of Carter Hawley Hale, who lost a rough fight to take over Marshall Field, would author probably the most severe scorched earth defense of all when he was pursued by The Limited in 1984. Hawley made plans to sell his best assets, place shares in the hands of friendly institutions, and buy back enough of Carter Hawley's own shares that shareholders would hardly get a chance to accept the tender offer if they wanted to. He won, with Joe Flom at his side. When The Limited returned with a bid in 1986, he beat them off again.

For the most part, however, these would remain exceptions. The antitrust laws continued to favor acquisitions over the succeeding years. The courts favored the shareholders' rights to higher bids. Targets for the next few years would have a very difficult time of it. But this handful of men proved that the takeover movement, for all its inevitability, could be defied, that strong men can turn a tide, at least for themselves.

12

One investment banker began to stand out as the tactical takeover battles became more sophisticated. Bruce Wasserstein, a twenty-nine-year-old with a commanding baritone voice, was hired by Joe Perella for First Boston in 1977. Wasserstein had been an associate at the prestigious law firm Davis Polk, which Perella had used as an adviser in several deals. Perella had been impressed with Wasserstein's work. The obvious articulateness of the young lawyer would impress many people. Perella, in fact, felt hamstrung because he would hire Davis Polk just to get Wasserstein. That was not done in the lofty circles of white-shoe firms. You hired a partner, not an associate.

On a plane trip, Perella and Wasserstein sat together and Perella broached the idea of his joining First Boston. It proved a match that would make history in Wall Street circles. In the early 1980s, First Boston would probably make more money in fees than any other investment bank. They would be involved in more of the giant mergers of the period. And by 1986, Perella and Wasserstein would be running the investment banking arm of what was once one of Wall Street's most WASPy firms. The Harvard-trained descendants of Jewish and Italian immigrants had surely arrived. Most would say they probably saved First Boston from going the way of White Weld or Lehman Brothers—of being gobbled up by a big brokerage firm and losing its identity altogether.

Wasserstein's interests were very much that of the bright upper-middle-class boy who did very well in school. Born in Brooklyn, he eventually moved with his parents to New York's posh East Side. Wasserstein's sister Wendy became a successful playwright. Bruce went on to Harvard Law and Harvard Business School. He was an honors student everywhere he went. By the late 1970s and early '80s, the takeover movement was sufficiently intricate that someone who was an excellent student could use all his skills to excel. Most would say that, in these terms, he was the brightest of the bankers.

But also in Wasserstein were many of the contradictions of his baby-boom generation. The leading merger investment bankers who were born in the mid-1940s had significantly different backgrounds. Geoff Boisi was an active lay Catholic and the son of a former vice-chairman of Morgan Guaranty Trust. Jay Higgins, who ran Salomon's mergers department, was a Catholic high-school graduate from the Midwest. Marty Siegel was born of Jewish parents in Boston and was apolitical. But Wasserstein's views were seemingly more traditionally liberal. He worked with Mark Green, a disciple of Ralph Nader, on corporate issues while he was a law student. He co-authored a study of the Federal Trade Commission under Nader. But when worldly success called, he answered quickly. If anyone fit into the simplified description of this generation found in the movie *The Big Chill,* it was Wasserstein. He had no hesitation about making money in aggressive ways. First Boston was one of the firms most frequently criticized for pushing bids by its clients very high. But Wasserstein also supported financially the New York race for the Senate of Mark Green, a politically liberal candidate and frequent critic of business.

In July 1980, J. Ray McDermott, having at last swallowed Babcock & Wilcox—and done moderately well with it—made a bid for Pullman Inc. that would ultimately help establish Wasserstein's reputation. (Pullman had already been on McDermott's acquisition list before the Babcock offer.) It would also be the deal that set the pattern for takeover strategies to come. Perella and Wasserstein had already set up a working relationship by which one would always act as the point man on a project, the other stay at home base. Eventually they would divide clients by geography. Wasserstein had Los Angeles, Houston, and England. Perella had San Francisco, Dallas, and the Continent. On this project, Perella was the point man, but

Wasserstein would provide much of the strategy. Perella would always argue that Bruce's strength was strategy and his was handling people and getting business. But, he would add, they could each easily fill in for the other. "We were very complementary," he says.

Pullman was a longtime client of First Boston's, and it was a company in rapid decline. Once the premier builder of railroad cars in the nation, its business had receded along with travel by train. It was now writing off, at a substantial loss, its passenger car business. At the same time, New York City was suing it for purportedly faulty subway cars it manufactured. In the second quarter of 1980, Pullman would actually show a loss of nearly $4 million. In the first quarter, earnings were way down. The possibility of more big write-offs was high, dividends had already been cut, and management had been turning over, to add still more uncertainty to a fragile situation.

The attraction of Pullman was not, on the face of it, apparent. Moreover, McDermott was having plenty of difficulties with its traditional business: oil rigs. Revenues continued to rise, but profits in the 1980 fiscal year were well below their level of three years before. What McDermott wanted was Pullman's Kellogg division. And the rationale was energy, once again. Kellogg was a thriving manufacturer of plants for petrochemicals and gas processing, as well as chemical fertilizer. For an energy company, this area seemed the place to be. Acquisition of Kellogg's parent company would fit into McDermott's overall strategy. McDermott had a commanding position in oil rigging in the Southwest, made boiler plants through Babcock & Wilcox, and now would be involved in gas and chemicals if it could take Pullman. It could sell off those businesses that it didn't want.

John Morgan, who had essentially masterminded the Babcock acquisition, was also running this takeover. And he thought he saw a bargain in Pullman. With troubles so widespread at Pullman, he would make a partial bid at a low price and see what he could bring McDermott. Except for the low bid it was very similar to the strategy he had applied in winning Babcock. Again, as in Babcock, he had McDermott buy a substantial position in the open market. The buying started in April, with Pullman selling at around $19. By the end of June, McDermott had about 500,000 shares, slightly under 5 percent of the total outstanding. Again, if McDermott was outbid, it would at least profit on its position.

On July 3, 1980, McDermott announced its plan. It would bid $28 for up to 2 million of Pullman's 11 million outstanding shares. With its shares in hand, that would give McDermott about 23 percent of all shares, enough to record part of Pullman's profits on its books, according to the prevailing accounting rules. But also enough, First Boston would argue to its client, to give it a fair amount of control over the course of Pullman, and ultimately a chance to take it all.

By then, however, Wall Street was accustomed to bidding contests. McDermott's bid looked very audacious to the Wall Street financial institutions and to the arbitrageurs, because it was so low. Only the day before, Pullman was selling for $27.25, just under the McDermott bid. Wall Street had long built up expectations for an offer, having detected big blocks trading hands. A bid at virtually no premium over the market price could not succeed, the financial community reasoned, even given Pullman's poor prospects overall. The book value of the company was $39 a share. A white knight looked like a shoo-in. Wall Street bid up the shares in the next few days to the mid-thirty-dollar range in expectation of a competing offer. McDermott's offer would not expire until August 11.

Inevitably, First Boston put out feelers for a white knight to buy all of Pullman. It also started a search for buyers for the individual pieces of the company, in case the search for a white knight failed. The arbitrage community was pretty certain that buyers would be found. But John Morgan had calculated correctly with his low bid. White knights proved hard to find. Pullman did not look like the hottest property on the Street.

The tactical key to the contest was the recent rule changes by the Securities and Exchange Commission concerning waiting periods for tender offers. The former rules required that an offer had to be kept open for seven days if it was a bid for any and all shares outstanding. A bid for only part of the shares would be kept open for ten days. The acceptance of shares would be made on a pro rata basis. If an acquirer bid for, say 25 percent of the shares of the company, the bid must be left open for ten days. At the end of those ten days, the bidder would pay for 25 percent of the shares of all those who tendered. Before the Williams Act, the bidder could accept shares on a first-come first-served basis, so that it paid to tender right away. A shareholder who tendered early would receive payment for all of his shares, not just some of them. Because that would coerce shareholders into tendering to the first bidder right away, the SEC disallowed first-come first-served offers.

But by 1979, the SEC also recognized that the seven-day and ten-day waiting periods were too short and unfairly favored the first bidder. It did not give a target company sufficient time to establish a defense or find a third-party bidder. At the end of 1979, the SEC lengthened the waiting period to twenty business days, but it did not change the period for proration. In so doing, it set up an enticing possibility. Any shares tendered within ten days would be prorated according to how many had tendered; if not all had tendered, the number of shares bought from those who did would be higher. The new rules would enable the bidder to apply pressure on shareholders to tender early. If they did, a larger portion of their shares might be accepted. "There was one basic idea," says Marty Lipton. "You could panic the shareholders into tendering."

In an offer for 25 percent of shares, for example, it was possible that fewer than 25 percent of the shares would be tendered. Any tenders in the pool before the ten-day expiration would therefore receive payment for all shares. Any shares tendered later would be prorated at a far lower proportion. If the bidder received just over 25 percent of the shares in the first ten days, it would accept almost all of them. Anyone who tendered later would not receive any compensation at all. An early tender could have another very important advantage. If the bid was raised, those already in what would be called the "proration pool" automatically received the higher bid. Shareholders who waited, therefore, were taking the risk of being left in the cold on several counts. There was a big advantage, then, in an early tender in order to be part of the proration pool.

The rules provided the takeover players with many tactical alternatives. They could raise the minimum or maximum number of shares they would accept, and thereby create greater or lesser value for their bids. A higher maximum meant more shares would be paid for. A lower minimum meant that a tender offer would be effected even if fewer shareholders tendered. The rules complicated the subsequent raising of bids, because that changed the timing requirements. And proration pools, more than ever, turned takeovers into contests designed for savvy arbitrageurs who understood how to evaluate competing offers, prorations and alternatives. If the arbs controlled enough of the outstanding shares, that would affect the way a takeover bid was played. The SEC would change the rules at the end of 1982, equalizing the proration and offering periods at twenty days. But until then, the use of proration pools dominated takeover tactics.

The most important result of the pools was the popularity of the two-tier bid, for which Wasserstein is given most of the credit. If an acquiring company bid high for only half of a company, it could entice the arbs and other shareholders to tender early. They might get most of their shares bought if they were part of the pool. The remaining 50 percent would then typically be bought for a lower price, and usually with securities, not cash. To many, the unequal treatment of the first and second steps of the deal were unfair, and First Boston was the target of much criticism for promoting the two-tier bid. Such tenders dominated takeover contests over the next few years, enabling many more bidders to acquire companies for less cash than would otherwise have been necessary.

What Joe Perella and Bruce Wasserstein immediately realized was that a bid for Pullman was relatively small, certainly under $500 million. The arbs would therefore gain a big enough position to decide the ultimate winners. Cash up front then would become important. The First Boston bankers also quickly realized that Pullman had few alternatives but to seek out a white knight. The reputation of the Pullman management was simply too negligible among shareholders to win their support against a hostile bidder. Pullman agreed, and First Boston launched the search for white knights, as well as potential buyers for the individual properties of Pullman. They also undertook the conventional lawsuits, in which they professed little faith. Indeed, Pullman would lose virtually all of them.

As noted, the search for a white knight turned out far harder than most people, including arbitrageurs, had anticipated. A Swiss investor took a very large position in the company, nearly 6 percent worth, provoking confidence that a bid would be made. But not until mid-August, nearly six weeks after the McDermott bid, did genuine white knights surface. One was Enserch Corp., a Dallas energy concern, which dropped out soon after. The other was Wheelabrator-Frye, an engineering firm built on acquisitions, with a very aggressive, financially oriented management.

Wheelabrator-Frye was started essentially as an investment holding company. Michael Dingman, with the help of other partners, bought Equity Corp. in 1970 for $1 million. Dingman, trained as an engineer, was a broker with Burnham & Co. when he spotted Equity. It was a closed-end investment holding company, a sort of private mutual fund, with interests in everything from casualty insurance to the waterworks in Athens. Dingman would divest Equity of all but two of its holdings: Wheelabrator, which made cleaning equipment, and Frye Industries, which made carbon paper and ink. Dingman then bought six companies in the next ten years. By 1979, Wheelabrator had $947 million in sales, and had increased earnings at a 25 percent annual pace in the preceding decade.

Dingman, however, had larger ambitions. In 1980, he made several acquisition attempts, all aborted. Interpace Corp., which manufactured building products, turned down his advances in early 1980, and Wheelabrator sold back its 7 percent stake. In a well-publicized failure, Wheelabrator was beaten out by BTR Ltd. of Britain for Huyck Corp. Wheelabrator offered $127 million for Huyck Corp., a North Carolina company which made equipment for paper manufacturing. Dingman, who had been quoted as saying he wanted to build a billion-dollar company, was not about to do it in 1980.

Joe Perella says that Dingman was at first hesitant to make a bid for Pullman. Having been burned in the contest for Huyck, he was wary. Pullman was also a very big bite. It would require heavy borrowing, and the company, except for the Kellogg division, was not obviously desirable. Krome George, the respected businessman and former chairman of Alcoa, the metals company, sat on Pullman's board and was an acquaintance of Dingman's. After a meeting on another Wheelabrator investment, he told Dingman that this was the acquisition that could *make* him and Wheelabrator. Dingman's reply to Perella was to prove to him how he could win. It turned out to be just what Krome George had predicted. Dingman would become a star of this takeover movement.

Perella and Wasserstein fashioned a package for Wheelabrator that they believed would be attractive to the arbitrageurs and take advantage of several defensive tactics meant to ward off McDermott. One participant adds that Joe Flom was also an important creator of the package, for which he would seldom get credit. "When I came out of that deal," he says, "I thought the best investment banker around is Joe Flom." The First Boston team insisted that Wheelabrator had to make a tender offer for cash, if only a partial offer. But the tender would also create a competing proration pool under the current rules, and immediately attract arbitrageurs and other sophisticated shareholders if the bid was higher than McDermott's. The offer, First Boston insisted, should top McDermott's $28-per-share bid by a sufficient margin. That was a strategy First Boston had long employed, and for which they would long be criticized because it produced very high prices in bidding contests. Wheelabrator would also announce what package of securities it would offer for the rest of the shares, the so-called backend. Contingent on that, Pullman agreed to sign a merger agreement with Wheelabrator.

Pullman would also agree to give Wheelabrator an option to buy the coveted Kellogg division if the merger failed. Such an option was known as a legs-up agreement, and was contestable in the courts. Eventually, Wheelabrator took a full-fledged lock-up on the division, which was an actual contract to buy it if the deal did not go through. Again, this defensive device had since been challenged in the courts, with rulings going both ways up to the mid-1980s. Pullman would also give Wheelabrator an option to buy 18 percent of new shares, another aggressive First Boston tactic. Selling shares during a tender again violated gentlemanly tradition. Both options were designed to give Wheelabrator an additional advantage over McDermott. It was a very tightly thought-through proposal, and epitomized the new tactical, aggressive sophistication of hostile takeovers.

Wasserstein was also generally given credit for devising the lock-up. But as with most innovations in takeovers, this, too, had been thought of before. One well-regarded takeover lawyer, for example, recommended a similar tactic that was turned down by a client back in 1978. The example again points up the fact that it is not so much innovative ideas that made history throughout the movement, but the boldness to undertake them, and the confidence and persuasiveness to see them through. Wasserstein surely had those characteristics.

Perella says Dingman took a lot of convincing. On August 16, however, Wheelabrator announced the following offer: It bid $43 a share for at least 2 million and up to 4 million shares of Pullman, potentially more than the number of shares McDermott bid for. It also offered to buy up the remaining 75 percent of the company—the backend—for a package of securities that would be worth approximately $43 a share, based on the trading prices of the respective stocks around the time of the consummation of the deal. The legs-up provisions were also agreed to, and Pullman and Wheelabrator would sign a merger agreement. The total package came to $479 million. It was clearly an offer that beat McDermott, who hadn't as yet even offered securities for the back end. Wheelabrator's bid expired in mid-September. But McDermott would act well before then.

The arbitrage community did not celebrate after Wheelabrator's bid. Wheelabrator was only half Pullman's size, to begin with. The debt the company would have to take on would be formidable. And to receive Wheelabrator securities—"paper," in the Wall Street argot— was not quite like a Treasury security, to say the least. The stock was selling at about twice book value, and Michael Dingman's reputation was by no means as high as it would one day become.

On Friday, August 29, McDermott came forward with its counterbid. It offered $43.50 a share for up to 6.3 million Pullman shares, topping Wheelabrator's offer of $43 for up to 4 million shares. McDermott also at last announced that it would buy the back end of the Pullman shares for about $43.50 in securities. If McDermott received all 6.3 million shares, it would have 61 percent of Pullman's common stock.

The McDermott offer was not as strong as some arbitrageurs would have liked, and probably not as strong as other investment bankers would have recommended. What it did, however, was to provide shareholders with a lot more cash—a lack of cash thought to be the weakness in the Wheelabrator offer. But it also set a high minimum. McDermott had to receive 51 percent of the shares or it could drop the offer. The high minimum gave pause to some arbitrageurs. McDermott also seemed to be baiting Wheelabrator, because its bid was only 50 cents higher in price. McDermott was certainly not blowing Wheelabrator out of the water. The company did realize, however, that Wheelabrator was strained for financing and that to come up with more cash might be difficult.

The McDermott bid was designed to force Wheelabrator's hand. It expired on September 12, and the withdrawal period for the proration pool, the point by which shareholders had to withdraw their money if they wanted to accept another bid, would expire earlier. Because Wheelabrator's bid expired September 19, McDermott might be able to force tenders into its own hands first. McDermott also thought it had backed Wheelabrator into a corner, because it might have to buy the 2 million shares it bid for, even after McDermott already had control of the company. The reason was that enough shares might have been tendered to it to meet its minimum and activate the offer. Wheelabrator would then be a powerless minority shareholder if McDermott then got control of the company. Perhaps Wheelabrator would drop out immediately, which would end all its obligations. The question was whether McDermott was able to raise its bid under the new rules without prolonging the original expiration dates. It gambled that it could.

A federal judge dashed McDermott's hopes for this coup. Pullman sued, claiming the McDermott offer was materially new and that the expiration period had to be reopened. Chicago federal judge Frank McGarr had already ruled against Pullman once on an antitrust matter, but this time, he ruled for Pullman, and forced McDermott to open its offer for an additional period of time. The expiration date became September 26, a date First Boston would now try to use to its tactical advantage.

Wheelabrator was preparing to raise the bidding in the meantime. On September 3 it pushed up the value of the package to $594 million, after the boards of both Wheelabrator and Pullman had met. In typical fashion, Perella went to the meeting of the Pullman board; Wasserstein attended the Wheelabrator meeting. Now, Wheelabrator raised the cash portion of the bid to $52.50 per share, and increased the minimum number of shares it would accept to 3 million. But it also specified that it would give 1.1 shares of common stock for each share of Pullman for the rest of the shares. That value came to only about $50 in the marketplace, and the value would obviously fluctuate with the stock price. The boards also then changed Wheelabrator's option to buy the Kellogg division to a definitive agreement for $200 million.

The initial reaction among the Wall Street professionals was that McDermott would now probably drop out. It would make a handsome profit on its position of 500,000 shares, which it had bought at an average cost of around $22. That would put its profit at around $10 million. But McDermott was not about to lie low. It thought it had detected a tactical advantage. If it did nothing, Wheelabrator would purchase 3 million shares. McDermott could then raise its cash bid for 5 or 6 million shares, receive those shares, and leave Wheelabrator stranded with the minority position. Behind this strategy was McDermott's conviction that Wheelabrator was strapped for enough cash to do the deal. Wheelabrator could raise the ante and bid for more shares for cash. But if that bid was not high enough, or for enough shares, McDermott might still be able to come in and sweep up a controlling interest.

The week of the Friday expiration date for Wheelabrator's offer, McDermott made the unusual announcement that it had not yet decided to raise its offer for Pullman. It wanted to see whether Wheelabrator would buy the 3 million shares. McDermott did suggest that it might then raise its bid, and here it was using the proration pools to their best advantage. By hinting that it might raise the price, it might be able to keep shares in its tender pool. That gave McDermott time, up to the last minute, to change its strategy. The arbitrageurs would keep their shares with McDermott until then, giving them a chance to up their bid before they withdrew and tendered to Wheelabrator.

The same, of course, was true for Wheelabrator. Enter Bruce Wasserstein. He argued forcefully that Wheelabrator had to up its bid before the expiration date. He also insisted that the Pullman shareholders' meeting be held by September 30. Even if McDermott received its shares by the September 26 expiration date, they would not be able to vote them. The Pullman shareholders, if they did not like the backend of the McDermott package, which would probably be priced very low, could vote for Wheelabrator, whose backend was more valuable.

Friday morning opened with the Wasserstein tactical blow. Dingman kept coming up with more money, enjoying a close relationship with Mellon Bank in Pittsburgh. Wheelabrator announced that it would accept up to 5.5 million shares of Pullman stock for the $52.50 cash price. That would give Wheelabrator 49 percent of the shares, which if received would just about wipe out McDermott's chances to get control with a higher bid later.

McDermott, surprised by the boldness of Wheelabrator's cash offer, knew it had to react. By three o'clock, knowing the professional investors were still holding out, McDermott came up with its new offer. It would pay $54 for 5.4 million shares, $1.50 more than Wheelabrator—but the backend value of securities would come to no more than $39.

The basic fear among arbitrageurs was that McDermott would not reach its minimum of 5.4 million shares. It then had the right to pull the offer altogether. Some observers say this was a key tactical error. Adding up the advantages and disadvantages, including the low-priced backend, the professional investors, and virtually all the arbs, tendered to Wheelabrator. It received 7.3 million shares. About 3.8 million shares were withdrawn from McDermott after the $54 offer and tendered to Wheelabrator. John Morgan says outright that Wheelabrator overpaid for the company. The final price was about $600 million.

But Wheelabrator was still not the clearcut victor. McDermott challenged the new Wheelabrator offer in court, claiming it had to be extended because a rise in the number of shares should be considered a substantially new offer. Again, Judge McGarr was presiding. This time he ruled for McDermott. That night, he ordered that both Wheelabrator's and McDermott's offers had to be extended until October 17. Wheelabrator still had the more attractive bid, but McDermott now at least had breathing room in which to amend it.

The hiatus would be short-lived. Wheelabrator immediately appealed the Chicago district court decision to a court of appeals. Early the next week, it got the decision it had hoped for. The three-judge court voted two-to-one that the Wheelabrator offer did not have to be extended. The battle was over, although McDermott tried another legal route, which Judge McGarr quickly quashed. By now, Wheelabrator had received 7.5 million shares. It would pay cash for 5.5 million of them, some 70 percent of those tendered and sitting in the pool. The arbs, all of whom tendered, therefore did very well. With 49 percent of the shares, it would then issue securities for the rest. Perhaps the most tactically complex battle of all time had ended. And this time, McDermott, who had once beaten out far bigger United Technologies for Babcock & Wilcox, lost to the smaller Wheelabrator-Frye.

The intricate maneuvering almost disguised the fact that Pullman, which was trading for a market value of less than $300 million a few months before, had now been bought for twice that, and by a company half its size in assets. The price was about twelve times 1979 earnings, and that ignored the likelihood of losses in 1980. But the Pullman acquisition would become a classic example of how to swallow a larger company. Wheelabrator's next step was to finance the acquisition by selling off parts of the company it had just acquired.

Dingman and his management team took over Pullman in November. By December, they had raised about $100 million in a convertible preferred stock offering. They took some companies off the books. They had reduced overhead substantially, paid back loans, and improved working capital sufficiently to raise another $101 million. They spun off Pullman's rail car and transportation business. In this way they kept their lead bank happy. Mellon Bank of Pittsburgh provided the wherewithal that allowed Wheelabrator to up its bid, especially on that last Friday. Dingman had been on its board, and so had Krome George. Eventually Mellon did very nicely, but it, too, provided a classic example of the important role of willing bankers in hostile takeovers. By the early 1980s they would be vying with each other to finance unfriendly acquisitions, an area they had once spurned.

Wheelabrator-Frye would eventually become a stunning success. Krome George was right. The Pullman acquisition would "make" Michael Dingman—with a little help from George, of course. Wheelabrator went on to more acquisitions, and eventually a merger with Signal Companies. Later, Signal merged with another acquisitions-built company, Allied, which boasted its own star takeover acquirer, Ed Hennessy, formerly of United Technologies.

In 1986, on the basis of reputation alone, Dingman and his management group bought about thirty companies from the newly merged Allied and Signal, and issued a stock offering. Together, the companies were reporting a loss, though they were bought well under their assets values. Some called the companies Dingman's dogs. But with them, the Henley Group was formed. The new issue market was strong that spring, and Dingman thought he could raise perhaps a few hundred million dollars. Confidence in what Dingman could do by buying and selling companies was high. The initial public offering was so successful that Dingman had to turn down money. Investors had pushed up the price of the Henley Group to a total of $1.3 billion. Dingman's Henley had become the largest initial public offering ever made by an American company.

Dingman did not hesitate to admit that he very consciously played the Wall Street game, selling companies that Wall Street, for whatever reason, deemed in fashion, buying companies that were cheap because they were out of fashion. "I think Henley is pure and simply," he said in a television interview with the author, "a mechanism to create value for our shareholders by participating in fads. . . . You know, the market has multiples just like you have hula hoops and seedless grapes and miniskirts. And multiples are established by analysts, and they say one company is worth seven times earnings, another is worth eight."

If a relatively smaller deal became the tactical model of the period, similar tactics would soon be employed in what would turn out to be the largest acquisition of all time to that date. And again it involved Joe Perella and Bruce Wasserstein. The relationship between the two at First Boston was an interesting one. It was complementary and it did not descend into rivalry. Perella was the organization builder and the "people man." To build a business at First Boston, it only reflected well on him to utilize the talents of Wasserstein. Yet both worked on all the major deals. To outsiders, Wasserstein was always seen as the supreme strategist. While Wasserstein gives Perella ample credit, even Perella concedes that Wasserstein's speciality was strategy. To Wasserstein has probably correctly gone the credit for waging the campaign for a giant takeover that, for its size alone, must be called the quintessential corporate contest of the period.

E.I. DuPont de Nemours & Co., the old-line chemical company, would buy Conoco, the oil company formerly known as Continental Oil, for nearly $8 billion in a frenetic three-way bidding contest. It would be the largest takeover of any kind to date, and it was decidedly hostile. To an important extent, its outcome turned on the same sort of tactics that had decided the Pullman contest. What is interesting is that this time around, Wasserstein and Perella fashioned a deal that was significantly different from the Wheelabrator strategy, because they recognized that something new was needed.

What triggered the takeover contest was a bid in May 1981 by Dome Petroleum of Canada for 20 percent of the stock of Conoco, then the ninth-largest oil company in the United States. Dome's real interest was Conoco's holdings in Hudson's Bay Oil and Gas Company Ltd., located in Canada, which they eventually got. But Dome's success aroused the interest in Conoco of other possible bidders. The U.S. subsidiary of Seagram Co., the big Canadian liquor company, held discussions with Conoco about taking a position in the company. Seagram made a hostile bid in June 1981 for about 40 percent of Conoco's stock, at $73 a share.

When Conoco rejected the bid, it immediately searched for a white knight. DuPont was very interested in doing the deal. Their appetite had already been piqued by their traditional investment bankers, Morgan Stanley, led by Bob Greenhill. Joe Flom had also already been brought into the possible battle. But Morgan and Flom were also representing Conoco, and according to Perella's account, DuPont also called on the services of Perella and Wasserstein. They ultimately came up with the package.

The key decision made by the First Boston team was that this battle differed from the Pullman contest in one important way. It was too big to be controlled by the arbitrageurs. To attract the arbs, it made sense to load up-front an offer with cash, to be paid as soon as possible. Financial institutions that manage pensions and profit-sharing accounts, however, would find stock just about as appealing, because they did not pay taxes on gains in stock prices when they sold. First Boston came up with an offer that included a simultaneous package of cash and stock. It was a two-step deal, but done all in one step, and according to observers, it had never been done before. On July 6, Conoco announced that they agreed to accept an offer from DuPont of $87.50 a share for 40 percent of all shares, and 1.6 shares of DuPont for each of the remaining shares. At the time, the DuPont stock was selling for about $83.

DuPont had raised the terms considerably over Seagram's bid, as was the penchant of both First Boston and Morgan Stanley. But Seagram still believed they could get the upper hand by coming in with a higher cash bid. Mobil Oil, the second-largest oil company, would become the third and ultimately highest bidder. But Mobil would eventually be beaten by the antitrust laws.

What the contest eventually came down to was a couple of weeks of frenzied activity in late July and early August. Seagram would raise its bid, to $85 a share in cash for 51 percent of the shares, in mid-July. It was going after the arbs, but it offered no backend yet to the institutions. Wasserstein and Perella thought this was the wrong approach. DuPont commenced its offer a few days later, now raising the bidding to $95 a share and 1.7 shares on the backend, about $85 a share of Conoco at then-market prices.

Now the proration rules would come into play. Those who tendered early could get all—or a higher proportion anyway—of their shares bought for cash. Because it bid for a higher proportion of the shares, Seagram counted on getting all the arbs, and maybe locking up its 51 percent, worrying about the backend only later. But some argue that Seagram then blundered. Having already received tenders, it raised the bid again, to $92 a share. The prorated value of that offer would be lower than the former bid, however. There were already many tendered shares in the pool. "You only raise the bid if the pool is empty or full," says Perella.

On the other hand, DuPont raised the shares it would buy for cash to 45 percent. Then, in early August, just before the deadline by which those who tendered could still withdraw their shares, DuPont raised the bidding to $98 a share, and it reduced the minimum number of shares it had to receive. These two maneuvers had the effect of keeping anyone from withdrawing the shares. First Boston was not looking to pick up new shares, but to keep those already in. The higher price would apply to everyone who had tendered. And the lower minimum would insure shareholders that the deal would go through. A high minimum is exactly what scared the arbitrageurs out of J. Ray McDermott's offer for Pullman. The shareholders went with DuPont, more confident in its bid and certain of its backend payment. The final value of DuPont's offer was $7.8 billion, a staggering sum, and the largest deal done to date.

Many other factors would be played out in what was the most important takeover contest to date (see Chapter 13). But for First Boston, it was a tactical feather in their cap. They were becoming the most successful takeover specialist team of this period, and also the richest. First Boston and Morgan Stanley would split 30 million dollars' worth of fees on this deal alone. Joe Flom's law firm would take home $4 million, small compared to the bankers and a constant source of irritation between lawyers and bankers. Nor would Seagram walk out a complete loser. They received about 30 percent of the shares in the tender, and wound up with 20 percent of DuPont in the end. Seagram, in fact, was now the largest shareholder in the chemical company, but it agreed not to exert any influence, or seek further control for at least ten years. It turned out to be a good investment for the liquor company.

One other takeover contest in this period would highlight the rising role of tactics in the merger movement. It again involved a stubborn, and perennially losing, Mobil Oil. It also marked the temporary end of the lock-up as a way of securing a white knight. And again, First Boston played a part in the events.

It took Mobile Oil only about a month to find another takeover target after it had lost Conoco. This time it settled on oil-rich Marathon, the nation's sixteenth-largest oil company as measured by sales. In late October 1981, Mobil bid $85 a share for two thirds of the outstanding shares. It also offered bonds that would be worth $85 a share for the backend of the deal, the remaining 33 percent of the shares. The total value of the bid was just over $5 billion. Just before the bid, Marathon was trading at about $67.

Marathon was particularly rich in oil reserves. It had a 49.5 percent interest in the second largest oil field in the nation, known as the Yates field, located in Texas. Oil analysts had figured its liquidation value at around $200 a share, maybe more, although these calculations are highly variable. The acquisition would make Mobil one of the nation's best-endowed companies in reserves.

Marathon rejected the bid quickly, however. Its investment bankers, First Boston, sought out a white knight. While the team filed an antitrust suit, all agreed they could not count on antitrust issues to carry the day. First Boston approached several large companies, including, as would someday become significant, Gulf Oil and Texaco. Three weeks later, U.S. Steel stepped forward. It had actively been seeking to diversify, and reached a merger agreement with Marathon. U.S. Steel offered $125 a share, topping Mobil's bid by $40, although for only half the shares rather than two thirds. The remaining 50 percent would be bought with securities worth only about $86, though that was equivalent to the current Mobil offer. The First Boston bid looked to beat Mobil handily.

What became significant, however, were the lock-up agreements that were also part of the merger. These lock-ups of the target's stock and, maybe, a key business—termed the crown jewel— had now become an integral tactic in lining up a white knight. It made it more difficult for the original bidder if the white knight had a lock-up on the crown jewel of the target, and on 18 percent of Marathon's stock as well (the maximum under the New York Stock Exchange rules).* U.S. Steel was given the option of acquiring Marathon's valuable Yates field interest for $2.8 billion and of buying 17 percent of Marathon shares for $90 a share. That gave it a hold on Marathon that reduced the value to the competing bidder, Mobil. A few days later Mobil challenged the legality of this tactic in

* As was typical of the evolution of this takeover movement, subsequent deals would simply ignore the Exchange restrictions.

court. It also raised its bid to compete with U.S. Steel's offer, being the richer company by a long shot, but only on the condition that the lock-ups would be invalidated.

Both lock-ups were ruled illegal by an appeals court. But Mobil's offer was stopped on antitrust grounds, and U.S. Steel's offer was allowed to go through, anyway. It took over Marathon in a deal valued at more than $6 billion.

Lock-ups would be employed successfully again, but their use would be much more circumscribed. In January 1983 the SEC would formally change the rules concerning the proration pools. And corporations had begun to adopt fair-price rules that required that the back end of an offer be equal to the front end. The rush to beat an opponent with a cash offer for part of the shares was no longer as advantageous. The tactical tools of the trade were being limited.

Tactics would always loom large in takeover contests, but they would never quite reach the sophisticated height of this period. The lesson for later acquirers, however, was that the tactically cunning takeover began to make anything look possible. If Wheelabrator could do it, so could just about anyone.

13

By 1979 or 1980, the shame of the hostile takeover had all but disappeared. Those who hesitated to make an unfriendly bid were now the exceptions. Just as important, every major corporation found itself part of the process. It was not necessary for a corporation to *want* to make an acquisition. The magnetic field that bound all companies to the takeover movement was the fear of being a target. The big investment banks, now armed with dozens of individual bankers in their "M&A" departments, combed the nation, instilling the fear of being a target in the heart of corporate America. Marty Siegel at Kidder Peabody built a business on signing up corporations to help build defenses before the raid.

The reach of the investment banks, as well as the law firms, was wide. The nation's thousand or even two thousand largest companies were easy to make contact with. But the real message the investment bankers delivered was not very subtle at all: Get your company in shape or someone will take you over. More to the point, put your assets to work. If you have a lot of cash, you're vulnerable. If your stock price is low compared to the value of your assets, you're vulnerable. If you're just a very good company in a thriving industry, you're vulnerable. Maybe better to extend your assets a bit too far. The bottom line of the message was that to remain independent, and for managers to retain their jobs, it might be better to make an acquisition now, better yet a very big acquisition, before you were taken over yourself. A big acquisition puts your money to work, and it's good to borrow plenty as well. More debt makes you less attractive. Most acquirers will want to use the target's own assets against which to borrow. If you're borrowed up already, so much less attractive are you as a target.

In this way, the takeover movement created its own momentum. That the threat of widespread takeovers even existed made other takeovers inevitable. Once a threshold had been passed—and that seemed to have happened around the start of the new decade— there was no escaping the hovering prospect of takeovers, either as a target or a raider, for any significant corporation. All had to respond.

Two barriers had been passed, then, by 1981, and arguably before that. Corporations had come to accept the undertaking of unfriendly takeovers. They eagerly adopted the sharp-edged tactics that developed in the late '70s, and most were quick to be aggressive. The second was the sheer breadth of the movement that by now involved, or threatened to involve, most major corporations. One major barrier did remain, however. While many deals were thought to be gigantic in 1980, very few reached the $1 billion level. To most, billion-dollar deals, and certainly multibillion-dollar mergers, still seemed far-fetched. In 1981, that final barrier would fall, and the reasons were largely economic, or at least were the result of what was perceived then as economic reality, the conventional economic wisdom of the period.

What had essentially happened by the late 1970s and early 1980s was that inflation had become accepted as a way of life. While many economists would argue that the severe recession in 1974 and 1975 should have killed rising prices once and for all, inflation raised its hydra head again in the late 1970s. The Carter administration had expanded the economy again with some vigor. The unemployment rate would go as low as 5.6 percent in May 1979. But with that expansion, the OPEC countries enjoyed sufficient demand for their oil that they raised prices two and a half times, now to more than $30 a barrel, in mid-1980. The inflation of consumer prices, which had fallen below a 5 percent annual rate in 1976, rose to famed double digits, averaging more than 13 percent in 1979 and 12 percent in 1980. And finally, interest rates would soar to their highest levels ever, the three-month Treasury bill hitting about 15.5 percent in 1980.

In this environment, stock prices would not keep up. Once

again, the central tenet of cash takeovers remained in place, and as
starkly as ever. Although prices had almost doubled since their lows
of 1974, they were still very low compared to the apparent value of
assets. Even compared to earnings, they appeared at rock bottom.
After selling at ten and nine times earnings in 1976 and 1977, the
market fell to seven and eight times earnings in 1979 and 1980.
Stocks looked cheap. Companies could still be bought on the
market far more cheaply than it would be possible to build them
from scratch. In 1980, six years after the movement started, stock
prices still looked like bargains, if not as low in absolute value as in
1974 and 1975. Given the length of time that it remained so, high
inflation took on an inevitability that was rarely questioned.

   Few bothered to doubt that these companies were worth the
stated value of their assets under these conditions, or to consider
that the value of assets was only as good as the future profits they
could produce. Conventional wisdom was tirelessly irrefutable. Moreover, when interest rates are high, it is less profitable to look to the
long run. A dollar received ten years from now is not worth very
much today if you can invest money now at a relatively riskless 12
percent. In fact, it is only worth about 30 cents in ten years. Even at
an investment rate of 5 percent it would be worth about 60 cents. Why
bother then about future earnings when interest rates are so high?
Worry instead, was the thinking, about assets that could keep up
with inflation. Furthermore, in times of inflation, it made eminent
good sense to borrow, and pay back later with far less valuable
dollars. Very few had the temerity to assert, no less live by, the
possibility that inflation might subside and interest rates come way
down.

   The lesson was clear: buy assets. These could include copper,
gold, or other minerals, but especially oil. At current oil prices, oil
companies were undervalued by a half and more. The analysis done
by Wall Street was frighteningly simple. Essentially, it involved
multiplying the number of barrels of oil in the ground by current
prices less the cost of production, which was relatively small. You
had to apply a high discount rate to future revenues, since the oil
would be pumped and sold over the years. But even so, the answer
pointed to extraordinary buys lurking in just about every public oil
company there was. Almost no one dared realistically suggest that

the price of oil might collapse, or even drop much. You ran the risk of being called a crackpot.

Add to this, one other factor that remained largely true throughout the takeover movement, only more so in the late 1970s and early '80s. The banks were eager to lend money. The Arab oil countries, awash in liquid assets, put cash in the banks in ever-greater quantities. The banks had to lend this money out. It was precisely during this period that Third World debt exploded, not on the basis of trade but in a period in which so much lending went merely to pay back former loans. And financial deregulation ended traditional ceilings on the availability of credit. So, banks had funds to spend on corporate takeovers. And similarly, they were eager to lend on the basis of the oil price, or the price for other mined assets, which was often related to the general level of inflation. There are few things to a banker the equivalent of assets in the ground. Inflation had seldom failed them in the past.

One final factor entered the takeover arena. The election of Ronald Reagan confirmed the dawn of a political era that looked favorably on business and the making of money. If this showed itself most explicitly in the lenient antitrust enforcement to come, it was also an important characteristic in a nation's judgment of who was worthy. In short, the election of Reagan nodded America's head in favor of business, and big business. It reflected an attitude that served to tear down what remnants were left from the idealistic '60s of the notion that making too much money or being too financially bold was somehow shameful. And it was confirmed in the dramatic tax cuts of 1981 which did much to promote takeovers by raising depreciation allowances. The election of Reagan, the social atmosphere it reflected and shaped, contributed significantly to the breaking down of the last major takeover barrier: size.

In early 1981, several giant mergers were under way. Standard Oil of Ohio would take over Kennecott. The price came to $1.77 billion. And in a hostile offer, Standard Oil of California bid approximately $4 billion for Amax Inc., the metals giant. The oil companies, cash-rich from inflation and the OPEC oil price hike, were eager to diversify. Inflation-oriented conventional wisdom pushed them in the direction of other asset-related companies.

But no deal of this period better represented, in the intertwining of several currents of the merger movement, the new rush to giant mergers than Seagram's attempt to take over St. Joe Minerals Corp. According to the prevailing investment wisdom of the time, St. Joe Minerals had just about everything. John Duncan, its CEO, launched what he called a diversification drive in the 1970s, having been brought in to run St. Joe from the conglomerate Grace & Co. St. Joe's basic business had been the mining of zinc and lead, but in 1972, the company bought CanDel Oil Ltd., an oil and gas producer in Canada. In 1977 it acquired Coquina Oil Corp., an offshore oil producer. In between, St. Joe took on A.T. Massey Co., a big producer of steam coal in the Appalachian mountains. And in 1981 it was deriving revenues from a new gold mining operation in Chile. In 1980, St. Joe's profit leaped more than 50 percent, to $117 million on revenues of $1.3 billion.

That John Duncan would call his expansion plans a diversification was noteworthy. All his purchases were for mined assets, all traditionally related to inflation. But to Edgar Bronfman and his advisers, St. Joe must have looked like just that, a company as well-positioned as any to benefit from the prevailing economic climate. Bronfman, the son of the founder of Canadian-based Seagram, one of the world's largest liquor and beverage companies, eagerly sought acquisitions. In 1980 he built a well-advertised war chest, also funded by the fast-rising value of oil. Over that summer, he sold Seagram's long-held oil and gas fields to Sun Company for $2.3 billion, at a stunning profit, after Sun lost its bid for Becton Dickinson (see Chapter 10). The original oil and gas investment was only about $200 million, all handled by Mark Millard, a highly respected banker at Loeb Rhoades. That extraordinary success must have prodded Bronfman. He also arranged, with the guidance of Millard, now of the merged Shearson Loeb Rhoades, a $3 billion credit line with a consortium of about thirty North American and European banks. In addition, Seagram had just come off of record earnings and sales in its second quarter. Bronfman had already announced he was on the hunt for acquisition candidates, and the size of that war chest put most companies on notice. Everyone on

Wall Street was waiting for Bronfman to strike. Bronfman would become one of the most important forces in the drive to giant acquisitions, all apparently sparked by the killing he had made a couple of years before on his oil and gas investment.

On March 11, Seagram, under the direction of Felix Rohatyn of Lazard Freres, announced its public tender offer for St. Joe. Bronfman said he tried to call John Duncan, who was on vacation, and instead spoke to several senior St. Joe executives. Rich Seagram bid $45 a share for all of St. Joe's approximately 45 million outstanding shares. The total cash bid would come to just over $2 billion. The day before the bid, St. Joe had been trading at about $30 a share, the Seagram offer representing an approximately 50 percent premium over the prevailing market price; but when trading opened the following day, arbitrageurs bid the price above the $45 offer, anticipating a bidding war. By then, such overpricing by the market of takeover targets had become an everyday affair. Bidding wars were now so commonplace that they were the rule, not the exception.

Also true to form, St. Joe management immediately rejected the offer as inadequate, despite the 50 percent premium. Bronfman, however, did go out of his way to praise highly St. Joe's current management, opening up an avenue for discussion. Seagram also immediately challenged in court the applicability of several state anti-takeover laws, conceding that if they were enforceable it would invalidate the offer. Seagram would indeed quickly nullify the effectiveness of the state laws, a sign that these laws had all but lost their bite by 1981, and another reason the takeover movement could roll along smoothly.

St. Joe hired the former foes, Smith Barney and First Boston, to manage jointly its defense. The two together would try to pull out all the stops. The immediate announcement from the St. Joe camp was that they would come up with an "innovative" approach on legal and investment banking fronts to block the offer. To many, that suggested a defense similar to McGraw-Hill's or Gerber's.

About a week later, St. Joe presented its defense. Its main objective was to push up the bidding price to Seagram aggressively, at the least to get the Canadian giant to raise its offer. But perhaps the higher price could scare Seagram away. First, St. Joe made a public offer to buy just over 15 percent of its own shares for $60 a share. St. Joe would also offer preferred shares for another 10 percent or so of the company.

St. Joe also acknowledged that it would search for a white knight. The Canadian CanDel could present a problem there, because Canada had adopted strict laws about who could now own Canadian companies. St. Joe offered to sell the oil and gas subsidiary to clear the way for a white knight bid from any comer. The sale would also have raised about $500 million in cash, which St. Joe could then use to buy back the shares.

St. Joe also made much of the fact that Seagram was able to analyze the company only on the basis of public documents. John Duncan now announced that earnings for 1981 would be even higher than he had forecast only a few short weeks earlier. He estimated earnings per share at $4.31, up from the $3.50 predicted a little earlier. He also said earnings would reach more than $7 a share in 1982. In 1980, St. Joe had only earned about $2.50 a share.

The exuberant announcement raised more than one skeptical eyebrow. The point was apparently to demonstrate that St. Joe shares were worth well more than $45. Finally, St. Joe management announced that rather than accept a $45 bid, it would consider liquidating the company. The stock price of St. Joe rose to $52.50 on the announcement.

Seagram chose first to challenge the St. Joe defense in court. Rushing for a temporary restraining order against St. Joe in a Manhattan federal court, Seagram quickly won the first round. The judge, Milton Pollack, expressed disapproval over St. Joe's threat to liquidate the company if the other attempts to stave off Seagram did not work.

St. Joe appealed, but several days later, that appeal was denied by the federal appeals court. St. Joe could not put its defense into gear. Its only alternative seemed to be a search for a white knight. In the meantime, it had successfully found a buyer for CanDel Oil: Sulpetro Ltd., based in Calgary, also an energy company. The company offered $545 million for CanDel.

The team of Smith Barney and First Boston was also combing the country for potential white knights. The first thought was that a deal this size would probably require a consortium of companies.

Among those they contacted was Fluor Corp., the immensely successful manufacturer of oil and natural gas facilities. Fluor's response was that it would rather bid alone, though in terms of earnings, St. Joe was almost as big as Fluor, and would probably top Fluor in coming years.

J. Robert Fluor and John Duncan came to agreement quickly. Fluor's offer looked very much like a classic two-step deal of the First Boston variety. Fluor offered $60 a share in cash for 45 percent of the shares, and 1.2 shares of Fluor stock for the remainder, which was then worth about $60 a share. The total value came to about $2.6 billion, the largest takeover battle to that point. The deal was announced on April 6. The next day Seagram dropped out.

Seagram claimed it could have won the contest with a bid of $55 a share. Others believe Seagram would have had to match the $60 offer, and probably for more of the stock. All those who tendered under the St. Joe offer, these observers contend, probably would have received cash for all their shares. What is clear is that Seagram, with Felix Rohatyn's advice, believed the price got too high. Edgar Bronfman was quoted as saying as much. If Seagram had won, Lazard Freres would have earned a fee of $5.5 million. Instead, it took home only $500,000.

The irony in the Fluor purchase was that it, too, described the acquisition as a means of diversification. But Fluor's construction and engineering business was already dominated by facilities for oil and gas. The two businesses would go up and down with oil. Within a couple of months of the bidding contest, there was already in the air the prospect of impending recession, and a cease in the lofty rise of oil prices. In fact, oil stocks had already taken a decided turn for the worse. Fluor's stock was among them, down to about $34 from the $50 level the shares achieved when the bidding contest was under way. By the time shareholders approved the merger in August, Fluor shares traded around $37, and holders of the backend of the securities, the noncash portion, were getting securities valued at only $51 or $52. As the escalation of bidding for so many oil companies continued, the seeds of a profound mistake were sprouting.

*   *   *

By the spring of 1981, then, the last major barrier had been broken. The $2.6 billion acquisition of St. Joe, in a hostile bidding contest, demonstrated to all that it could be done. Billion-dollar hostile mergers could be completed. The banks were willing to stand behind the bidders. Fluor borrowed $1 billion from the banks, paying only $200 million or so out of its cash reserves.

There would be other barriers to be broken over the years. No one in 1981 would ever have guessed that CBS Inc. could be seriously threatened with a hostile bid, for example. No one would have guessed yet that even the largest oil companies were vulnerable to unfriendly acquisition. No one would have guessed that financial entrepreneurs could have raised financing in low-quality debt markets to launch a hostile bid. But by 1981, no company but the very largest could ever feel safe again.

That did not mean, however, that Wall Street fully anticipated the size of the deals still to come. In the spring of 1981 it was generally assumed that the nation's biggest oil companies would do the acquiring, the smaller ones being the targets. Few would have guessed that any of the big ten oil companies was possibly a target.

The eventual $8 billion takeover of Conoco, then the nation's ninth-largest oil company, did not begin with a direct, audacious assault. The culmination of the major trends in the takeover movement to date, including the tactical one already described in the last chapter, it had a fittingly slower evolution. Conoco was almost inadvertently put into play, a phrase not yet in wide use on Wall Street, by a tax-motivated offer from the giant Canadian oil company Dome Petroleum Ltd.

Dome was based in Calgary and had oil and gas assets of about $5 billion which had been aggressively acquired over its history, mostly with borrowed funds. Its debt totaled more than $2.5 billion. What Dome wanted from Conoco was its 53 percent holding of another Canadian oil company, Hudson's Bay Oil and Gas. To Dome, the oil company looked very attractive, in part because it was debt-free. Also, as a Canadian company, it could probably benefit more from favorable tax laws for new exploration, as well as more easily be granted exploration rights in the country. Conoco, on the other hand, found itself hampered by stringent Canadian laws governing the rights of non-Canadian companies.

The mutual benefits were sufficient that John Gallagher, the aggressive head of Dome, and Ralph Bailey, chairman of Conoco, had discussions about the sale of Hudson's Bay in early 1981. For Bailey, it would turn out to be a tactical mistake even to have opened the door that wide. In addition, one of the conclusions they reached was that Conoco could sell Hudson's Bay to Dome free of taxes if Dome took a stock position in the company and then swapped it for the Hudson's Bay share—in effect, a tax-free exchange.

The talks were not resumed, and on May 6, Dome launched an unsolicited tender offer for 22 million Conoco shares, 13 to 20 percent of the company, at $65 a share. Conoco had been selling under $50 a share. Dome's objective was to force Conoco's hand and win Hudson's Bay for itself. Dome announced that it did not want control of Conoco. Conoco's board met quickly and opposed the offer, publishing a strongly worded letter to shareholders that in effect accused Dome of using the nationalistic Canadian laws to force a sale. Conoco even called on the U.S. government to consider what actions it might take so that "U.S. citizens are not victimized by Canada. . . ." There is little argument that those Canadian laws, which so favored its domestic companies, would provoke the larger mergers in the United States. Seagram was also Canadian. But the boldness of Dome also ranks as one of the key factors in the takeover movement. No one had thought before of taking on one of the big ten.

Conoco's defense included searching for other potential Canadian buyers for Hudson's Bay. Bob Greenhill of Morgan Stanley, long Conoco's investment bankers, swept through Canada. He did come up with Husky Oil, but the negotiations would eventually peter out. Apparently, Conoco's asking price was too high.

If Conoco did not sell, Dome might well go through with its tender anyway. Conoco was not about to sit tight and call Dome's bluff. In response to that, Conoco proposed a bylaw that would restrict foreign ownership to 20 percent of the company, and scheduled a shareholders' vote to approve it in early July. Conoco also asked Dome to indemnify it against any tax liability that might accrue in the transfer of Hudson's Bay, though Dome refused. The tax-free nature of the stock swap that Dome attorneys had contemplated was by no means assured, as the IRS was already investigating similar cases. Moreover, as it turned out, Hudson's Bay was owned by a subsidiary, which further jeopardized the tax consequences.

The day before the withdrawal rights were to expire on the Dome offer, an Oklahoma court where Conoco had sought a temporary restraining order issued its ruling. It went against Conoco. The courts' march to protect shareholder rights was well along by this time. The irony is that Bailey's takeover team was by then urging him to sell Hudson's Bay for cash. Morgan Stanley was convinced that a large number of shareholders would tender to Dome. Institutional investors and arbs were by now too sophisticated. They would go with the highest bidder. But to Conoco's chairman, Ralph Bailey, this simply defied common sense. He did not believe his institutional shareholders would abandon the illustrious and long-lived Conoco to a relative upstart just for a quick profit. Many observers believed the same. After all, a tender for an oil major had never occurred. Bailey took off for London on business.

It would turn out that more than half the shares, some 55 million, were tendered to Dome. Many people were shocked. And another point of the takeover movement was driven home: Institutional investors would indeed sell out, and very willingly. It put Dome in the remarkable position of having the option, if it could afford it, of taking all the shares and controlling Conoco outright. Ralph Bailey, absurdly ensconced in London, could have returned to find himself the employee of the company he was tirelessly criticizing. He had indeed turned down a cash offer from Dome the night before for Hudson's Bay.

Dome bought 20 percent of the shares, the maximum it had committed to. Conoco management was stunned by the willingness of shareholders to cash in. Again, another tie to past business manners was crushed by the weight of the bottom line. Times had surely changed now. The message to the rest of corporate America was clear. And if it wasn't, the investment bankers seeking new business would sound it. The ninth-largest oil company in the nation was up for sale to the highest bidder. Several would heed the call. And in the process, several other giant oil companies would get their first taste of the takeover process.

Because it was willing to pay the price to a market now willing to sell to the highest bidder, Dome Petroleum would soon get its way. It would certainly not be able to afford to take the full 50 percent. The 20 percent share would cost it $1.43 billion, an astonishing sum for a company with more than $2.5 billion in debt and little cash to come up with. But the banks were willing to lend stunning amounts against oil company assets. What troubled Conoco's advisers, however, was that this web of companies they had helped create, both potential raiders and targets, now made Conoco vulnerable to many other potential raiders. If Conoco did not sell Hudson's Bay to Dome, Dome might turn around and overnight sell its 20 percent holdings to a wealthier bidder who could afford to buy control of Conoco, and achieve it with hardly a fight. Conoco management was now painfully aware it needed a merger partner to be absolutely certain it would remain independent.

To the Seagram company, fresh from its failure to take St. Joe, and sitting on a pile of unused billions, the Dome success read like an open invitation. Edgar Bronfman would soon conclude that he was interested in Conoco even if he, a Canadian, could not get reserve-rich Hudson's Bay. His analysts would no doubt run the numbers at current oil prices, assume that those prices would rise along with inflation, and demonstrate with almost no demurrer that Conoco was worth more than Dome offered for it.

Bronfman's president and top financial officer were both intrigued by the newspaper reports of Dome's successful tender that day. They contacted their chairman. Within two days, with the cash virtually sitting in the till waiting to be used, Bronfman, in a move reminiscent of the speedy David Mahoney, was ready to make an offer. Seagram considered first approaching Dome to buy its 20 percent. Instead, Bronfman went directly to Conoco's Bailey, who had returned immediately from London, with his proposal.

Bronfman's first intention was to make a friendly investment in Conoco. He even hired Goldman Sachs, who still followed a practice of not initiating unfriendly bids, as advisers. Bronfman offered to buy a large chunk of Conoco stock, enough to keep Bailey independent, and was willing to sign a standstill agreement that it would always vote with current management and not acquire any more stock.

The discussions between Bronfman and Bailey had taken place, and Bronfman put the proposal on the table. All this had occurred before Bailey and Gallagher at Dome had gotten together to work out a deal between themselves. They planned to meet that weekend in Connecticut, at Conoco's headquarters. And Bailey was working on another possible merger, this time with Cities Service. It was another indication of how interrelated the takeover movement was, how one deal would lead eventually to a chain of others. Cities Service Co., the nation's twentieth oil company, was in exactly the same circumstances as Conoco. Prodded by the new Canadian tax laws that provided so much incentive for oil production, Nu West Group Ltd., another Canadian oil and gas company, had made a partial bid for Cities Service. The objective was to swap its stake for Cities Service's Canadian operations. After talking to Bronfman, Bailey quickly headed for Oklahoma City to talk about a merger with Cities Service. In terms of sales, a merger would have made it the seventh-largest oil company and, it seemed, would have protected both companies from takeover. At that size, they figured they were safe.

Seagram had still wanted a Conoco that included Hudson's Bay. On Sunday, Conoco conducted negotiations in Connecticut with both Seagram and Dome. What Conoco's advisers cleverly extracted from Bronfman was a promise that if Conoco management did not agree to take the proposed offer, Bronfman would go away and not return with a hostile bid.

On Monday, June 1, Conoco announced that it had agreed to sell Hudson's Bay to Dome. The price was a return of all the 22 million shares Dome had bought, plus another $245 million in cash. The total value of the package was just under $1.7 billion, and for only slightly more than half its stock. Conoco would put the cash in the bank, retire the stock, which would raise its earnings per share by about 18 percent, and surprisingly also open a line of credit with a group of banks for $1 billion. The funds, of course, would be useful for a defensive merger with Cities Service, if it did materialize.

It took more than two weeks of negotiation before Conoco came back with a decision for Bronfman and Seagram. In the meantime, the negotiations with Cities Service—guided by Marty Lipton— were under way. On June 17, the Conoco board rejected the Seagram offer. By the next day, Bronfman, infuriated, broke his promise. In the following two days, Seagram would buy more than 140,000 shares on the open market. Because of the activity, the stock exchange suspended trading in Conoco, and the oil company was forced to make a statement. Conoco said it had turned down an offer from a "foreign company," meaning Seagram, and that it was discussing a merger with another oil company.

One week later, Seagram announced a hostile tender for almost 41 percent of Conoco's outstanding shares. The price was $73 a share, but Seagram did not make an offer, even in securities for the backend. Goldman Sachs, mindful of Bronfman's earlier promise not to go unfriendly, dropped out as adviser, giving up fees potentially in the millions. Seagram announced earlier in the week that it was considering such an offer, and that it had filed the appropriate papers with the Federal Trade Commission, according to the prenotification requirements of the Hart-Scott-Rodino Antitrust Improvements Act.* That same week, public reports emerged that Cities Service and Conoco were talking actively. Just hours after Seagram's announcement, Cities Service called off the merger discussion. The total cash value of Seagram's offer was about $2.5 billion, making it the biggest takeover offer ever by a non-U.S. company for a domestic company.

However big, its weakness was that it was not big enough; the offer was not for the whole company, nor was there any indication that Seagram would eventually buy the rest of the shares. Several days later, on July 1, the Conoco board announced that it had rejected the Seagram offer. It also announced a $1 billion lawsuit against Seagram, among other charges accusing Edgar Bronfman of backing off the explicit promise that he would not undertake a hostile tender. Conoco called it a breach of contract. Eventually, Conoco would also accuse Seagram in court of violating state liquor laws. Nothing worked. It turned out that Conoco's only recourse was to find a white knight.

Eventually, DuPont, the old-line chemicals company, stepped forward. Long a Morgan Stanley client, DuPont also asked to bring

*This act required that the antitrust authorities be given a period of notice within which they could decide to investigate the antitrust implications of a merger.

in First Boston, Morgan now representing Conoco. Perella of First
Boston had called on DuPont in the spring, a year before. He says
that Joe Flom and Bob Greenhill suggested that a bid for all
Conoco's stock could win, even if the offer entailed only securities.
Perella told DuPont management there was no way that could win.
He and Wasserstein then came up with the package of cash up
front, and stock for the backend, that would so appeal to the
financial institutions (described in Chapter 12). It was the first time
that a two-step deal was announced simultaneously. It was a package, Perella insists, that Morgan Stanley did not know how to
improve upon. Another banker says bluntly, "First Boston beat the
pants off of Morgan."

DuPont and its advisers worked on the offer over a frenetic
July Fourth weekend. On July 6, DuPont announced a merger
agreement with Conoco. The offer was for $87.50 per share for 40
percent of the outstanding shares, and 1.6 DuPont shares for the
rest. An appealing alternative would have been to bid for 51 percent
of the stock for cash, the remainder in stock, probably for a lower
value, but that would have required DuPont's paying more cash.
Other alternatives might have required shareholder votes, which
would have taken too long. The offer the First Boston team had
fashioned seemed to have intelligently met all the objectives. And it
had clearly topped Seagram's bid by a wide margin. Now it was
Seagram's call.

The bidding and counterbidding that ensued would be a strategic match (see Chapter 12) that utilized the proration pools to their
best advantage. Seagram would indeed top DuPont's offer a few
days later, offering $85 a share for 51 percent of the stock, and
would abandon its minimum requirement for number of shares to
be tendered. The round of bidding between the two would escalate
once again. DuPont raised its cash bid to $95 and its securities offer
to 1.7 shares, about $77 based on the current price of DuPont
stock. It commenced its offer on July 14. On July 23, Seagram
would raise its offer to $92. Cities Service had long since dropped
out.

In the intervening period, however, a new bidder entered the
fracas. Mobil Oil, with Merrill Lynch as adviser, bid $90 per share,
in cash for slightly more than 50 percent of the shares, an extraordi-

nary cash bid of nearly $4 billion. And no one doubted that Mobil could afford it. The second-largest oil company in the nation, with $64 billion in sales in 1980 and nearly $3 billion in profits, Mobil was easily the richest player in this game. Mobil also offered 90 dollars' worth of debentures for each of the rest of the shares, in addition to $90 in cash for the first half. It was the offer that many thought DuPont should have made to assure it victory.

But the highest bidder would not prevail. The three-way contest for control of Conoco did not merely pivot on finances. It also demonstrated how far the nourishing attitude of the courts and federal government toward big mergers had come. Mobil lost in the end because the investment community, and Mobil itself, had not caught up to the reality that the courts and the antitrust authorities had virtually opened the chute even for a merger between two oil giants. Many still cringed at the prospect of the nation's number two oil company taking over the nation's ninth-largest oil company— but the courts and the administration did not.

The battle for Conoco demonstrated the evolution in the courts better than did any other deal. First, there was the outcome of the flurry of litigation Conoco and Seagram hurled at each other to neutralize each other's bids. At most, each gained only the most temporary of restraining orders over the other. A very testy Judge Edward Weinfeld, who reigned in New York City's southern federal district, threw out Conoco's contention that Seagram had violated a contract by initiating the hostile bid. Judge Weinfeld kept reminding the parties that it is the good of the shareholders they should be working for, not management's or the board's. He rejected the Conoco contentions on July 16. Moreover, Seagram easily neutralized the state anti-takeover laws with a series of suits. By then, the state takeover laws were ineffective, only awaiting their final demise with the Supreme Court decision in 1982.

Seagram's battery of lawsuits to stop Conoco's offer also failed. The only litigation that did work, and then only briefly, were several barriers Joe Flom tried to throw up at the last minute to block the Seagram offer. Several Conoco gas stations sold liquor, and a Seagram takeover could violate the state prohibitions against a liquor distributor owning a retailer. Flom won a restraining order in Florida—a bit of dirty pool, according to his competitors. Conoco did not even inform Seagram of the suits. But Seagram was able to go to the judge to reverse the decision. Then Seagram discovered that Flom had won a similar restraining order in North Carolina. Seagram lawyers could not even find the court that issued the order. Ultimately, they took the case to a federal court and the judge held a Saturday hearing in which he cleared the Seagram offer. The speed with which these, too, were overturned showed just how far the courts had moved toward accepting hostile takeovers, and the courts' unwillingness to get in their way.

That driving philosophy would also eventually show its benevolent face at the offices of antitrust officials. But not until Mobil Oil, despite making the highest offer for Conoco by far, some $120 a share, would indeed lose partly on fear by Wall Street that the Justice Department would not allow numbers two and nine to join. There was still some antitrust muscle left, if it was wilting fast.

The Hart-Scott-Rodino legislation, passed in 1978, proved the key to Mobil's loss and DuPont's victory. The legislation requires that any takeover offer be filed with the two antitrust authorities, the Federal Trade Commission (FTC) and the Justice Department. They would decide who would have jurisdiction between themselves and have fifteen days to rule on whether a merger would be challenged. The ruling agency can ask for more information from the companies involved and get another ten days to reach a decision. In the case of securities offerings, rather than cash, however, the waiting period is a full thirty days, and another twenty days if more information is requested.

The three competing offers lined up as follows: Seagram had already passed muster with the antitrust agencies by early July, but every time it raised its bid, it delayed its offer, in accordance with the law, another ten days. DuPont first filed on July 8, making its offer eligible at the earliest on August 7. Mobil was thought to have a clear advantage because it was offering all cash. The offer could be approved by July 31. But if it got a request for more information, it would be delayed to August 10.

Most analysts assumed that both DuPont and Mobil would get

requests for more information from the antitrust agencies. It didn't turn out that way. According to an exhaustive account of the legal aspects of the contest in *The American Lawyer,* the Justice Department assigned a separate group of its staff to each case. Both groups felt compelled to come to judgment quickly. Why the need to rush, one may fairly ask, especially given that this would be the largest merger in history? And here lies the crux of an entire takeover movement, an entire ethic that dominated the times: The Justice Department did not want to get in the way; it wanted to let the market decide as freely as possible who should win a takeover contest. In other words, don't obstruct. What a long way this takeover movement had now come. That dominating philosophy in President Reagan's Washington would allow the Justice Department to clear the DuPont transaction, which was for securities, in less than the required time—in fewer than the thirty allotted days.

The political influence of DuPont in Washington no doubt played a part in the stunningly quick decision to clear the merger. By contrast, a second request for information was made of Mobil only a few days before.

The American Lawyer would argue that Wall Street misread the way the Justice Department interpreted the antitrust laws. Two years later, Wall Street would have been confident that the Justice Department would have eventually cleared Mobil. The fact was that however huge the big oil companies were, the market was the biggest single-product market in the world. In very few regional markets did Mobil have more than several percent of sales. In the national sale of gasoline, it had a 6.3 percent share and Conoco a 2.5 percent share. The antitrust guidelines would allow a combination only up to a point where both parties had 5 percent of a market. Still, the number two and number nine companies could stir fear among the Wall Streeters, because it was the first such test. And DuPont's public relations team kept emphasizing the point.

When DuPont got its clearance on July 30, a few days after a second information request would delay Mobil another ten days and, in Wall Street's eyes, possibly end the bid altogether, the contest was essentially over. Mobil's bid at that point was $105 per share, and it raised it twice, to $120, in order to show its determination (though Mobil also lowered the backend value, which probably did not sit well with Wall Street). It also went to court. But the courts were seldom a source of relief anymore, and investors traveled to Conoco. By this time, Seagram, too, knew that it had lost the bidding contest with Conoco. It would not go any higher. DuPont finally bought Conoco for just under $8 billion. Seagram took a 20 percent position in DuPont in exchange for the shares tendered to it.

The chain reaction of giant takeovers, the web of interest and relations and bank-financed war chests, would result in other giant takeovers. Texaco had sewed up a $5.5 billion line of credit when it made its friendly offer for all of Conoco. Rejected, it was biding its time, eventually to engineer an even larger merger. And Mobil, led by a couple of aggressive, energetic, and proud executives, Rawleigh Warner and William Tavouloureas, was not about to give up its search for an oil company. Only a couple of months later, Mobil made its bid for Marathon Oil, a reserve-rich oil company already the sixteenth-largest in the nation in sales. It offered $2.5 billion in cash and another $2.5 billion in debentures for the company. When U.S. Steel was enticed to be the white knight, a bidding contest was under way. But Mobil's eventual loss (see Chapter 12) was an example of the fact that the obstacles to giant takeovers had not all been erased. The FTC did challenge the merger and asked that Mobil sell certain operations, to which it agreed. But a Cleveland district court stopped the merger temporarily anyway. On appeal, the Sixth Circuit court affirmed the lower court ruling. U.S. Steel went ahead to buy Marathon for about $6.4 billion. The administration might have loosened its antitrust policy significantly, but an occasional court ruling could still throw a wrench into the well-laid plans of takeover specialists. For the most part, such barriers were temporary.

In 1981 there were initiated mergers that would total nearly $83 billion. The year before, a very active one, the total dollar value of merger transactions was only $44 billion. There were 94 mergers of $100 million or more compared to 113 in 1980 and 83 in 1979. Of the 25 largest deals ever undertaken to that point, 21 were done between 1979 and 1982, and 15 of the largest 25 were done in 1981 and 1982 alone. The takeover machine was running full speed.

In the bidding contest for Conoco, the evolution of the takeover movement could be seen on its fully mature scale. Chief executives realized that if they were going to fight, they had to fight to win. The use of legal and financial tactics had been honed to an aggressive science. Virtual armies of takeover specialists were now available on Wall Street.

And size was no longer a barrier. The credit lines established with major banks in 1981 would total in the tens of billions of dollars. Antitrust considerations were narrowing. The conventional wisdom, which claimed that the stock market itself badly undervalued corporations, was rarely second-guessed. It was cheaper to buy than to build, pure and simple.

Wall Street speculators had discovered one of their hottest plays ever. Every bidding contest was now a magnet for money. The takeover bankers raked in undreamed-of amounts. First Boston earned a handsome $3.5 million, as did Smith Barney, when Fluor bought St. Joe. But they earned about $15 million, as did Morgan Stanley, when DuPont bought Conoco. All this for the services of a handful of professionals, no capital ever having been put at risk by the investment banking houses. First Boston would earn nearly $18 million on the U.S. Steel purchase of Marathon.

The insular life-unto-itself of takeovers was now evident. The U.S. economy was just then entering recession. And even before that, the demand for oil products had begun to slacken. If the point needed any more bringing home, Conoco, even while under siege, reported disappointing earnings in the second quarter of 1981. By early 1982, the evidence of recession could not be denied. By 1983, the oil price would crack dramatically.

In 1982, the movement would reach excesses that would constitute its darkest hour. Many thought the takeovers on any broad scale would end that year. But the machinery proved far too developed, the process far too lucrative. Takeovers would continue despite evidence of mistakes everywhere.

14

It would turn out that the court rulings against the U.S. Steel lock-up and Mobil's bid for Marathon on antitrust grounds would only momentarily give pause to the takeover movement. Both decisions, it became apparent, were out of the mainstream of prevailing legal opinion. Lock-ups would be tailored more carefully in order to circumvent the ruling. And observers accused Mobil of not cooperating sufficiently with the antitrust authorities in its fight for Marathon. Otherwise, says one lawyer who had been close to the case, there's a good chance Mobil could have taken Marathon.

By 1982 the takeover mechanism had been so finely crafted that even the most delicate push could get the system moving. It was as if it had reached a critical mass. So many potential buyers and sellers were lined up, and the techniques fine-tuned enough, that a chain reaction was inevitable once an aggressor launched an attack. Contributing to this process was the way corporations now thought about takeovers. Takeovers were part of the environment. Hundreds of companies had adopted golden parachutes for their top executives, for example. If the company was taken over, these executives had the option to leave and be compensated at several times their annual salary. In some cases, golden parachutes, which often included stock, amounted to several million dollars. They would become in 1982 one of the most frequently cited abuses of the takeover movement.

Corporations were also adopting methods, known as shark repellents, to try to keep raiders away. If a corporation had only a minority of its board of directors elected every year, an acquirer could not come in and sweep the board away in one proxy election. These staggered boards became a favorite among the anti-shark techniques. Another was the adoption of what were called super-majority rules that required as many as 90 percent of the shares to approve any merger. Before this shark repellent, the corporate bylaws typically only required that a simple majority of shareholders vote.

If the environment literally shouted *takeover* at the corporations, the evidence suggests that corporate raiding also became an end in itself for many. The question had changed from *whether* the chief executive should make an acquisition to *whom* should he acquire. For some, it was not so much a question of whom to acquire, but how much could he afford to pay.

Every market fad is difficult in itself to pin down precisely. The participants continue to say the right things, the rhetoric designed to appease critics and probably fool oneself. The language of takeovers seemed intelligent and rational by most business terms. So it did in the late 1960s as well. It described decisions in terms of *return on investment* and *corporate fit* and *strategic big pictures* and *industrial restructuring*. But the language would increasingly disguise another world altogether, the world of competing at takeovers. Winning became the real goal. To some, that was always the case. But winning as an end in itself became widespread by the early 1980s. Business meant long-term objectives of growth and profit. Winning meant the short-term objective of getting the company. When Mobil lost its bid for Marathon, it immediately turned around to make a tender for 25 percent of U.S. Steel—almost, it seemed, to get even. When Mobil abandoned that effort, it announced that now it would make forays into the movie business. To investment bankers, playing Iago to these vulnerable Othellos, winning meant something far more real than the pride of victory. It meant huge fees, and reputations that would win more business and still more fees. The fine mechanism would tilt, however, in 1982.

If the rhetoric of takeovers still reflected a more rational and cool way of thinking, the conventional wisdom that provoked them was clearly several years behind events. If politicians and economists and soldiers, as well, can be accused of fighting the last war, so certainly can corporate chieftains and their Wall Street lieutenants so eager to get ahead. The truth is that by the early 1980s, the plush rug that supported so many of the biggest acquisitions was being pulled out from under the acquirers.

The economy had begun to slow rapidly in 1981. This had followed a mild but nevertheless real slowdown in 1980. Oil companies had already begun to see a drop in their demand, showing up quite clearly in subsiding profits. But the inevitability of inflation had sunk very deeply into business's way of thinking. Few believed that inflation could fall sharply. The props of inflation, however, were about to crumble, including the most important of them, oil.

The price of crude oil had risen only a couple of dollars between the end of 1973 and early 1979. Of course, in one year, 1973, oil prices had been nearly quadrupled, to about $12 a barrel. That year, U.S. gasoline prices averaged about 38 cents a gallon. The most severe recession in the postwar period followed; nevertheless, inflation reached above 12 percent in the United States. In 1974 the average price of gasoline was 55 cents. Soon, new oil fields were discovered. The first North Sea crude was pumped in June 1975, for example. Mexico began to increase production sharply over the next few years. Oil importers also began to cut back on the use of oil. The United States reduced the nation's driving speed limit to fifty-five miles per hour in 1973.

The effects, however, were not yet apparent, even by 1980. The economic expansion, prodded by government policy, in the mid- and late '70s, helped keep oil demand high. The next round of OPEC price hikes began in 1979. By the end of that year, the benchmark oil price was $24 a barrel. Early in 1980 the price of Saudi light crude was raised to $26 a barrel; by December, to $32 a barrel. U.S. inflation reached 13.3 percent in 1979. In 1981, gasoline prices, still climbing, would peak at an average of $1.35 a gallon. It was the double rounds of oil price hikes—in 1973 and again in 1979—that drove home the assumptions that oil could only go up. Even the severe recession of 1974 and 1975 did not kill the inexorable rise. Some did speculate that an oil bust was possible, but to most that sounded like nonsense.

What went less noticed, however, was that U.S. oil imports in 1979 fell for the first time since the recession of 1975. The world output of crude dropped by 5 percent in 1980. OPEC's output for the year fell to its lowest level since 1972. In early 1981, Sheik Ahmed Yamani, the Saudi oil minister, declared that his country had purposely created a glut of oil in order to keep prices from rising. It would turn out that 1981 would be OPEC's last good year. That October, OPEC posted a price of $34 a barrel for Saudi light. Early in 1982 the price would drop sharply.

The recession of 1981 and 1982 supplanted the 1974 contraction as the most severe since World War II. At the same time, however, the use of oil throughout the world had stopped expanding. Moreover, new oil discoveries would soon make OPEC a minority supplier of oil. The general level of inflation was closely linked to the price of oil. Not only was oil one of the most widely used commodities in an industrial economy, but the same factors that would reduce its prices would also affect many other prices. In 1980, consumer prices in the United States still rose at double-digit rates. By 1981, inflation fell to 9 percent. By 1982 it would fall to under 4 percent.

To a takeover movement whose backbone was the acquisition of companies with assets in the ground, the drop in inflation should have been the warning signal. It went unheeded. In fact, it simply went unbelieved. The very biggest oil acquisitions only began to take place in 1981. The experts—heads of major oil companies, heads of smaller drilling companies—chose to believe that oil was high-priced to stay. Even though OPEC could not come to terms in July 1982 on prices, the heads of oil companies for the most part bought the old assumptions. Certainly, so did Wall Street. Perhaps if the disarray among OPEC that was to come in December had taken place earlier, the mistakes of 1982 would not have occurred. Then, oil prices in other markets were several dollars cheaper than OPEC's posted prices. The OPEC members themselves were discounting prices widely. An era was ending for oil. It was also ending for mergers and acquisitions, or so it would seem for a while. But the conventional wisdom about inflation would persist, it turned out, for several more years.

*   *   *

T. Boone Pickens made two gifts to the takeover movement. The first was living by his firm conviction that most oil companies were worth more dead than alive. He believed that at current world prices, it was best to at least partially liquidate an oil company—to sell off the oil reserves—and distribute the proceeds to the shareholders. What made little sense to him was to plow profits back into new exploration. He felt that would simply run companies into the ground.

His second gift was an audacity that was very different from Wall Street's. Boone Pickens had already come to understand the financial mechanisms of the takeover movement when Mesa Petroleum made its bid in 1976 to take over Aztec Oil. He did not buy shares beforehand, but he learned that you should because you could provoke a higher bid for the target. The practice went far back into the 1960s, and probably earlier than that. But Pickens had the kind of free-wheeling spirit that probably sprang from his southwestern wildcatter background. Wall Street was very careful when it broke new ground. The march of the takeover movement was one of very clever, well-educated Ivy Leaguers picking loopholes in the law, pushing accepted procedures a little bit further. Even Carl Icahn, Pickens's only rival for his particular throne, was cautious. He seemed to choose his targets because he knew he could defeat them. Pickens spoke and acted like Don Quixote. The difference was that he did defeat knights. To the press, it was a refreshing mixture of ingenuousness and guts and seeming unsophistication. Pickens had one other public relations calling card: He talked to just about anybody from the press who called him.

In 1982, Pickens knew you could press a button and put a vast and efficient machinery in process. Pickens decided to push Cities Service's button. Cities was already a takeover player by virtue of having had serious discussions with Conoco about a defensive merger. Brought to everyone's attention by those discussions, Cities was not about to escape the takeover web.

Pickens saw Cities as a company that was not good at finding oil and gas. Its reserves of oil and gas had fallen by about one fifth in the preceding five years. On the other hand, its capital and exploration budget had risen by about the same percentage. Nevertheless, Cities had substantial proven reserves of both commodities, and plenty of unexplored land in oil and gas territory. Pickens also saw a vulnerable management team. They had made unsuccessful diversification attempts and were selling out of them. The potential for taking over this company and then liquidating its assets was inviting.

Where Pickens would come up with the money was another matter. In assets, Mesa was about one-third Cities's size. But Pickens had several things on his side. The first was that Wall Street believed he had financial allies. Southland Co., which owned the retail chain 7-Eleven, was rumored to be one. A closed-end investment company, Madison Fund, was said to be another. Second, Mesa had already bought a stake in Cities, just over 5 percent of its shares.

In short, Cities had to take Pickens seriously. With First Boston and Lehman Brothers at its side, it decided to make a preemptive offer for Pickens's company, Mesa. But it bid only $17 a share, just 25 cents above Mesa's current market price. The bid was announced on May 28 and the offering was mailed on June 1.

The possibility of tendering for the company that tenders for you had long been considered an option in the takeover wars. Geoff Boisi, for example, says Goldman Sachs considered and discarded it several times. Conoco considered a countertender against Seagrams. That spring, NLT countertendered for American General. But to adopt the PacMan defense—named after the popular video game— meant sailing on uncharted waters. No one quite knew what would happen if two companies bought controlling interest in each other. There were no precedents. The logical culmination would be a combined entity loaded with debt and virtually no equity. By 1982, however, the takeover specialists had grown far bolder.

Boone Pickens temporarily decided to ignore Cities's $17 bid. On May 30, he presented its management with a friendly cash offer for just over half the stock, the remainder to be paid off in securities. The bid came to $50 a share. On June 1, Mesa announced that Cities's management rejected the offer.

Now, the play would get rougher. On June 6, Pickens turned down Cities's $17 bid and responded with a surprise tactic of his own. The next day, he reaffirmed his friendly offer at $50 a share, but now he made an unfriendly tender for only 15 percent of Cities's shares at $45. He was sending a message to shareholders. If your management turns down $50 a share, the best you'll get is $45 a share. He counted on the shareholders to put pressure on Cities. Pickens also reasoned that he would receive 15 percent of Cities, because the arbs were not about to turn down the offer. Then he would be in a stronger position. He held out the possibility that he might then tender for more.

The very next day, Cities made a new friendly offer that bore the First Boston signature. It was a two-tier bid, amounting to $21 a share in cash for the first 51 percent of the shares, and securities worth about $16 a share for the backend. Cities management also turned down both Mesa's $50 offer and its $45 hostile bid.

Now, Cities Service was bidding for Mesa, and Mesa in turn for Cities. No one was quite sure how the deal would turn out. Who would gobble up whom? The problem for Cities was that it was paying a lot for Mesa. On a per-barrel basis, Cities was buying Mesa's reserves at more than $6 a barrel. Mesa in turn was buying Cities's reserves for only a little over $4 a barrel. Nor would Cities's balance sheet sit comfortably if it did succeed in winning Mesa. It already had some $2 billion in debt, and had lost nearly $50 million the year before. By contrast, Mesa earned more than $100 million. Wall Street also knew that Pickens would probably sell off much of Cities's assets if he got control.

Cities knew it was vulnerable. It might have beaten Pickens, but it might also have lost. And Cities's management did not want to take that chance. They began to search for a white knight. Cities would find it relatively easily among the many players already lined up, bank credit in hand, to stalk acquisitions.

Gulf Oil had often been approached by investment bankers as a white knight or acquirer in the past. Given its track record, Gulf needed to do something. It had been lagging behind its rivals in many categories for up to a decade at that point. Still the sixth-largest oil company in the nation in sales, it ranked only ninth in income. About half its reserves were overseas, and it eagerly sought new domestic oil and gas reserves. The addition of Cities Service would increase its U.S. reserves and nearly double its U.S. acreage. Cities's single refinery would increase by nearly one third Gulf's capacity. In all, acquisition of Cities would put Gulf back into the ball game—that is, if you ignored the debt they would have to take on to pay for it. On June 17, Gulf offered $63 a share for 51 percent of Cities, the rest in securities. The total value of the transaction: about $5 billion.

It took only about a day for Boone Pickens to fold his tent and steal away. Obviously, Mesa was no match for towering Gulf Oil. The offer of $63—some $18 above his bid—was clearly meant to scare Pickens away. Gulf obviously meant business. Both Mesa and Cities agreed to drop their tender offers for each other. The PacMan defense would not go to the mats. Instead, Pickens sold Mesa's shares back to Cities for $55 a share. Given the average cost of $44 at which it purchased the shares, Mesa pocketed more than $40 million of profit. To Wall Street, which had bid Mesa stock up to the high teens on the basis of Cities's $21 bid, as well as the prospect that Pickens would get Cities, the agreement was a disappointment. The stock dropped to the low teens. But what no one doubted was that Pickens would be back to fight again. Nor were there many doubts that Gulf Oil was the new owner of Cities Service, and soon to be the third-largest oil company in the nation. As of June, it was hard to argue any other way.

Few believed that Gulf was paying anything but a high price for Cities. In an earlier period, perhaps, that woud have cast immediate doubt on the likelihood that the merger would indeed be completed. But in the heady days of the early '80s, anything having to do with takeovers was by and large credible. This time, however, it was going to go too far.

Gulf's long-term debt as a result would rise from about 20 percent of equity to nearly 50 percent. But even the price Gulf was paying in terms of Cities's reserves was high. Part of those reserves was still regulated by controls. Taking this into account, one estimate made at that time had Gulf buying reserves at an average value of $8 a barrel. Discounting that cash flow over time, at current oil prices, that left little leeway if prices fell. One analyst suggested that Gulf would have done better to buy back its own stock. If it bought its own shares, it would be getting reserves at a cheaper price.

There were other doubts raised. Some analysts were dubious about the value of Cities's millions of acres of undeveloped land. The sizable chemical operations of both firms did not seem to many an obvious fit. Cities Service management had not been given high marks by Wall Street, either. Add to all that a falling oil price. In March 1982, Britain cut its price for North Sea oil from $36.50 a barrel to $31. By July, OPEC could not come to agreement on production controls. James Lee, the Gulf chairman, had taken on a lot of adverse factors.

For all that, many arbitrageurs and other investors bought plenty of Cities Service stock. The takeover movement had come so far, momentum alone would carry it on. What gave them most confidence, no doubt, was the newly articulated antitrust policy of the Reagan administration. Under William Baxter, the antitrust division of the Justice Department was now willing to negotiate what changes it believed necessary to make a merger work, rather than impede prospective mergers for an unnecessarily long period of time. Baxter himself said to an SEC study committee that he believed "takeovers and the market for corporate control in general are socially beneficial." In April he announced a new policy that would do its best not to obstruct unfriendly takeovers. Essentially, beginning in 1982, the authorities would allow a merger to take place as long as the parties agreed to divest businesses under question at some later date. There was no longer any ambiguity to the administration's viewpoint on hostile mergers. The antitrust rules would not be an impediment in most situations.

The professional investors were mostly convinced, therefore, that Gulf and Cities Service would encounter no serious antitrust obstacles. What is less obvious is why the arbitrageurs were so confident the economic benefits of the merger would also prevail, and Gulf would go through with the merger. The best answer is the simplest one: Gulf would take over Cities Service because U.S. Steel had done so with Marathon, and DuPont with Conoco, and many smaller companies had done the same thing. It was in fact the thing to do. And if the price seemed a little high, everyone by then agreed that it was appropriate to "pay up" for a property you wanted badly. The arbs bought "big." Eventually, the professional community was reported to own 15 million shares, and Cities stock rose to $55 a share.

In a jilt felt 'round the world, Gulf Oil dropped its bid for Cities Service on a hot Friday afternoon in August, while much of Wall Street was lying lazily around their pools in Long Island's

Hamptons. Ivan Boesky was in his office. There had already been concern that Gulf would drop out. Boesky's position was reportedly as many as 2 million shares. It could amount to a loss between $30 million and $40 million. One observer says that after the end of trading, Boesky simply walked out of his office in rare silence and went home.

The first step in the Gulf pullout came in late July. The Federal Trade Commission did challenge the merger. The legal and Wall Street communities did not take the FTC action seriously. There were three markets the regulators were concerned about. In all three cases, it seemed likely Gulf could sell businesses that would reduce its market share. The most clearcut problem was retail gas sales in the South and along the East Coast. The combination of the two companies could give the new entity up to 50 percent of the market in some regions. Even here, however, most theorized that the new entity would sell gas stations to meet the objections. Gulf might also have had to sell a refining operation.

The FTC action did scare less-sophisticated investors away. At the least, it would delay the bid, costing some interest expense. Other oil stocks also fell after the FTC announcement. Still, the professional arbs believed this deal would go through, given Baxter's explicit statements. Some analysts even urged buying oil stocks now that they were down a bit. But by the next Monday, doubts were rising, not because of the FTC but because Gulf was now said to be worried about selling any operations to satisfy antitrust objections in a weakening oil market. It would be like selling at distress prices. Furthermore, a revision of a tax bill in the Senate Finance Committee would increase the cost of the merger to Gulf. Some estimated it could raise the price $250 million. Could Gulf be looking for excuses to back out?

The facts were that these risks were small in comparison to the size of the transaction. Aggressive investors stayed with their investment, though Cities Service stock did fall. Early that week, Gulf announced that it was extending its offer and that it hoped to settle the FTC objections soon.

Few believed Gulf's explanations when it suddenly bailed out of the bidding contest. It had been negotiating with the FTC for a couple of weeks and claimed it could not come to an agreement.

Gulf said the cost of the FTC requests was too high. Others said that Gulf's aggressive response to the FTC actually provoked the agency's stance. When Gulf had pulled out, Charles Waidelich, Cities's chairman, called the action "reprehensible." What Wall Street really believed happened was that James Lee, the Gulf chairman, got cold feet. The price was high to begin with, oil was falling, and now the FTC was inadvertently offering Lee a face-saving way out. The pullout on August 6 helped burst the takeover bubble that had been expanding for a couple of years by then.

Cities Service stock had already dropped to the mid-forty-dollar range after the FTC announcement. At that point, many experienced arbs considered it a bargain. On the Friday of the Gulf announcement, Cities stock continually lost ground as rumors spread that Gulf might pull out. Trading was then halted. Gulf made its announcement after the market closed. By Monday afternoon, Cities was down to $30. The average cost of stock to the arbitrageurs was probably $52 or $53. Losses for the arbitrage community could run as high as $250 million.

The immediate objective was to find another buyer for Cities. It is likely that in the first few days, some fondly hoped that a major oil company would scoop Cities up with scarcely a penny lost. With all that stock ready to be sold, it did not seem that impossible a task. Cities announced on Sunday, before trading resumed, that it would buy back up to 25 percent of its shares, thereby helping to protect its shareholders. The announcement helped stabilize the market. And the search for a white knight was on.

By any standard, the savior Cities would eventually come up with was a disappointment. Occidental Petroleum, a controversial loser in its outing to take over Mead four years earlier, was too deep in debt to be a financial powerhouse. Now, it was being represented by the investment firm that had defeated it last time, Goldman Sachs. A little more than a week after Gulf dropped out, Occidental came up with an offer valued at about $3.8 billion. It would buy 49 percent of the shares for cash at $50 a share, and offer Occidental securities for the remaining half.

Cities Service would turn down the Occidental bid, and the relationship almost turned unfriendly. But with a slightly sweetened offer at $55 a share, and a better package of securities for the backend, Cities accepted. The FTC raised no objections. But Wall Street was left seriously scarred. Many professional investors made back a good portion of their losses. Others, such as Boesky, had bailed out quickly and did not fully recoup. The losses, even for those who did recover somewhat, were substantial enough to puncture the Street's confidence. Some big deals actually might not go through. Wall Street had grown accustomed to easy profits on hostile acquisitions; now Gulf had thrown cold water on their games. Could the bubble burst altogether? The professional investors had a narrow escape when Occidental turned up.

The history of a social movement is in an important way marked when its members become household names. Until 1982, probably no participant in the takeover movement had become the subject of conversation in an average American home. Surely, Ivan Boesky, T. Boone Pickens, Joe Flom, and Marty Lipton had become dinner conversation for most active readers of the business press. But the big step to broad public recognition had not yet been taken. Few businessmen had ever made that spectacular rung on the ladder, in any case.

What placed takeovers on the popular map of America was Bendix Corp.'s presumptuous offer for Martin Marietta Corp. It precipitated a round robin of bidding that ended in Bendix's being acquired and its chairman, William Agee's being out of a job. It was a takeover contest that degenerated into burlesque, and that is what it took to capture the public's attention. But what also helped was that at its center was a love affair between a boss and his former employee. Here, too, there is a social irony. The only woman of note in the years of hostile takeovers that began in 1974 was a wife. Coming as it did in 1982, on the heels of Gulf's abandonment of Cities Service the near farcical Bendix–Martin Marietta takeover contest would mark the low point of the acquisition wave. That it was tragicomedy rather than stark tragedy was worthy of this movement.

The impetus of financial excess, whether it be the conglomerate rage of the late 1960s or the tulip craze of the 1630s, is that it develops its own mythology. The man who would bring this takeover movement to its absurd extreme was one who could apparently buy this mythology almost whole. William Agee, one day to be chairman of Bendix Corp., one of the nation's hundred largest companies, and at only 38 years of age, was apparently such a man.

Agee grew up in Boise, Idaho, earned a degree from the University of Idaho, and went to Harvard Business School. His good fortune was to enter the job market in the soaring, gilt-edged early '60s. He got a job with Boise Cascade Corp., the forest products company, with the help of the same Harvard dean who had helped to get him accepted at the graduate school. Boise, on its way toward conglomeratization, was the perfect place for takeover mythology to take hold. It began acquiring companies at a prodigious rate. In those days of rapid economic advances—there was no economic recession between 1960 and 1969—a company could seemingly do little wrong. It was a time for the young and bright, bursting with new untested ideas, so many of which would work as long as the economy and the stock market were booming. Wealth breeds super-fluousness, and almost certainly bad decisions. By the early 1970s, Boise would be recording losses from a variety of businesses other than paper. By then, Bill Agee had been chief financial officer for several years.

There is little reason to think that Agee did not sincerely believe in the conventional wisdom of the time, which included the theories of conglomeratization and the notion that a managerial elite could handle just about anything. On the other hand, he left Boise in time. Michael Blumenthal, one day to be Jimmy Carter's Secretary of the Treasury, hired him in 1972 as an executive vice-president, director, and member of the office of the chief executive of Bendix. Bendix was a highly successful manufacturer of auto parts, such as ignitions and brakes, and aviation products, largely for defense. Blumenthal wanted to diversify away from his two main lines of business and he hired Agee to help do that.

Despite one disastrous purchase that Agee supported, made from Boise Cascade, Bendix made money over the next few years and Agee was named president in 1976. Agee had a talent for acquiring mentors. First a Harvard dean, then the chief executive of Boise Cascade, now Blumenthal. When Blumenthal left to join the

Carter administration, Agee was named chairman, after serving only one month as president—and at the age of thirty-eight. Nowhere in his record did Agee have much actual experience at running a business. But he was a chairman before he was forty.

What gave Agee his confidence, and in the minds of colleagues his credibility, were the sales of several Bendix businesses in the early 1980s. In one notable example, Agee capitalized on a partial purchase of Asarco, the big copper and silver refiner. Bendix had bought just over 20 percent of Asarco in 1978 for only about $125 million. Agee sold it two years later for nearly three times the price, at about the peak for mining companies.

Agee partly lucked into this sale. He was not so lucky when he successfully bought all of Warner & Swasey, the Cleveland machine tool maker, in a bidding contest in 1980. Bendix came in as a white knight, paid $300 million, and was showing losses in its machine tool business by 1982.

Mary Cunningham, the household name to be, joined Bendix in 1979 as executive assistant to Agee, who was then chairman. Also a graduate of Harvard Business School, she worked closely with Agee in devising a new strategy for Bendix. She was a good student. She was articulate, ready with answers, quick with conceptualizations. The takeover movement was a model playground for the facile strategies of business school students. By the early 1980s, corporate deal-making and huge takeovers could be fit into a personal romantic philosophy. Surely, Agee and Cunningham, who, according to one witness, would occasionally sit holding hands at a meeting during the takeover contest that was to come, were utter romantics wrapped up in a cause. Could two such lovers have found a common cause in business in the 1960s, for example? No better proof that takeovers had developed their own life and mythology can be found than that they seemed to bring Mary Cunningham and Bill Agee together.

Cunningham's role brought her national attention, not the least of it over her stout denials that she and Agee had an intimate relationship while she was at Bendix. At first, much of the press took up her cause as an executive mistreated because of her sex. Later, the press would be less kind. How ironic, this romantic image of two star-crossed lovers riding off into the sunset to undertake a hostile acquisition together. Because of the controversy over their relationship, Cunningham was forced to resign from Bendix. She took a planning job at Seagram. She and Agee were married in June 1982.

By early 1980, after the Asarco sale, Agee had built up nearly $800 million in cash. It was no secret that he was seeking to make a major acquisition, and that, like so many others, he had decided—with Cunningham's strategic help—to buy a firm in technology. The rising cliché was now to sell cyclical basic industries that were victims of foreign competition and big swings in the economy, and move into the front edge of growth through technology. To chief executives who managed business as though they were portfolios of stocks, such concepts made eminently good sense. Gould International, under William Ylvisaker, was particularly aggressive in transforming itself from a machinery to a high-tech company. That the same concepts had often failed in the conglomerate era a decade earlier was an issue seldom raised. Gould had mixed results at best.

Agee had been compiling a list of possible takeover targets. By the summer of 1981, they included Lockheed, RCA—which owned NBC—and Gould itself. There were other candidates as well. Agee would make approaches to several companies, including RCA. In the spring of 1982, he would consider a hostile tender offer for RCA, but his investment banker, Salomon Brothers, advised against it.

Soon, Agee had set his sights on Martin Marietta. Marietta had a very strong aerospace business, which included the manufacture of several missile systems. Salomon had already accumulated nearly 4.5 percent of Marietta's stock for Bendix between April and July. The question now was how to devise a strategy that would win. Agee had apparently made up his mind. He wanted Marietta.

Most analysts agreed that Marietta was cheap at its price in the low thirty-dollar range per share. Its aerospace business was very strong, though cement and aluminum, two cyclical businesses, were holding the company down, suffering as they were in the recession. What Agee may have misunderstood was how tactics had come to dominate takeover contests at that time. He was using several investment bankers, including Goldman Sachs, Lehman Brothers, and Salomon. Some would blame Jay Higgins, who headed Salomon's takeover team, for not being aggressive enough. Others blamed Agee's intransigence.

By 1982 cautious tactics were necessary, because it was becoming increasingly obvious that the first bidder often lost. For one thing, a target company could frequently find a white knight now. Second, as Whittaker Corp. recently discovered when it tried to take over Brunswick, a target could also sell off its most desired business in an attempt to thwart a takeover. Whittaker was a medical and chemical products company that found Brunswick's Sherwood medical division especially attractive. Brunswick, which made both leisure products and medical supplies, sold Sherwood to American Home Products before Whittaker could complete the acquisition. Whittaker then dropped out.

There was also now another defensive possibility: the PacMan defense. In devising a takeover strategy, Agee and Salomon agreed that the popular and effective two-tiered offer, so frequently used by First Boston, should be ruled out. It was considered unfair by many in the profession, because it paid heavily for the first half of the company and left remaining shareholders on a string. On the other hand, it was often successful because it attracted the arbitrageurs to the stock for a quick profit. "We thought it was coercive," says Higgins. Agee may have also felt vulnerable. He had already been called out publicly by Thornton Bradshaw of RCA when he approached the company with an offer. Bradshaw had openly stated that Agee should learn to manage his own business first. And Agee's already known personal life could now be easy fodder for a vitriolic public relations battle. Agee ruled out a two-tiered offer.

What Bendix lawyers did discover while they were preparing for the tender offer was that Marietta would have a significant advantage should it choose to countertender. Incorporated in Maryland, Marietta enjoyed a statute that required ten days' notice before a new majority shareholder could call a meeting to remove the board of directors. In other words, if Bendix bought Marietta's stock, it might not be able to remove the board for ten days. If Marietta countertendered—the PacMan defense—and got a majority of Bendix, which was a Delaware corporation, it could kick out the board almost immediately. Theoretically, Marietta could win a PacMan showdown.

Aware of this, both Salomon and Agee nevertheless dismissed the likelihood of a countertender, because it would remove one of Marietta's potential defenses. They would not be able to cry anti- trust violation if they were in turn trying to take over Bendix. Agee also realized one other conventional fact. The first bidder might lose the contest, but he usually came away making a lot of money. Often, at worst, a white knight bought out the raider's stake, or the target itself bought it back. It must have looked to Bill Agee that he had little to lose. And so, on August 25, Bendix bid $43 a share for Marietta. What Bendix had underestimated was how determined Marietta would be to fight it.

The Bendix battle for Martin Marietta exemplified the state of the takeover movement by 1982, and it was something like this: Many of the nation's five hundred largest companies were on each other's hit lists. According to several public reports then, Bendix had Gould and Marietta on its list of targets. But Gould had Bendix and Marietta on *its* list. And Marietta in turn had considered making a bid for Bendix. Similarly, everyone now believed almost anyone was acquirable. Agee's audacity had gone so far as to consider a takeover of RCA, much bigger than Bendix, and the owner of NBC, which most still believed would make it relatively immune from takeover, given the government regulatory bodies that must scrutinize such an acquisition. In addition, bank credit lines were there for the grabbing. Banks, too, learned that acquisi- tion loans could be profitable, a small fee being charged that, in the case of multibillion-dollar credits, significantly enhanced the bottom line.

Similarly, the circle of white knights had enlarged, as had potential buyers for pieces of companies. This multiplied the possi- bilities in every takeover enormously. Shortly before Agee bid for Marietta, he called Gould to sell back the block of Gould stock he had bought. Marty Siegel, head of Kidder Peabody's mergers depart- ment, represented Gould and was told of the buy-back. To him, it was a clear signal that Bendix was building a war chest. In addition, he knew large chunks of Marietta stock were being bought. He warned Marietta, an obvious target, immediately. It was all legal—it did not constitute illegal use of inside information—but it characterized the advantage the merger professionals enjoyed, and why they could command so much in fees.

Moreover, by 1982 the best of them knew one other thing, either by their own nature or through experience. Boldness and the single-minded desire to win were necessary once a contest began. Any shortcomings, any hesitation to be aggressive, could spell doom. That advice, that outlook, was worth a lot. Agee did not fully understand this.

Finally, the romance of takeovers was at a high point. Agee designated allegorical code names for the takeover players: Earth, Wind, and Fire. The secretness was more self-delusion than dictated by need. That *Newsweek* would publish a rumored list of Agee's targets shortly before he made the bid—and Marietta was on the list—made a sham of his efforts at maintaining secrets. In fact, no deal had ever received nearly as much press before, for both its personal and its business interest. That truly was the mark of the state of the takeover movement.

For the economy, only one issue mattered, and it was hard to believe this contest would decide it properly. Who deserved to own the assets and business of Marietta, either for the good of the employees, or shareholders, or corporate America? The battle would not be decided on those grounds at all. Marty Siegel argues that those who made bad takeovers did not survive to make others, that the process, in effect, provides its own weeding. But how many bad deals are done in the meantime?

What finally did happen was this: Marty Siegel urged Martin Marietta to countertender for Bendix—a PacMan defense. He argued that Marietta was big enough to scare Bendix away. A key in what was to happen was that Marietta steadfastly took Siegel's advice, and held to their bid. The PacMan defense was being put to its most serious test. But it became clear that Marietta's bid needed more financial credibility with Wall Street; otherwise the investment professionals would assuredly tender to Bendix. Siegel set out to find a white knight who might share the Bendix assets with Marietta, once Bendix was acquired.

Marietta made its counterbid for Bendix, but a white knight

was in the making. Felix Rohatyn coaxed none other than Harry Gray of United Technologies to take a look. By early September, Gray and Tom Pownall, head of Marietta, had cooked up a deal. United would tender for Bendix, and Marietta would pay United some $600 million for several of Bendix's assets. Now there were two offers outstanding for Bendix. Marietta had tendered $75 a share for the first half and a much lower $55 a share in securities for the backend. United also offered $75 in cash for the first half of Bendix shares, but slightly less than Marietta offered for the backend. Unlike Bendix, neither company had qualms about the two-tier deal. Bendix had raised its offer for Marietta to $48 a share.

As of September 8, then, Agee was stuck. While he might have been able to fashion a deal with Marietta to have them both drop their tenders, he could not be sure that United would also agree to drop out. Agee felt he now had to go ahead with his bid and buy the Marietta shares tendered to him. What would surprise him was that Marietta, when its deadline approached, retained its resolution to buy the shares tendered to it as well. If both companies had succeeded in buying each other—if the PacMan went ahead—the resulting company would have a ridiculous debt load, more than two and a half times its equity.

Agee had dropped Salomon and hired First Boston to represent Bendix soon after the United bid. Bruce Wasserstein led the team. United raised its bid for Bendix on the condition that Bendix agree to a friendly deal. But negotiations were never completed. To the great surprise of the Marietta camp, Agee went ahead and bought the Marietta stock tendered to him. It looked as if PacMan was close to its first real-world test. Few ever thought it would go this far.

In the meantime, Ed Hennessy, Harry Gray's former chief financial officer and now chief rival as head of Allied Corp., had told Agee he was interested in buying Bendix or some of its assets, even after Agee had bought the Marietta stock. Hennessy became Agee's white knight and only out, or else both Bendix and Marietta would be swallowed up by each other. The only consolation was that Agee's lawyers did get a court to keep Marietta from voting the stock it owned to overthrow the Bendix board. The early advantage that made the PacMan countertender look reasonable to Marietta was overriden anyway.

In the end, Agee decided to sell Bendix to Allied, and Marietta with it. Marietta's bid had not yet expired. If Allied bid for Bendix, it would automatically delay Marietta's bid and Bendix would own Marietta clear. Allied did bid $85 a share in cash for half of the shares, and about $75 in securities for the rest, topping United Technologies's bid. Gray would go no further. But through an unusual series of miscalculations, the bid came too late to stop Marietta. Nor was Bendix able to convince the arbs not to tender. When he realized what had happened, Hennessy, now in control of Bendix, made a deal with Pownall of Marietta to exchange shares. Marietta would get back its own shares and Bendix its shares. Because Bendix had spent more, Allied received an additional compensation in the form of Marietta stock. But Allied also agreed to a standstill that kept it from making any attempt at control of Marietta. In all, the final deal cost Hennessy less than he had expected. Bill Agee would remain as president of Allied, but only until June 1983. Hennessy says that when he saw him and Mary Cunningham on the cover of *People* magazine, he had had it.

To the public, which had watched this takeover battle more intently than any other, the outcome was very simple. Bill Agee bid for a company and wound up losing his own. It was ironic, and maybe fitting. To the takeover community, it was an embarrassment—"the low point," says one investment banker. To other chief executives, it was a stern warning about takeovers. They were playing with fire. And maybe more important, the Agee debacle took the glamour out of the battle as well. Once considered romantic and perhaps a sign of business machismo, becoming a corporate raider no longer seemed so attractive; no chief executive wanted to look as foolish as Agee.

Allied won Bendix in September, close on the heels of Gulf Oil's pulling the plug on its bid for Cities Service. It was easily the worst year for the eight-year-old takeover movement. Activity would slow in the next few months. And now the stock market was moving higher, a sharp bull rally igniting in August. Potential target companies no longer looked nearly as cheap. Many observers were saying that the takeover movement had ended.

The most remarkable part of the story is that they were completely wrong.

15

Talk was widespread after the four-way battle for Bendix and Martin Marietta that takeover volume was sure to decline. Because the Bendix-Marietta confrontation came soon after the Gulf pullout, the investment community realized that corporations would get wary of bidding. Though arbitrageurs did well on the Bendix-Marietta battle, there were signs of decline elsewhere. Most important, stock prices were starting to rise again, and the Dow Jones Industrials reached 1200 in mid-1983, a jump over the period of nearly 50 percent. What helped propel the rise was a drop in oil prices, which should have stood as a warning.

But the Bendix-Marietta deal did in fact mark a turning point. Comparatively fewer large companies would make hostile bids again. Not only did Agee's loss take much of the glamour out of the bidding. More important, it became obvious that if you bid first you could lose. "Martin Marietta represented the end of the road for most hostile takeovers made by major companies," Marty Lipton says categorically. In addition, corporations moved diligently to shield themselves from the effective two-tier bid by adopting fair price amendments that required that any bid be more or less equal for all shareholders. Other shark repellents also became widespread. In addition, the SEC changed the rules for proration pools in early 1983, in effect diminishing the striking power of the partial cash bid.

Takeover volume dropped significantly in 1982. Instead, divestitures were sharply on the rise as company after company that had succumbed to the lure of diversification began to sell pieces off. In 1981, there were 366 divestitures worth less than $17 billion. By

1983, there were 24 billion dollars' worth of divestitures, and by 1985 that would rise to $46 billion. It looked as if mergers had gone too far.

For all that, the largest mergers of all time were still to come, just two years after the 1982 low point. Oil companies were again the target of these huge acquisitions. Total takeover volume in 1984 would reach a record level—$122 billion. And that record would be topped again in 1985 with 180 billion dollars' worth of mergers. Wall Street investment bankers would make more money than ever before, and so would arbitrageurs. Yet it was not major companies that would lead the way. The takeover mechanism had reached so refined a state that a new brand of takeover specialists would emerge, soon to be called financial entrepreneurs or takeover artists, or, to most, corporate raiders. They could push a button that now put into action a chain reaction of cause-and-effect that left no company with sufficient protection. In reaction, poison pills and other extreme defense mechanisms would be developed. In 1982 and 1983 the takeover movement began to take a turn that no one could have predicted. It no longer took another big company to make a raid. Now, just about everyone was vulnerable to a sort of professional acquisition specialist—some called them gunslingers. The leader of this new and most extraordinary phase of the takeover movement was Boone Pickens.

Many of those at the forefront of takeovers over these years were not men driven by mysterious or outsize needs. The most influential, Joe Flom, learned his aggressive trade at the knees of elders in the late 1950s and during the 1960s. He no doubt excelled out of ambition and talent, but those qualities in turn were fostered by growing opportunity. He was bred along the way; he had no vision that preceded it all. Marty Lipton, Flom's closest rival in influence, was a man in part motivated by intellectual curiosity, drawn to takeovers almost as if he enjoyed the game. And he was Flom's disciple as much as his competitor. Arthur Fleischer, of Fried, Frank, Harris, Shriver & Jacobson, was an intellectual, drawn into the contest by his knowledge. Felix Rohatyn, over the years one of the most influential of the investment bankers, was also a man of intellectual curiosity and bred by experience during the 1960s. Harry Gray, the most influential acquirer among corporate chief executives, had learned his trade during the rise of the conglomerates in prior decades. The men of Goldman Sachs were products of their well-run and driven investment banking house, not individual entrepreneurs who set out to take on the world. Even Carl Icahn, Boone Pickens's closest rival, had a long pedigree of financial training, growing bolder slowly as he gained more experience and had more success.

But there were a few participants whose sheer ambition and turn of mind need more explanation. Charles Baird's drive to win had set the movement on its course when Inco stalked ESB, but Baird had little other takeover experience. Bob Greenhill scrapped his way through an elite and satisfied group of managers at Morgan Stanley to make that house perhaps the most aggressive of the banking institutions in the earlier years. His assurance and drive have no obvious forebears. One senses he would have ground his way to success no matter what the circumstances. Joe Perella, who built First Boston into a major takeover player, and in some periods the most sought-after of the houses, had an edgy ambition and confidence that preceded any experience that would justify them. Ivan Boesky could see no boundaries to his world. He pushed the potential of risk arbitrage further than anyone could have imagined in the mid-1970s. An outsider by every standard, he feared no Goldman Sachs or Salomon Brothers in his passion to get more, get bigger, get just about everything. None of these men was ambivalent about his role. All had personalities that defined success in terms of money, or at least social prestige that was very closely aligned to money, the social prestige of Ivy League schools and Wall Street titles.

But of all the players on the takeover scene, Boone Pickens, with his commitment and talent and understanding of the financial system, must have looked to these Wall Street men like something of a miracle rising out of the West. Even after he had succeeded in taking on the nation's largest oil companies, everyone always speculated on what Boone was really up to. When asked, he always gave the same answer. He was out to get the shareholders their fair value.

A more cynical financial community did not buy it. Pickens was making a lot of money in the meantime. He had figured out better than anyone, this Texas wildcatter, how to exploit the takeover mechanism. It was popular simply to believe he was just plain smart. People always have a tendency to believe others are essentially like themselves. It is hard to know someone who may not be. Pickens would always talk innocently about his representing the shareholders, especially to the press. But Wall Street thought it knew better.

The truth seems to be somewhere in between. Pickens surely liked to make money for himself and his investors. He also seemed to have a mission. But that mission was probably not quite what he said it was. To Pickens, the enemy seemed to be the management of the major oil companies. This man, who started his career as a geologist for Phillips Petroleum in Bartlesville, Oklahoma, viewed those who rose to run the major oil companies as an insensitive and undeserving elite. He has said so time and again. The track to the top, as in many stable, large corporations, was fastest for those who could be docile in the face of bad decisions, flatter their bosses, and bide their time until the opportunity was right—in other words, classic organization men.

Pickens was not a member of that club. He left Phillips after four years to strike out on his own. He would hit oil enough to eventually build himself a fortune and a company. Perhaps what drove him was a need to prove himself against the oil establishment. Now, he could take them on, if not as equals, at least more directly. The name of his crusade became to defend the shareholders, but the reality seemed to be a deeper-seated cause. The boldness of Mesa Petroleum, with $400 million in sales, taking on a giant with $30 billion in sales, could better be understood in light of that. Pickens was willing to risk more, because he had something to prove to the oil establishment.

Pickens typically claimed that oil companies' reserves were far more valuable than the stock market was crediting them for. He proposed that for the most part the big oil companies should sell their reserves and pass the money on to the shareholders. He proposed that they form so-called royalty trusts to do this, a method that would circumvent the double taxation of dividends, since income earned in a royalty trust was not taxed if passed on to the shareholders, though shareholders would then be personally taxed for the dividends they received. The Pickens proposal would also, of course, serve to dismantle the major companies at the same time. Management would get theirs. And the only reason they weren't doing what he proposed, Pickens claimed, was that they were afraid to lose their jobs.

Pickens had, by the end of 1982, become a very sophisticated student of the financial markets. His battle for Cities Service was carefully calculated. But because Pickens waited, Cities actually got the opportunity to bid first. Yet Pickens was also well versed in the advantages of taking a position in a company, then bidding. If you succeeded, you owned the target. If you failed, it was almost always because someone else bailed you out at a higher price. Pickens had earned Mesa Petroleum $40 million when Gulf bid for Cities Service. And he had watched the same phenomenon occur time and again with countless companies. Moreover, he was not put off when it backfired on William Agee. Pickens was a true gambler, careful and on guard. For the right price, many analysts said, he also would have sold Mesa.

General American Oil Co., based in Dallas, was long one of the most coveted independent oil and gas companies in the United States. It had been built up by Algur Meadows, who had died in 1978. Ever since then, it had become the subject of takeover rumors, Meadows's lock on some 35 percent of the stock a clear deterrent until his death. Pickens had Mesa buy a large piece of the company in the 1970s.

After Mesa cleared its Cities Service profit, Pickens was ready to strike again. Oil company stocks were down. The oil price was weak, and most oil stocks had not bounced up with the rest of the market. Were oil companies in trouble, or just selling for bargain prices? Pickens said they were a bargain, certainly a lot cheaper than drilling for new oil directly.

General American had some 80 million barrels of proven oil reserves in the United States and Canada, and a like amount of natural gas. A conservatively run company, it had virtually no debt. Mesa boasted more revenue and profit, about $400 million and $100 million respectively, but its proven reserves amounted to only 28 million barrels. General American was not as big a target as

Pickens had already proven he was willing to take on. Cities Service was much bigger. But Pickens's attack would prove the start of a new phase of the takeover movement.

In a typical move, he waited until Sunday evening, the beginning of Christmas week, to start. With Morgan Stanley as an adviser, he bid $40 for enough shares to get 51 percent of General American, a total in cash of $520 million. The stock had closed at $35 the Friday before. If he got the 51 percent, he would offer to buy the remainder of the shares with a package of securities that analysts speculated might be worth less than $30 a share. To many, it looked like a bid that could be beaten. Some claimed Pickens bid low just to entice a competitive offer. But in those days, after Gulf had dropped out of the Cities Service deal, the confidence in oil takeovers was not high. Nevertheless, after Pickens announced, the arbitrageurs drove General American higher, eventually up to $46 a share.

What was pretty certain was that General American would not sit by idly and let Pickens grab them up. They went right to First Boston for advice. Marty Lipton was their lawyer, and he launched the obligatory lawsuits. General American, smaller than Pickens's Mesa, did not need convincing that Pickens could acquire them.

General American management reacted swiftly. By Wednesday night, they adopted a sweeping golden parachute that provided all their employees with at least three months' pay if control changed hands. They set First Boston off to find a white knight. And they launched a tender offer for about one third—which could be raised to more than half—of their own shares at $50 each. They also planned to sell key assets. The takeover procedure seemed well worn by now. A bidding contest was brewing.

First Boston did not have an easy time finding a white knight. Confidence was low, if only temporarily. Several major oil companies, including Mobil, Texaco, and Gulf, were all approached. But by the first week of January, only Phillips Petroleum stepped forward with a higher bid. The attraction to Phillips was General American's domestic oil reserves. Phillips's own domestic reserves were declining, and nearly half of its reserves were overseas, where politics could be unstable.

The Phillips offer amounted to $1.2 billion. Essentially, it would pay $45 a share in cash for half of the shares.

Pickens decided to drop out, satisfied with the Phillips bid. General American also agreed to pay Mesa $15 million for expenses. In all, Mesa claimed a profit of approximately $45 million on the deal on its original stock purchases.

For the takeover movement, however, there was now a little light at the end of the tunnel darkened by Gulf's withdrawal and William Agee's boondoggle four months earlier. What set the stage for the new takeover phase was that this acquisition was initiated by a lone raider. CEOs might now hesitate to make bids, but the corporate raiders would not. Mesa pocketed more money. The irony is that some analysts claimed that Phillips had so strengthened itself with the General American purchase that it was now probably immune to a hostile raid. Soon Phillips itself, Pickens's alma mater, would become the target of his pursuit. But there were a few deals to come before that fateful day.

Among those who would become known as corporate raiders, Carl Icahn was Boone Pickens's closest rival. But their similarities ended with that label. In his early years, Carl Icahn made little show of any larger mission. He was an opportunist, if by almost everyone's acknowledgment an honest one. Boone Pickens denied that he was a greenmailer. Icahn denied that it was a moral issue, though he eventually testified before Congress that greenmail should be outlawed on the condition that corporations were also to be deprived of anti-takeover weapons such as the poison pill and scorched earth defenses. In the meantime, however, Icahn says he would accept greenmail, and he certainly became its most successful practitioner. Despite his reputation, Icahn was less of a gambler than many others in the business. He weighed every move very carefully and rarely came up a loser.

Where Boone Pickens could swagger a little, a confident man, even a college athlete, Icahn appears clumsy. He is a man who, if courteous, seems to have few natural graces. Pickens always aimed big. Icahn, by far the taller of the two, was a small businessman in attitude, the small businessman of the takeover movement. In one way, he and Pickens were very similar. They were both more or less outsiders to their respective establishments.

Carl Icahn got his training in the 1960s with several Wall Street firms until he founded his own small brokerage firm in 1968. But he lived by his wits, exploiting profitable opportunities as they arose. He was not out to build an institution. He traded in options on stocks. He practiced classic riskless arbitrage, trading on small differences in securities that arose in different marketplaces. He made money for his investors. When New York Stock Exchange firms were still charging fixed commissions to their customers, Icahn followed a few leaders into the discount brokerage business. When options trading formally started on exchanges, Icahn got a boost. The appeal of options was that it gave the investor an inexpensive way to play swings in stock prices. You could buy a call for a few hundred dollars that would enable an investor to own one hundred shares of a stock at a given price. But the stock had to move within a fixed time period or the call expired worthless. Once formalized on options exchanges, trading became very popular.

Icahn followed money. When takeovers heated up, Icahn became a small risk arbitrageur. But his real love was riskless arbitrage. He was more analytical than Ivan Boesky, and far more careful. But what many friends say about him is that he was a very good company analyst. And they always say he was very honest. He was a strict believer in the conventional wisdom of the time, which argued that the stock market was severely undervaluing corporations. He also claimed, arguably less sincerely, that bad management was the culprit, and he believed it was often better to sell off parts of a company, or liquidate it all, than keep it running. By the late 1970s, Icahn started to move away from being a passive investor to taking an active role. He began to see the purchase of low-priced companies as almost the equivalent of a riskless arbitrage. Characteristically, he started off small.

Perhaps what got Icahn rolling is the seldom remembered fact that he actually won his first contest. Icahn bought up the shares of Baird & Warner, a real estate investment trust based in Chicago, when those shares were trading very low in 1979, then launched a proxy contest and gained control, renaming the company Bayswater

Realty and Investment Trust, after the Queens neighborhood where he was born.

The winning-by-losing strategy that would make Icahn famous, however, scored its first success later that year. Icahn and his investors bought about 1.5 million dollars' worth of the stock of Tappan Co., the well-known maker of kitchen ranges. With 5 percent of the company, Icahn again launched a proxy contest. Elected to the board, he demanded the liquidation of the company. Frightened by Icahn's threats, Tappan found a white knight in the Swedish company A. B. Electrolux. Icahn's group walked off with a profit of $2.7 million when it sold out to A.B. Electrolux for the higher price. He had discovered that he did not have to take over the company to make a profit.

Icahn would duplicate his success in an investment in Saxon Industries in early 1980. But these targets were small compared to Icahn's next assault.

Hammermill Paper Company had been a premier manufacturer of writing and printing papers for more than eighty years. Despite Icahn's oft-stated philosophy about how takeovers motivated management to improve itself, it was very hard to make the case that Hammermill's management had been lax. In 1979 it had sales of just over $1 billion and profits of $35 million, about double its 1975 levels. It had upgraded its plants, and was planning more expansion. The company still had a reputation for sluggishness, but it was certainly moving in the right direction, by most current assessments. Still, the stock market valued Hammermill at about $25 a share, well below its stated book value of $37. Moreover, Hammermill's timberland was generally considered understated on the books, and if calculated at its market value, analysts said it would add $25 or more to Hammermill's stock price. This was the kind of value Icahn loved. Liquidation sounded like the best way to get the values out of the company.

In March 1980, Icahn announced that his various investment companies owned more than 10 percent of Hammermill's stock. Typically, Icahn stated that he might suggest that Hammermill be liquidated. In this way—with an investment of only about $20 million—Icahn was able to get the ball rolling. Hammermill did not take the Icahn threat lightly. Each group filed suit against the other, and Hammermill braced for the proxy contest that was to come.

Icahn's election campaign rested essentially on his proposal to sell Hammermill. Hammermill's management stood by its recent record, and actively solicited proxies. The outcome of the contest was not clear until July. Icahn had lost, and due to the expenses of both the proxy fight and his pursuit of legal remedies, he says he accepted a settlement with Hammermill to drop out. Hammermill paid him $750,000.

But Icahn and his investors enjoyed the last laugh. One year later, Hammermill, still intent on ridding itself of this thorn in its side, agreed to buy back Icahn's shares. It paid $36 a share for Icahn's 865,000 shares. On its $20 million investment, Icahn's group cleared about $9 million in profit. It was classic greenmail. Icahn's reputation was growing.*

The investment killing that would raise Carl Icahn to a kind of institutional status, and produce many imitators, would take place in 1982, when Icahn threatened a takeover of Marshall Field. This move, along with Pickens's bid for General American, marked the new phase of the takeover movement.

To those who maintain that the threat of takeovers is an incentive to better management, Marshall Field offers a case study in contrary lessons. Its management did not improve under the threat of takeover. On the other hand, good management did not keep Hammermill out of the hands of acquirers, just as it did not keep Carborundum out of the hands of Kennecott or ESB out of the hands of Inco.

Marshall Field, as we have seen, had been the target of an aggressive takeover attempt by Carter Hawley Hale in late 1977 and 1978. CHH, the West Coast retailer and owner of the Neiman-Marcus department store chain, had built itself up through acquisitions and well-run retail stores. Philip Hawley had apparently long coveted Marshall Field, Chicago's best-known depart-

*Several years later, Hammermill would succumb to an acquisition, again provoked by a hostile bid from a group of independent investors, this time not including Icahn. Hammermill eventually sold out to a white knight, International Paper, for $64.50 a share.

ment store, with fifty other stores throughout the nation. When
Marshall Field's chairman, Joseph Burnham, suddenly died of a
heart attack, Hawley approached a Marshall Field director and
suggested a merger.

Angelo Arena, the man who was put in charge of Field after
Burnham's death, was a former Carter Hawley executive who had
successfully run Neiman-Marcus for CHH. There was little doubt
he and his board would resist Hawley. On December 12, 1977,
Hawley made a hostile offer for Field at $36 a share, which repre-
sented a handsome premium over its prevailing price of about $23 a
share. Marshall Field, under Arena, chose to fight.

To most, Field was vulnerable because of its ineffective management over a full decade. Earnings were no higher than they had
been ten years earlier, while some retail chains had expanded and
thrived. Even within its home territory, Marshall Field was being
beaten by the competition. Arena's charge was to build up Field.
Under the takeover advice of Joe Flom and Goldman Sachs, retail
expansion could serve as an effective anti-takeover device. Arena
announced plans to open a southern division, with new stores in
Dallas and Houston, Neiman-Marcus territory. He planned to buy
five stores from Amfac Inc. in the nation's Northwest.

Hawley raised his bid to $42 a share, but Field continued to
resist. The FTC had also begun to investigate. Facing Field's expensive expansion plans, and an FTC that still exercised power back in
1978, Hawley dropped out of the contest in February. Eventually,
he acquired Wanamaker's instead. And Marshall Field lived
independently—only to fight Carl Icahn four years later.

Marshall Field had the sort of brand name that had always
attracted Carl Icahn. Tappan and Hammermill Paper also enjoyed
well-known product names. Marshall Field was still the best-known
department store in Chicago, and ranked among the major chains in
the nation. But under Arena, it had not fared well. The takeover
scare provoked it to expand too quickly. It now boasted triple the
number of stores it had when Arena took over but it also added
nearly $120 million in debt, which would produce additional inter-
est expenses of $21 million in 1981. In the fiscal year ended January
1981, Field earned under $21 million, still less than its record
profits earned in 1972, a decade earlier. Carter Hawley Hale's

hostile bid had provoked no renaissance at Marshall Field—indeed, had made matters worse.

To Icahn, however, the conditions were ripe for his type of investment play. Marshall Field's stock was actually below the level of 1978, when Hawley had made his bid; it was now under $20 a share. Criticism was renewed that Field had turned down the Carter Hawley $42 offer. Field's real estate properties in Chicago were also very valuable, as were other properties in the nation. These, Icahn knew, could be sold off at a handsome profit. The weak Field could probably be bullied by the Icahn offensive, a consideration colleagues say Icahn always took into account. One friend recounts how he suggested to Icahn going after a particular company, only to have Icahn come back with a firm no, claiming the board of directors was too strong.

Icahn by now had a significant pool of capital to work with. Early in February 1982, he announced that his investment group, which included a Netherlands Antilles company, owned nearly 11 percent of Marshall Field. Icahn said he might try to get his own slate of directors elected to the board in a proxy contest.

With Goldman Sachs again as its adviser, Field fought back. It filed the conventional lawsuits against Icahn, adding a new, contentious charge of racketeering. It was testing a new defense based on legislation known as the Racketeering Influenced and Corrupt Organizations Act (RICO) designed to make it easier to fight organized crime. Field claimed the investor group was financing its purchases with past profits that were made in violation of securities laws. The innovative defense, while tried several times, never proved effective.

By 1982, the takeover mechanism was far easier to put into play than when Icahn had started only a few years before. Arena was quoted in *The New York Times* as follows: "There are at least 15 options that Goldman Sachs could pursue for us." On the other hand, as Arena conceded, the options mostly required more purchases of companies by Marshall Field, or sales of assets, or finding a white knight. Field did announce that it considered selling real estate properties in Chicago and Seattle.

In the meantime, Icahn had found new sources of capital. In early March, he let it be known that a Paris bank, Banque Commercial Privée, would make up to $40 million available to his group in the pursuit of Marshall Field. And by the middle of the month, Icahn's holdings in Field were nearly 30 percent of its stock.

Ultimately, Marshall Field believed it had no recourse but to find a white knight. The candidates even included Carter Hawley again. But the Field management chose to go with Batus Inc., the American subsidiary of B.A.T. Industries of London, formerly the British American Tobacco Co. The United States subsidiary had 1980 sales of $4 billion. It owned the nation's third largest tobacco company, Brown & Williamson Tobacco, maker of such cigarettes as Kool and Viceroy, and it had acquired ten years earlier Gimbel's and Saks Fifth Avenue. Even at that time, Gimbel's was not paying off, and Batus would dismantle it in 1986.

In mid-March, Batus offered only $25.50 for Field, topping slightly offers by Carter Hawley and May Department Stores. (Batus made an equivalent offer for Field's convertible preferred shares.) Icahn was irate at the low price. After all, Hawley had offered $42 a share four years earlier. Icahn sued, claiming that a lock-up agreement between Field and Batus was illegal, on much the same grounds that U.S. Steel's lock-up with Marathon was overthrown. Ultimately, a federal judge ruled against him. With First Boston as advisers, Batus sweetened its offer, the final offer being in two steps. Icahn's complaints may have paid off. Batus eventually paid $30 for both the front and back ends of the offer, the total price some $365 million. The FTC did investigate, but by 1982 many anticipated that the government would merely request some changes that could be easily made. Batus was indeed barred from building stores in some areas, and had to sell a couple of Milwaukee units. Complaining all the way, Icahn eventually cashed in. His group scored a $30 million profit on an investment of about $60 million.

In 1982 and 1983 Icahn would profit with similar raids on Dan River and American Can, again well-known names in their fields. And by then, the corporate raider had gained a place on the roster of those who were making big reputations and fortunes in the takeover movement. The word *greenmail*—the actual payoff of an investor to go away—had not yet come into wide use. But Icahn was its artist. He did not bother to explain away how it hurt other shareholders. A company bought back Icahn's shares at a premium, but it in effect used the other shareholders' money to do it. One shareholder, Icahn, benefited at the expense of others. These new methods became a growing source of controversy.

In following years, Icahn would enjoy similar successes pursuing the likes of Viacom. He also spawned a host of followers, such as Irwin Jacobs, Asher Edelman, and Saul Steinberg, all of whom bought up stock and threatened takeovers, only to sell their shares back to target companies at a substantial profit. By 1983, the takeover movement had entered the new phase that required a lesser role from the nation's large corporations. The corporate raiders would be in charge for the next few years. Only one piece of the puzzle was missing: big financing. And that would soon come.

There is one other important change in the environment that made the rise of the raiders possible. What gave men like Boone Pickens and Carl Icahn credibility was the growing acknowledgment that the sale of parts of a company made good sense. In the wake of so many mergers, it became recognized that diversification was not necessarily good; that individual businesses, especially if unrelated, could be managed better if independent and not part of a large conglomerate. Indeed, separate businesses were more valuable if managed independently, and a corporation could produce higher share prices by selling these individual businesses off. Private investors, or another corporation, would be willing to pay more for an individual business. The whole was worth less than the sum of its parts. In this lay the substance of bids by men like Icahn and Pickens, who usually intended to liquidate the companies they bought, and raised financing on that assumption in order to buy them.

The failure of many of the acquisitions of the previous eight years or so inspired the turn against diversification. Mobil's experience with Marcor, Exxon's bad investment in Reliance Electric, Schlumberger's regrettable results with Fairchild, Standard Oil's piggybacking of a poor acquisition of Kennecott Copper, after Kennecott had bungled its acquisition of Carborundum, were all readily visible examples of the failure of diversification.

But two corporate events marked the period very clearly. General Electric, under new management, swallowed its enormous pride and sold Utah International to Broken Hill Proprietary Company for $2.4 billion in 1982.

The second event was a proxy fight for Transworld Inc. in early 1983. The dissidents demanded that TWC consider selling off each of its five separate divisions, which included TWA, the airline, food services, hotels, and other operations. The challenge was engineered by Odyssey Partners, an investment company created by the former senior partners of Oppenheimer & Co., a leading brokerage firm, after it was sold to a British company. The idea was Leon Levy's. Levy and Jack Nash were the principal partners of Oppenheimer, and subsequently of Odyssey. With little taste for blood, Levy chose not to undertake a hostile contest for the company, but instead to initiate a proxy fight and use the tools of persuasion. One of his partners recalls receiving a call from Geoff Boisi of Goldman Sachs—who was defending TWA—that shocked him at the time for its bellicosity. Boisi, of course, was just doing his job, one that had become increasingly and acceptedly aggressive. Odyssey lost the proxy contest, TWC having vigorously lined up its institutional investors. TWC remained together. But Levy's message was sent to Wall Street. A company was often worth more broken up. Transworld eventually spun off part of the airline, which Carl Icahn acquired in early 1986 (see Chapter 17). Other Transworld operations would also be sold off. Levy as prophet turned out to be far-seeing.

The popularity of divestitures and the growing market for subsidiary companies, among both private investors and corporations, would, one would naturally assume, reduce the number of big mergers. But the propensity for making mergers, for growing and utilizing the readily available capital, remained as high as ever and was abated only for a short time. Corporations would acquire under most circumstances. It was the main if frequently forgotten lesson of the takeover movement.

Most ironic of all, the acceptance of liquidation and divestiture gave substance to the claims of corporate raiders like Pickens and Icahn that these companies were being poorly managed. In each Pickens and Icahn assault, the selling off of assets, or the liquidation of the entire company, was the underlying purpose. It was how they intended to finance the acquisition. Borrow, and sell off the parts to pay down the debt. Pickens and Icahn raised capital on the assumption that they could sell off the pieces at high prices. Marty Lipton dubbed these mergers *bust-ups*, and because they were done on a shoestring, so to speak, he added the epithet *bootstrap*. Bootstrap bust-up mergers became all the rage.

For oil companies, the concept of selling off pieces, selling off reserves, was growing more popular under the prodding—and success—of Pickens. The reverse also became more acceptable. If an oil company had to pay so much on the open market to buy reserves, why not simply buy public oil companies on the stock market? If the concept was not new, it needed more justification in 1984 than earlier, in the '80s, when U.S. Steel bought Marathon and DuPont bought Conoco. The oil price had fallen. Yet to big oil companies, buying oil in the stock market was so much cheaper than drilling for it that they did not hesitate to undertake the biggest mergers of all time. No one seemed to ask the basic question. It might be cheaper to buy than to drill, but what price would the oil fetch down the road? It might still not be cheap enough. It would probably turn out that it wasn't.

The monumental 1984 battle for Getty Oil that would result in Texaco's purchase of the company for more than $10 billion demonstrates clearly how the logic worked. Texaco's appetite for acquiring oil reserves was among the most ravenous of the major oil companies. The entire industry was finding it more expensive to come up with new reserves. But Texaco had been very bad, or very unlucky, at it. Between 1978 and 1983, Texaco's oil reserves declined by 1.4 billion barrels, leaving them with less than 1 billion. At that rate, Texaco could cease to be an oil company at all, and very soon. The drop in gas reserves was almost as rapid.

Though Texaco found very little oil or gas, it did continue to spend on exploration. The result was that, according to one ranking, its average cost for finding a barrel of oil was second-highest of the sixteen major oil companies. On average, the cost for Texaco to find new oil or gas came to about $21 a barrel over the five previous years. The eventual purchase of Getty at $128 a share, for $10.8 billion, meant that Texaco was gaining a couple of billion barrels of reserves for less than $5 a barrel. As one expert testified, replacing reserves is the "lifeblood" of an oil company. It would have taken Texaco fifteen years at its current rate to come up with that much in reserves. And it would have cost four times as much.

If the logic seems compelling, it also ignores the basic question: What will the oil sell for? The simple fact is that Texaco might have done better to sell off its oil, pack up its offices, and steal away. If it costs $20 a barrel to find oil, that does not mean you will get $20 a barrel over time in the market. You may not even get $5 a barrel.

The battle for Getty between Texaco and Pennzoil resulted in an extraordinary suit. Pennzoil charged that it had an agreement to purchase Getty that had been usurped by Texaco. In trying to assess damages, Pennzoil called on expert witnesses who gave an inside look at how such values are calculated.

Few talents are as overrated as the ability of financial experts to assess the future. The Pennzoil trial proceedings make this starkly apparent. The analyses of the future value of Getty during the trial took little account of the possibility that the price of oil might fall. The most conservative assumption made was that the price of oil might not rise any further. At the time, the price of oil fluctuated between $25 and $30 a barrel. One expert witness, Thomas Barrow, who headed Kennecott when Standard Oil took it over, calculated that Getty was worth nearly $16 billion if an investor sought to make a minimum of 12 percent compounded return on that investment. What price assumptions did he make? "I looked at the price and nobody can guess what price is going to be in the future," he testified. "And I wouldn't pretend that I'm going to be able to do it. So I took the Getty numbers and looked at their projections and compared them with other projections I'm aware of, some that Getty itself had done, and they were reasonable assumptions made by competent personnel as far as I could determine." The "reasonable assumptions" were that the price of oil would continue to rise or at least not fall. The fact was that the price of oil fell to about $15 a barrel in mid-1986.

Texaco's purchase of Getty was in truth a $10 billion bet on the price of oil. And Texaco lost. At one point in its 1986 fall, the price of oil dipped below $10 a barrel. The windfall profits tax ate into revenues above $17 or $18 a barrel. The reduction in revenues is not a straightforward calculation, but leading analysts at the time figured reserves in the ground were worth, in 1986, only 50 percent to 60 percent of their market valuation in mid-1984. One respected appraisal service reduced the value of Standard Oil of Ohio by 50 percent between 1985 and 1986. Murphy Oil's appraisal was cut by 40 percent. These reductions are also based on other factors, such as adjustments to the amount of oil and gas reserves. But they give a rough idea of how quickly oil companies' values had fallen, and how far.

One analyst attended a 1986 meeting where even the Texaco management conceded they had paid too much for Getty, but argued the investment would at least break even. And when Texaco's lawyers argued about damages that Pennzoil might win in its suit against them, they brought with them an argument they would have done well to abide by before. They claimed that the value of Getty was no higher than what the free market was paying for it—in which case it was no higher than Texaco's bid of $128 a share—and that any damages should be based on that. Apparently gone was the idea that Texaco had saved billions of dollars in replacement costs, and that Pennzoil had lost some similarly computed amount because it was deprived of the Getty reserves. Gone was the idea of doing a cash-flow calculation based on an ever-rising oil price. The only value that Pennzoil lost, Texaco now claimed, was the difference between what it offered to pay for Getty—$110 a share—and what Texaco offered: $128 a share. The implication, says Texaco, was that Getty was worth no more, because if it was, the market would have bid up the price of the shares.

16

If the new conventional wisdom called for the breaking up of companies and acknowledged the limitations of diversification, it did not result in any cutback in mergers. Now, instead of an oil company's buying a retail company, it bought another oil company. Newspaper companies bought newspapers, while timber companies bought paper companies. Airlines swallowed other airlines, and TV companies bought more TV stations. Stick to your last, was the philosophy. But mergers rolled on.

Nor did diversification entirely stop. The rationale of these mergers also relied on the growing ability to sell off bits of a company; the parts were worth more than the whole. When the big tobacco companies saw only barriers to future growth, they bought giant packaged-goods companies, in part rationalizing the high prices by presuming they could sell off the individual businesses to a ready market. Individual groups of investors bid for TV stations or movie studios or even airlines, certain they could help finance the acquisitions by selling off chunks here and there.

The prevailing rule of thumb over more than a decade would be just one: Mergers would continue until they were stopped by the government or the drying up of available capital. Under changed circumstances, even including a sharp rise in stock prices which made target companies far more expensive, or scandal, the takeover machinery still ground on.

There was no doubt, however, that its lifeblood was access to capital. Originally, the recycling of OPEC oil monies in the mid-1970s provided the spur. But the banks soon learned on their own that financing takeovers was enormously profitable. The process became institutionalized. In 1981, according to a Securities and Exchange Commission sample, banks supplied more than 70 percent of the funds used in takeovers. That level got as high as 80 percent in 1983, receding to the 70 percent range in the following years. Among hostile takeovers, banks supplied on average even more funds, up to more than 90 percent of the SEC sample in 1983.

But the new phase of the takeover movement was fueled in significant part by a relatively new kind of financing. In the vernacular of Wall Street, they would be called junk bonds. Essentially, they were the bonds issued by less credit-worthy corporations. By definition, the ratings services, themselves the source of constant criticism, rated such bonds lower than BBB. In other words, by conventional measures they were considered riskier, and they required a significantly higher interest rate to be paid to investors as compensation for that risk.

The advent of junk bonds is what gave the corporate raiders sufficient capital to mount the stunning assaults that were to come, beginning in 1983. Banks, while much bolder by 1982 than they ever imagined even five years earlier, still could not supply capital at the level of risk that junk-bond lenders could. The first important user of junk-bond financing was Boone Pickens in his raid of Gulf Oil, a company with $26.6 billion in sales compared to a mere $422 million at Pickens's Mesa.

The rise of junk bonds is a dramatic and controversial piece of financial history in itself, and one that emanated from many of the same causes as did the takeover movement. But the two did not serve each other until 1983. Moreover, seldom in financial history can a major financial tool be ascribed largely to the efforts of one man. But Michael Milken, hired as a bond trader in 1973 by Drexel Burnham Lambert, built the market to the point that there was an estimated $120 billion dollars' worth of junk bonds in 1986.

Milken was a prodigious worker and an intense man. His vision was simple and direct, but went very much against the grain of his time. In graduate school, Milken updated a long study on the lower-rated junk bonds. The study had suggested these bonds yielded a higher interest rate than they should have. In the 1970s, such notions were fairly heretical in academic circles. The financial markets were for the most part thought to be very "efficient." It meant that profitable opportunities were exploited so quickly that the prices of stocks and bonds reflected almost immediately any news about the underlying companies or the marketplace. In other words, it was very difficult to beat the market.

Milken set out to prove that there were actually systematic advantages to buying low-rated bonds. The advantage in yield over a high-rated bond, he demonstrated historically, more than offset the risk that these companies would not meet their interest and principal payments. The market, he concluded, was not efficient. Occasionally, one of these companies would default or go bankrupt, but not often enough to offset the overall group's high yield. Moreover, some of these companies would do very well over the years, raising their credit ratings. High-rated bonds could only lose their luster, went the argument. Lower-rated bonds held the hope of improvement.

While a high-rated bond might pay 10 percent, a low-rated bond would pay as much as 13 percent or 14 percent. Milken concluded that it paid to invest in these bonds, provided you could diversify—that is, as long as an investor could buy enough issues from different companies to reduce the penalty if any single company defaulted. In addition, the investor needed enough money to ride out the dangerous side of the business cycle, when defaults were most likely. Milken's study covered the twenty years after 1946.

Milken's thesis got its biggest boost, however, from the markets themselves. When stocks and bonds bounced back after the deep recession of 1974 and 1975, junk bonds performed outstandingly. It was the kind of substantiation Wall Street understands best. The most profitable kinds of bonds over the period were junk bonds.

Drexel Burnham got its first junk-bond investor in 1972. It was the pension fund of a major industrial company, which committed 5 percent of its total funds to junk bonds. The number of investors grew, largely through Milken's diligence. In addition, traditional bond funds converted in large numbers to higher-yielding investments to make up for severe losses in 1974. In the next couple of years, all these investors did exceptionally well. The junk-bond revolution was under way.

Drexel Burnham itself decided to launch bond funds. These funds are, like mutual funds, a pool of capital that is invested in particular types of securities. Unlike mutual funds, they don't continue to accept new investors. Drexel's new funds would invest in a diversified portfolio of lower-rated bonds. The first fund was launched in early 1977 and raised only $15 million. But Drexel's third fund, started late that year, raised $85 million. In addition, bonds of real estate investment trusts bounced back sharply after their plummet in 1974. At that time, these bonds could be bought for 25 and 30 cents on the dollar. In the recovery that followed, their values surged, and their success again attracted attention to the entire lower-rated bond area. A new pool of individual investors who were open to this kind of investment had been developed.

Drexel had all this time been building a broad client base. But its major breakthroughs came in the late 1970s, when it at last got the giant insurance companies—which control the largest pools of capital in the nation—to buy junk bonds. The argument Drexel made was that the insurance companies already bought low-rated bonds as private placements. These in effect were loans made to corporations privately, rather than through a public marketplace. Drexel argued that insurance companies would be better off buying similar bonds sold on a public market. In this way, they could more easily find buyers for their bonds if trouble arose. With private placements, insurance companies were generally restricted to renegotiation if problems endangered repayment.

Tapping into the insurance market also attracted major money management firms. Soon, the pension funds of the nation's largest corporations were also buying junk bonds in big numbers. Financial institutions—including the newly deregulated savings and loan associations, which could now buy all kinds of securities, not merely make mortgages—also put them into their portfolios. Critics charged that these investors were now taking on significantly more risk than they once had. The high yields on the junk bonds, which typically exceeded those on Treasury securities by 3 percent to 4 percent, were now becoming all too popular, said the critics.

What added to the controversy was that a thriving market was also developing for new issues of junk bonds. Historical studies measured only low-rated bonds already issued, and some academic critics claimed the conclusions were oversimplified. With new issues of bonds for lower-rated companies, critics claimed the same historical relationships did not apply at all. Supporters maintained that junk bonds were an important new means of financing for upcoming or reviving corporations.

The first new issues of junk bonds were undertaken by Lehman Brothers in 1977. They were for Zapata International, an energy and shipping company; Pan American, the airline; and LTV, which had revamped itself into a steel company. With Wall Street's deepest foothold in the junk-bond market, Drexel eagerly climbed aboard the new issue wagon. In the next few years, about $1.5 billion a year in new junk bonds were issued annually. Drexel was the leader. The fast growth began in the early 1980s. Drexel had succeeded in creating a large market for the bonds. The economic recovery, and falling interest rates, made the economic conditions right. In 1982 there were $2.5 billion dollars' worth of new issues. By 1983, that jumped to $7.5 billion. By 1985, it was almost $15 billion. And Drexel Burnham had risen with the market to become one of Wall Street's largest underwriting firms. Eventually, all the major investment banking houses were issuing new low-rated bonds, and Drexel insisted *junk* was not the right word to describe them.

One other criticism arose over this period that Drexel would have a hard time shaking. To some, the buying and selling of low-rated bonds had the look of an investment ring. While Drexel and others could point to a large number of buyers, much of the buying, critics asserted, had been done by a relatively few institutional investors and corporations who bought each other's bonds. In a recession, such a house of cards, the critics claimed, could tumble easily.

Nevertheless, by 1983 the market for junk bonds had been well established. Leveraged buyouts were also growing in popularity along with takeovers. In such transactions, banks and financial institutions put up debt capital to take a company private, usually with the participation of management. The popularity of leveraged buyouts (LBOs) also rested on the tax law that allowed corporations to deduct depreciation for taxes. Depreciation was an annual charge that took into account the wearing out and obsolescence of machinery and plant. But it was not a cash outlay. The federal government nevertheless allows it as a tax deduction. Moreover, the Tax Reform Act of 1981 raised the depreciation allowances markedly. When a company was bought, the acquirer could often write up the assets and depreciate them at a higher annual rate, gaining a bigger tax advantage. LBOs were almost always structured to take advantage of this. The 1986 tax reform legislation reduced depreciation allowances, and therefore also the attraction of LBOs.

Raising the money for LBOs, as always, was the key. Banks would lend up to 60 percent of the cash flow of a corporation, but seldom any more. The banks, seeking low risk, felt this was a safe limit. The additional debt capital then had to be raised at higher interest rates. Firms like Kohlberg, Kravis & Roberts, and Forstmann Little, pursued insurance companies and other financial institutions. This "mezzanine" level of financing, at first very difficult to raise, became much more available over time. The debt was sweetened by giving investors a participation in the equity as well. Like Mike Milken, these LBO specialists soon developed a thriving market source for the riskier debt capital. Eventually, they tapped the junk-bond market as well.

At an annual conference sponsored by Drexel Burnham in California, where Milken was based, the proposal was made in 1983 that Drexel could raise capital to launch a hostile acquisition. It now had a broad-enough marketplace. The question was whether Drexel could move fast enough. The daring Boone Pickens would be Drexel's first big taker.

The major oil companies had suffered a difficult year in 1983. Prices for oil started to fall, but demand fell even faster. Revenues at giant Standard Oil of California, for example, peaked in 1981 at $44 billion. In 1983, they hit $28 billion. Profits fell from a high of $2.4 billion in 1980 to $1.6 billion in 1983. Corporations with big refinery operations were particularly hard hit. Those profits depended entirely on the amount of oil refined, and the demand for oil was still far below levels a few years earlier. The surplus oil-refining capacity in the nation was growing.

By the end of 1983, however, a ray of light appeared at the end of the tunnel. It was all the takeover community needed. Prices had firmed, and demand for oil products was rising slightly. By the first quarter of 1984, virtually all major oil companies would report sharp increases in profits. Executives found it possible, if not exactly easy, to believe that the glut was over. Given the fixation on comparing the replacement cost of reserves to stock prices of the oil companies, it was easier to convince oneself that the stock market was seriously undervaluing oil and gas reserves. For Boone Pickens, the conditions were ripe to attack once again.

The document that was to start the ball rolling on the largest merger ever was less than fifty pages long. It was bound in blue and marked *confidential*. It had the name of no investment banking firm on it. It did not mention the name of a target company. The only names listed at all were those of the investment group, which was headed by Boone Pickens of Mesa. Others in the group included the wealthy Belzberg family, which made its money in Canadian oil. They participated in the name of their corporations, First City and Far West Financial. Other corporations in the group included Sunshine Mining and Wagner & Brown. Beyond that, anonymity ruled.

In fact, the document was a sort of offering memorandum put together by Drexel Burnham. It proposed to raise money for a hostile tender offer to be engineered by an investor group. The investor group was code-named the Gray Investor Group, or GIG. The target company was code-named Gray Oil Company. The document was generally called the Gray Memo, and it became a classic. Drexel Burnham was using it to sell a hostile-takeover financing to its junk-bond investors. The initial offering memo sought to raise more than $1.5 billion.

The memo is fascinating in several ways. It fully reflects the optimism of its times. In other words, it presented essentially an optimistic outlook for the price of oil. High returns also depended on Pickens's ability to sell the oil and gas properties of the acquired company quickly. Sales of such extraordinary size would certainly disrupt the market. The secrecy behind the code names defies common sense. It says much about the true nature of information sharing on Wall Street. No oil analyst would not have known that the target under question was Gulf Oil, based on the financial analysis included in the memo. Moreover, the Gray Memo was dated January 28, 1984, and by that time the Pickens investment group already owned more than 13 percent of Gulf, had waged a proxy contest for it, and lost. The point of the secrecy was not to let anyone know Pickens was contemplating a hostile bid for Gulf Oil. In reality, it must have done just the opposite, and indeed would become a subject of controversy in the insider-trading scandal to come.

Drexel Burnham was trying to raise $1.5 billion for the Pickens group to make a bid for 50 percent of Gulf Oil. The remainder would be bought with debt securities at a future date. The Drexel group initially would raise the money with preferred stock that would be exchangeable into subordinated debt, a junk bond.

The financial structure of a deal is very important to the potential return for investors. Investors must know how much equity they are entitled to, and this can often get complex. The Gray Memo outlined the flow of potential profits carefully.

The conventional measure for a bond's risk is to compare cash flow to the payment of interest and principal. Drexel's assumption about cash flow must have looked very conservative at the time. It assumed that oil prices would not rise from their level, then in the mid twenty-dollar range. It then used Mesa Petroleum's assumptions about the actual level of Gulf's present and future reserves. On this basis, Drexel derived what is called cash flow coverage of debt payments; how much higher annual cash flow is than annual interest and principal payments. For the senior subordinated debt, it came to nearly two times for the first five years, a respectable level of risk—but respectable only if one assumes the oil price will not fall.

The second set of assumptions had to do with the sale of the oil and gas assets. The Gray Memo assumed that the assets would be sold by the end of 1986 at substantially higher prices than they were being bought for. With such assumptions, Drexel then computed the potential rates of return for investors at anywhere from 30 percent to 40 percent a year.

By the beginning of 1984, the battle for Gulf Oil had already been under way for several months. Pickens had been a buyer as early as August 1983. Gulf's record for finding oil had been very poor and it was rapidly losing reserves. One of the so-called Seven Sisters, it had revenues in 1983 of nearly $30 billion and earnings of nearly $1 billion. Oil reserves came to about 2 billion barrels. Only Boone Pickens would have dared to believe it could be taken over. Pickens maintained that companies with such poor records at discovering oil should be returning money to shareholders through the royalty trusts. Though not subject to corporate taxes, these trusts were required to return a very high percentage of their income to shareholders as dividends. That would be Pickens's principal recommendation for Gulf.

By October 1983, the Pickens investor group, recently formed, had nearly 9 percent of Gulf Oil stock. When Pickens had made his holdings publicly known, Gulf Oil responded quickly. The Pennsylvania state laws would allow Pickens to get a seat on the board fairly easily, given his holdings. Holders of only 20 percent of the common stock could call a special shareholders' meeting. In early October, the Gulf board of directors adopted a plan to reincorporate in Delaware, where the 20 percent provision did not exist. Mesa began to solicit proxies itself in order to stop the Gulf move.

Gulf set its special shareholders meeting, to approve the reincorporation in Delaware, for December 2. By only a narrow margin, the shareholders voted with the Gulf board. Ironically, Pennsylvania changed its law anyway. Nor did the move seriously deter Pickens. Pickens knew, perhaps better than James Lee, Gulf's chairman, that it was money that now talked to investors, not loyalty or old ties.

The Christmas season is apparently a favorite time for Pickens's dramatic forays. At the end of December, Pickens formally proposed to Gulf management that they should establish a royalty trust. "We like to keep them working," Pickens says. He argued that the new trust would have a value of $35 to $38 a share; the remaining value per share of Gulf, he figured, would have a value of about $32. In short, each current common share of Gulf would be worth $65 to $70 a share. Gulf was then trading in the mid-forty-dollar range. In early January, Gulf's board tersely rejected Pickens's proposal.

According to several insiders, the Gray Memo, which was making the rounds by the end of January, was a success. But Gulf sued the investor group, as well as Drexel Burnham, for not disclosing the plans of a tender offer in the 13D filing that acknowledged the group's holdings. In addition, Gulf announced that it would acquire companies, significantly raising the level of its debt—a scorched earth defense. This could stretch the Gray Memo's financing proposals too thin.

Pickens never called on the Drexel financing. Instead, he found a new investor, Penn Central, which provided Mesa with an additional $300 million in equity through a complex transaction involving the purchase of Mesa securities. He was able to borrow several hundred million dollars on top of that. Pickens was not about to bid for the whole company at $55. The reason is that potential white knights were volunteering to save Gulf from Pickens. This time around, it would be far easier to find one than during the battle for General American. The environment for oil had improved.

In late January, Robert Anderson, the chairman of Atlantic Richfield, met with Boone Pickens. He offered to buy the shares of Pickens's group, and then planned to make a friendly offer to Gulf for all its shares at $70 apiece. Pickens turned him down. By mid-February, Gulf dug in even deeper. It publicly announced its opposition to any new tender offer by Pickens. Then on February 17, it announced that it had established a $6 billion line of credit with its banks and offered to buy back Pickens's shares for $70 apiece. It also offered to buy 20 million to 30 million of its own Gulf shares for $72.

With such high prices, Pickens—who says the price was too high—decided on a partial bid that could force a proxy fight. On February 23, Pickens bid for an additional 13.5 million shares of Gulf at $65 a share. Now, James Lee was apparently trapped. With the $70 offer from Atlantic Richfield having leaked out, it would be difficult to maintain the fight for independence. Some chief executives would have fought hard anyway, leveraging the company to the hilt in order to defeat Pickens. But Lee, who had already gained a reputation for weakness by dropping out of the Cities Service bidding, chose to get the shareholders as high a price as possible. He put the company on the block the day after Pickens's bid. He offered to provide confidential information on the company to all bona fide white knights.

Three bids surfaced. Atlantic Richfield would bid $78 a share in cash, or a total of $12.9 billion. Kohlberg Kravis arranged a complex leveraged buyout transaction that involved cash, preferred stock, and debt, and which was worth between $75 and $79 a share. But it would put the new company deeply in debt. Standard Oil of California (whose retail brand was Chevron), represented by Morgan Stanley, bid $80. Though George Keller, the Socal chairman, had declared a few years before that he would never acquire a big oil company for its reserves, he now decided to go for giant Gulf. In truth, Pickens had probably gotten up his ire. The oil establishment was finally beginning to understand that Pickens was going after them. And they were fighting back. The total value of Socal's offer price would be almost $13.5 billion, the largest merger in U.S. history if it went through. On March 5, at a meeting in Pittsburgh where all the bidders made presentations, Gulf accepted Socal's offer. Pickens dropped his bid. The largest merger ever was made.

The amount of capital mobilized for this transaction, all sparked by the potential sale of several hundred million dollars' worth of junk bonds, was staggering. Bank of America led a group of banks in lending $14 billion to Socal. At the same time, Arco had rounded up $12 billion of financing for its bid from sixty-five banks. Kohlberg Kravis, the LBO specialists, also arranged $6 billion dollars' worth of financing. Banks showed little trepidation then in lending against oil, firm in the belief that by lending only up to 60 percent or so of the current value, they were protecting themselves against any feasible downturn in the oil price.

Boone Pickens would become the big winner. Throughout the contest, he steadfastly maintained that he was not a greenmailer. He did not accept a buyout of his investors' shares from Atlantic

Richfield. In the process, on the basis of a feared bid for Gulf shares, Pickens drove the price of Gulf from the 40-dollar range to $80 a share, putting nearly another $6 billion in the hands of all the shareholders. Pickens's group bought its 22 million shares in 1983 for an average price of $45, netting the partners a profit of more than $750 million on the transactions. Mesa itself was entitled to about $500 million of that, giving Pickens the war chest he'd always wanted in order to hunt for more oil companies.

The investment bankers, too, had incentive aplenty to recommend the giant oil mergers. Morgan Stanley earned a fee of $17.5 million for advising Socal, all for the work of perhaps a dozen employees, and with no capital invested. Merrill Lynch and Salomon Brothers were Gulf's advisers. They split a fee of $45 million. James Lee may well have had the average shareholder in mind. But he certainly did well for his own account. The profits on his stock options reportedly exceeded $10 million.

With Gulf under its belt, Socal would now be the third-largest oil company in the world in terms of oil revenues. It had increased its oil reserves by two thirds. In sales of retail gas at the pump, it was first, exceeding even giant Exxon. To George Keller, as to all oil executives, these acquisitions must have seemed a dream come true. Certainly, in terms of sheer financial size, such deals had looked impossible only a few years before. No one believed then that the federal government would allow such combinations. After all, Socal and Gulf were two of America's largest corporations at the time. How could the government, ever since the trust-busting of the 1890s, even consider allowing such a merger to take place? But the state of antitrust enforcement was never more permissive. No oil company executive would look this gift horse in the mouth. More oil mergers were surely to come.

In fact, by this time, no one really doubted that the federal antitrust authorities would let the Socal-Gulf merger go through. Public comments of antitrust lawyers at the time were very confident. The Federal Trade Commission was reviewing the case, and judging by its former criteria, the oil market was simply too large to claim these combinations were anticompetitive. It did not matter to this administration that the companies were giants. Exxon, the largest, had nearly $100 billion in sales, but that still amounted to less than 10 percent of the oil business, the argument would go.

The only antitrust vulnerability was in local regional markets where the number of gas stations controlled by one company might amount to a highly concentrated monopoly; local refineries might do the same. In Kentucky, for example, the combination of Socal's Chevron gas stations and Gulf's gas stations would have nearly 24 percent of the market. The government, of course, was now only too willing to propose the appropriate sales of assets in order to overcome their concerns. Socal even announced publicly that it was willing to sell any operations, other than oil and gas reserves, in order to meet government objections. The Federal Trade Commission made its requests within a month. It asked Socal to sell about $1 billion in assets, including 4,200 gas stations in the Southeast. Socal was also required to sell a refinery, two pipeline operations, an oil warehouse, and thirty wholesale supply terminals. With that relatively painless divestiture, the largest merger in history received Washington's approval.

Congress would not sit back so idly, though whatever action was taken to stop the giant mergers was eventually defeated. In early 1984, three giant oil mergers would be consummated. At about the same time that the Socal-Gulf merger was under way, the $10 billion contest for Getty Oil was being fought. And only a few days after Socal took over Gulf, Mobil Oil announced a $5.7 billion purchase of Superior Oil.

Pickens's influence could clearly be discerned in the fight for Getty. The restless wildcatter's constant attacks on oil companies apparently aroused the natural concern of Gordon Getty, J. Paul Getty's son, that he was not getting his fair share out of his huge ownership in the Getty Oil Company. As the only trustee of the Sarah C. Getty Trust, he controlled more than 40 percent of Getty's shares. Speculation was that he wanted to run the company. He decided to act, and precipitated a hostile contest for the company.

Gordon Getty began to suggest ways to raise the value of stock for the shareholders. The suggestions included buying back shares on the market, forming a royalty trust, or the sales of assets outright. In October 1983 the infighting came into the open. Getty and Getty Oil's management announced that they had signed a standstill agreement. Getty Oil would not issue new shares and dilute Gordon Getty's ownership. Gordon, and the Getty Museum—which had another 12 percent of the shares—agreed not to sell their shares to an outsider. Why sign a standstill agreement if all is well? To Wall Street, it already looked like war.

By December, Gordon and the museum had entered a public agreement to give each other the right to buy their respective shares before a third party did. It looked as though they were preparing for battle, and together they had more than the majority of Getty. Then they announced that they wanted to change the company's bylaws. Something was clearly going on.

By late December, however, Pennzoil would enter the fracas. Pennzoil, built by Hugh Liedtke largely through acquisitions of oil properties, made a surprise partial tender offer for Getty. It would buy 20 percent of the shares for $100 each. In midyear, Getty was selling in the mid-sixty-dollar range, by the end of the year in the mid-seventies. After the bid, Liedtke approached Gordon Getty about forming an alliance. When they were through meeting, they together bid $110 a share for all the Getty shares, financed through a leveraged buyout. Over the New Year's weekend, 1984, Getty management had apparently approved the Getty-Liedtke proposal. Whether or not they had formally approved the sale would become the subject of the controversial lawsuit that threatened the corporate life of Getty's ultimate buyer, Texaco.

It took only two days after the announcement of the $110 offer for Texaco to make a competing bid. Several companies, including Texaco, had been interested in buying Getty. Goldman Sachs assiduously sought a buyer after the Pennzoil–Gordon Getty bid that New Year's weekend. And First Boston, advising Texaco, urged them to do it. Texaco broke in with a $125 bid in the early days of January. Eventually, it would raise the bid to $128. First, the museum accepted. Then, Getty management accepted. Ultimately, Gordon Getty sold the Sarah Getty Trust shares to Texaco. The antitrust laws were barely a concern. By mid-February 1984, the deal was complete. For all of three weeks it would stand as the largest merger ever. Texaco paid more than $10 billion. By the following month, Socal, of course, would surpass that.

By the standards of the Getty and Gulf takeovers, Mobil Oil's purchase of Superior Oil at less than $6 billion was modest. Nor did it contain the fireworks of the previous deals. Mobil Oil had long been trying to buy another oil company, and had been considering a bid for Gulf Oil, along with several other major firms. Superior Oil, in turn, with huge domestic reserves, had basically been on the selling block. The announcement that Mobil and Superior had come to a $5.7 billion agreement caught virtually no one by surprise. It would be a package of cash and securities, and Mobil in this friendly deal had the luxury of deciding over time how to finance it. When completed, it gave Mobil a tighter hold on its position as the nation's second-largest oil company.

The Superior acquisition did rile some Senators and Congress-men, already disturbed by the $13 billion Gulf takeover. In an unusual alliance, Senator Bennet Johnston, a Democratic friend of oil from Louisiana, and Senator Howard Metzenbaum, a liberal merger critic, also a Democrat, jointly sponsored legislation to put a six-month moratorium on all mergers among the fifty largest oil companies. This was a watered-down compromise from a more severe bill originally proposed by Senator Metzenbaum. The Senate Judiciary Committee also held hearings, at which the industry's major CEOs defended their recent mergers. Fears of congressional action were strong enough to keep the stock prices of Gulf and Superior somewhat depressed. By the end of March, though, it was becoming clear that Congress would take no action. Giant mergers had won even *their* acceptance. Now all the speculation was over which companies were the next targets, though nothing would quite equal the activity of the first three months of 1984.

The rise of the new sources of debt financing gave every major independent entrepreneur the opportunity to make acquisitions, and changed the face of the takeover movement. The criteria for bidding changed as well. Where once corporations were bought because they were cheap on the stock market, now they were purchased for subtly different reasons. The parts of a business could be sold off to help finance the takeover. The corporate raiders earned a new name—asset strippers. Slowly and surely, companies were now being bought not as a function of price, but because they were valuable, no matter what the price. Franchises were valuable because they had little competition. A successful newspaper, for example, or a TV station, had a franchise in its market. Indeed, there was frequently only one newspaper in a region now.

Name brands were franchises of sorts also, monopolies in the sense that their trademarks could not be duplicated. The rhetoric was still the same. It was cheaper to buy a brand name than build a new one, for example. But in fact, the definition of desirable take-over targets expanded broadly. If capital was available, rationalizations to justify takeovers were easy to come by. More likely, unless takeovers were stopped, someone would find a way of raising the capital to make them.

No one deal quite represented this better than Pantry Pride's junk-bond bid for famed Revlon Inc. Ronald Perelman, the young, ambitious chief executive of Pantry Pride and its diversified parent, MacAndrews & Forbes Holdings, must have seen the legendary Revlon cosmetics company as too tempting to let go by. Perelman was already considered by some an asset stripper. He began on the acquisition trail in 1978, after leaving his father's successful metals firm in Philadelphia. MacAndrews & Forbes was his second acquisition. Cohn-Hatfield, a jewelry company he had bought 40 percent of in 1978 for $2 million, in turn bought MacAndrews in 1979 for $45 million. The company was a supplier of chocolate and licorice. In the following years, Perelman, a Wharton School graduate, bought several bigger companies, including Technicolor, Consolidated Cigar, and a controlling interest in Pantry Pride, a successful retail chain. In 1984, MacAndrews had $750 million in sales.

Revlon was built by Charles Revson into one of the nation's largest cosmetics companies. But in 1974, nearing retirement, Revson believed the giant firm had to take a different turn. He reached for a financial man, Michel Bergerac, then head of ITT International, and a protégé of Harold Geneen. Bergerac's business philosophy developed in the 1960s. He believed in conglomeration. As chief executive, he engineered acquisition after acquisition, building up Revlon as a health care company, including drug and hospital-supplies operations. Within ten years, two thirds of Revlon's $2.4 billion of revenues came from drugs.

Perelman saw in Revlon a company ripe for stripping. Its earnings had been sliding since 1980, down from $192 million to $112 million. Perelman believed he could sell off most of the health care businesses and keep the glamorous brand-name cosmetics, which had been floundering. Perelman had recently married a well-known New York gossip reporter, and was something of a man about town. It was also Perelman's shot to enter the big-time world of takeovers. It was a $2 billion takeover, by far Perelman's largest.

Enter Drexel Burnham, led by Dennis Levine, who only a few months later would be convicted for profiting from inside information. (Revlon was one of the companies he illegally invested personal money in.) By July 1985, Drexel had built Perelman's war chest up by $750 million with an offering of junk bonds. Perelman first approached Bergerac with a friendly proposal. Bergerac turned him away. In July, Perelman was ready to act. With Drexel's financial muscle, Pantry Pride bid $47.50 a share for Revlon, whose stock had then been trading in the low forty-dollar range. Few believed Perelman would pull it off. Even when the deal was under way, one *New York Times* headline read: A VICTORY BY REVLON SEEN NEAR.

Michel Bergerac traveled in a Boeing 727 that was lavishly decorated, with a separate bedroom, a kitchen, and a gun rack for hunting. Observers agree he was among those who did not believe that Revlon could be acquired by the smaller and financially weak Pantry Pride. Pantry was taking on an enormous debt load to consummate the deal. Some arbitrageurs claim Bergerac's cockiness may have gotten in his way. They say he did not act fast enough, avoiding the harsher defenses, or even a search for a white knight, until it was too late.

Pantry Pride continued to sweeten its offer through the fall, raising its bid into the fifty-dollar range. That Perelman kept coming is what made him successful ultimately. Bergerac, with such advisers as Felix Rohatyn and Marty Lipton on his side, adopted the appropriate defensive measures, and eventually offered to buy back some Revlon shares. In response, Perelman at first lowered his bid to $42. But when Perelman raised the bid to the mid-fifties, Revlon began to look vulnerable.

One trouble for Bergerac was that he waited until there was less than a week to find a friendly buyer. At last, a small leveraged buyout firm, Adler & Shaykin, agreed to buy the cosmetics business for $900 million. Forstmann Little would arrange to buy the rest in a leveraged buyout. Low-rated debt financing of junk bonds was coming up against the low-rated mezzanine financing of LBOs.

Who would prevail turned out to depend on the courts. As the bidding intensified, Forstmann Little finally upped its bid to $57.25 a share. Now, both sides were committing about $1.8 billion to the purchase. But for its raised ante, Revlon gave Forstmann, represented by Arthur Fleischer of Fried, Frank, a lock-up designed to keep Pantry away. Forstmann won the right to buy two valuable divisions of Revlon for a discount price of $525 million. If Pantry Pride took over Revlon, Forstmann could buy those divisions for perhaps half their real value. That, figured Bergerac and his advisers, would be enough to keep Perelman away, even though he raised his bid to $58 per share.

On October 23, the Delaware Chancery Court disallowed the Forstmann Little lock-up. Revlon appealed. On November 1, the Delaware Supreme Court upheld the chancery court's decision. The Forstmann Little bid was killed. Perelman bought up the shares tendered to him. Revlon threw in the towel and announced that management, too, would tender its shares to Pantry Pride. But the path was not smooth for Pantry. Revlon had contracted to sell the beauty products division to Adler & Shaykin. Pantry insisted it was not bound by the contract, and the parties brought the issue to court. Forstmann Little would also put up a legal battle to acquire the two divisions it had options for. Finally, Pantry probably had paid a lot more than it had anticipated, a minimum of $1.83 billion, $1.5 billion of which was raised by Drexel, and perhaps as high as $2.7 billion when everything was done.

Pantry immediately set itself the task of selling off some of the assets. By early December it made its first serious sales. Rorer Group, a medical company, agreed to buy the prescription drug businesses for $690 million. Perelman was already on his way to whittling Revlon down to size. And he now owned the legend that

Charles Revson built, Adler & Shaykin having agreed to drop their pursuit of the company for a settlement.

The amount of money made in the Revlon contest was staggering. The fees, *The Wall Street Journal* calculated, topped the $60 million or so earned by the small group of advisers who had handled the giant Gulf Oil contest. Drexel may have earned as much as $60 million for financing the acquisition as well as advising Pantry Pride. Morgan Stanley would garner as much as $30 million, also as a Pantry Pride adviser. Felix Rohatyn earned Lazard more than $11 million as adviser to the losing Revlon. Goldman Sachs got $3 million for advising Forstmann Little. Nor did Forstmann come out behind. Pantry Pride agreed to pay it $20 million for losing the options to buy the two Revlon divisions. Finally, Michel Bergerac resigned—but not without pulling down a golden parachute worth more than $35 million, which included stock options of $15 million. The takeover movement had come a long way from the days when Fred Port of ESB was content to walk away with $250,000 when Inco took his company over.

If any Wall Street outcry gave the lie to the rationale cited by protagonists of takeovers to justify acquisitions, it was the criticism that hounded James Lee, chairman of Gulf on selling out to Socal. Lee's reputation had declined when he suddenly pulled his bid for Cities Service in the late summer of 1982. The arbitrageurs took a bath, and Lee's name was bandied about with little regard after that.

When, in the estimation of many observers, Lee did not fight Boone Pickens hard enough, Wall Street again rose in criticism. He could have undertaken a PacMan defense and bid for Mesa. He could have adopted a scorched earth policy and built up his debt until the Pickens junk-bond group couldn't take any more. Instead of all this, instead of toughing it out and remaining independent, he ran into the arms of a white knight.

But if protecting and benefiting the shareholders is really the objective of Wall Street, and the acquisitions it undertakes, James Lee did a very good job indeed. A company that typically sold in the low forty-dollar range got $80 a share in cash for all its shareholders. Moreover, Lee probably sold out at the top of the oil market. How much smarter he looks in selling at the top than in buying at the top, as so many of his colleagues did.

The criticism of Lee was a giveaway to the double standard of Wall Street. Winning was really the game at bottom, not enhancing shareholder values, as was now commonly proclaimed by the Wall Street establishment.

17

The state of the takeover movement by the mid-1980s was easy to misinterpret. If a man like Ron Perelman could succeed almost miraculously, other corporate raiders were beginning to lose, including Boone Pickens. Large hostile deals had been dominated by the corporate raiders, and some commentators would claim the days of unfriendly acquisitions were ending. Such comments had been heard before. But the fear of unwanted acquisitions had also seeped into the everyday thinking of every major corporation. Mergers of giant firms were technically friendly, but were at bottom the reaction to a long history of hostile takeovers. Companies knew they were vulnerable and acted before they became targets. And the acquisition philosophy of the raiders also penetrated conventional business strategy. Now, corporations would analyze merger candidates in terms of their ability to sell off assets, or at least according to what the value of a corporation might be if they did liquidate it.

The troubled tobacco companies were among the leaders in this type of thinking. Their revenues had stopped growing for the most part due to the nation's long antismoking campaign. Subject to lawsuits and advertising restrictions, they sought other kinds of companies as new sources of growth. RJR, the former Reynolds Tobacco, bought Nabisco, maker of brand-name cereals for $5 billion. Philip Morris bought giant General Foods for $6 billion. Nestlé S.A. may have pointed the way when it bought Carnation in 1984. All three paid the equivalent of fifteen to twenty times future earnings, very handsome prices.

The tobacco companies had swallowed the argument of the

takeover specialists. They sought value not so much in earnings as in assets. They bought companies with brand names—"franchises," or small monopolies, in Wall Street parlance—that appeared to be invulnerable to competition. And now corporations, just like raiders before them, were willing to bid up the value of these companies. Newspapers and TV stations with locks on their regional markets became favorite acquisition candidates. Often, the purchase was not cheap; but it was a franchise. The hostile takeover movement pushed all of business toward this strategy.

If one group of companies was truly unassailable, however, it was the TV networks. Granted their franchises by the federal government more than a generation before, they always had thought of themselves as partly responsible to the public in general, not merely to the bottom line. After all, they operated on the public airwaves, of which there were only a few with far reach. They had in effect had their monopolies bestowed on them by the federal government. And they had long been run by men who believed they often had to sacrifice profits to another purpose. The takeover movement would knock down this barrier as well.

As late as 1985, few thought the Federal Communications Commission would easily approve a hostile bid for one of the three networks, CBS Inc., ABC Co., or RCA Inc., which owned NBC. But when Ted Turner raised money, again through junk bonds, to raid CBS, it did not look as if the FCC would protect the target. The ultimate acquisitions of ABC by Capital Cities Communications and of RCA by General Electric were at least in part motivated by the fear of hostile acquisition. CBS took on $1 billion in debt to buy up its own stock and keep Turner away.

In 1985, there were a record $180 billion of mergers made. In 1986, that would go higher. And at bottom, the hostility had not altered. More and more corporations were open to the thought of friendly mergers as a result.

What was different in 1985 and 1986, however, was that target corporations learned how to fight back. This tug of war between raider and target had gone on through the preceding dozen years. The new corporate raiders were defeatable. But the new defense often came at a big price. It left a company as weak and debt-ridden as a takeover by a junk-bond-financed raider would have.

*   *   *

The poison pill was invented by Marty Lipton. It was probably the only takeover weapon that had no obvious antecedent. It produced enough controversy to break, at least temporarily, the longstanding friendship between Lipton and Flom. To Lipton, it stopped the poorly financed takeover artists who could bust up any company in sight. To Flom, it usurped shareholders' rights because it made it harder to find a bidder. What was clear was that, after a period of testing, the poison pill achieved in large part what it was intended to.

Marty Lipton remembers it as a very hectic December 1982. He was simultaneously defending General American Oil from the raid by Boone Pickens's Mesa Petroleum, and El Paso Natural Gas from Burlington Northern Railroad. In each case the bids were for half of the company. Lipton first flew to Dallas to advise General American. The objective was fairly straightforward. The Meadows family, the largest shareholders, essentially wanted to sell. The issue was how to get the highest price. General American, with little debt, could afford to make a tender for the other half of its shares at a handsome price. In the meantime, Phillips Petroleum entered the contest as a white knight and bought General American for $1.2 billion.

Defending El Paso was more difficult. Highly leveraged, it could not afford a self-tender, and its advisers realized it was vulnerable. In reading over the El Paso financial statements, Lipton noted that the company had authorized the issuing of preferred stock, but had not issued it. Such preferred stock is typically issued to raise capital with a provision that it can be converted into common shares at a set price. He cannot remember exactly when the idea occurred to him, but Lipton devised a preferred stock offering that would make El Paso less attractive to Burlington. The preferred shares would be issued as a dividend to current shareholders, who would then get the rights to vote separately for a large number of directors. This could prevent Burlington from getting control of the board.

It was not yet a poison pill, but Burlington Northern challenged its legality in a Delaware court. The court, however, did not grant Burlington a temporary restraining order. In the end, Burlington and El Paso negotiated a friendly merger. By now, the idea had taken hold in Lipton's mind. He developed a form of this shareholders' rights plan using warrants rather than preferred shares. Though he recommended it, no one bought the idea. It was a hostile contest in mid-1983, however, that became the testing ground for the first full-fledged poison pill.

In 1983, Brown-Forman Distillers Corp. was being run by the great-grandson of the founder. The fifth Brown to run the company, based in Louisville, Kentucky, William Lee Lyons Brown presided over the making and marketing of such products as Jack Daniel's whiskey, Martel cognacs, and Korbel champagne. The company had about $900 million in sales, a little less than $100 million in profits, making it the fourth-largest distiller in the country. It also had a lot of cash, and little debt. It had acquired liquor brands before, but never any other kind of product.

In June of that year, with takeovers everywhere, Lee Brown decided to branch further afield. Lenox Inc. could boast a brand name as well known as Brown-Forman's. Its china was once used in the White House, and it had recently acquired Hartmann luggage. Brown thought he saw a fit. Both companies made products for the higher-income consumer. Lenox was about one quarter Brown's size, earning under $20 million in 1982.

Lee Brown was not shy about the offer he would make. On Tuesday, Lenox shares were trading under $60 a share on the New York Stock Exchange. The next morning he offered $87 a share, more than twenty times earnings of $4.13 a share the year before. The total price was more than $400 million. One analyst was reported to say that the bid was too high. But as a takeover strategy, it may well have been right.

Lenox's immediate reaction was to fight, though the high bid created ambivalence among its directors. It hired Marty Siegel of Kidder Peabody to defend it, as well as Lipton. Lipton soon discovered that the Brown family held more than 60 percent of Brown-Forman's voting stock. In this fact lay the key to a new defense, for anything that jeopardized that control would certainly scare the Browns away. Lipton proceeded to invent the original version of the poison pill. Siegel in fact gave it its name.

What Lipton conceived was not that far a jump from the El Paso preferred shares. Rather than issue preferred shares he wanted to issue shares that could dilute control by the Browns. But he also wanted to be able to redeem the new issue of preferred shares if the target company so wanted. In that way, they could be free to negotiate an acquisition by a white knight and not activate the pill.

The result was an issue of preferred stock, each share of which would be convertible into forty shares of Brown-Forman if Brown took over Lenox. The preferred issue would be distributed as dividends to all Lenox shareholders. When converted, it would give so many shares of the newly merged company to other shareholders that the Brown family would see its control seriously diluted. It was ingenious, and Brown-Forman challenged it in court, but it could not win a restraining order.

Lee Brown was bending over backward to make the offer for Lenox appealing to its chairman, John Chamberlin. He offered him a seat on the board, and assured him the offer was basically friendly. When Brown upped the bid by $3, to $90 a share, Chamberlin relented. He urged shareholders to accept the bid. Brown-Forman avoided having to swallow the poison pill, but Lipton and Siegel could now argue that the pill forced a higher bid.

In the ensuing months, the new pill would be challenged several more times in the courts. To many, it still seemed too far-fetched to work. But in August 1983, a Delaware court ruled in a case that involved National Education Corporation's attempted takeover of Bell & Howell that the pill was not invalid. It was still early in the development of the defensive tool, and more important court rulings were to come, but that ruling gave corporations more confidence in the defensive tool. Slowly, the pill began to catch on.

Lipton contends that the poison pill was never intended to stop a cash deal for all the shares of the company, nor could it. It was aimed principally at poorly financed two-tier offers or partial tenders that, in effect, borrowed against the assets of the takeover target in order to finance the acquisition. These of course were the specialties of the corporate raiders like Pickens and Icahn. The pill did not really come to full popularity until late 1985. Over the next two years, the pill evolved into a more potent weapon, aided by one very important court case.

Lipton and other lawyers continued to perfect the pills. There would soon be several versions. For example, issuance of preferred shares could complicate a firm's balance sheet. The poison pill replaced the preferred issue with an issue of rights, which were really a form of warrants. The flip-over provision was the term used to describe the conversion of rights into shares. A plan designed to protect targets from partial tender offers, with no planned second step, was also developed. It added enormous debt to the balance sheet if triggered, and made any future borrowing to finance a second step very difficult.

One adept corporate raider slipped through a poison pill defense. In 1985, James Goldsmith, the British entrepreneur, bid for Crown Zellerbach, the forest products company. Crown distributed its poison pill rights, but Goldsmith boldly ignored them. He bought up enough shares of the company to control it. But he did not merge it into his own company. The rights could not then be flipped over into the newly merged company and dilute the ownership. Instead, Goldsmith sold off parts of Zellerbach to others, the largest chunk going to James River. He kept the valuable timberland for himself. No one wound up with 50 percent of the company; there was no company to dilute. A pill was soon devised that would allow rights-holders to convert into a very large number of shares of their own company, once an acquirer has bought, say, 20 percent of the company. This so-called "flip-in" provision would dilute the target company, whether or not the acquirer merged it into his own.

The court case on which the future of the basic poison pill hinged was brought by a dissident director of Household International who was represented by Joe Flom. With the help of a poison pill, Household warded off a takeover bid. In the most comprehensive court decision on poison pills to that date, the ruling in November 1985 found that the pill was indeed legal. The court found that the pill did not necessarily keep bidders away. Rather, it gave management an opportunity to seek still higher bids if they could.

By the end of 1986, nearly four hundred corporations had adopted the basic poison pill. And Lipton could claim with some legitimacy that they served their purpose. They did not stop cash tender offers for a company. They did make it more expensive for those who made partial bids and then expected to use the assets of a company to finance the rest of the acquisition. That was the way the corporate raiders had long worked. Now, it had become far harder to make a hostile raid unless the raider was very well funded.

But poison pills were not the only way corporate America was now fighting back. Some argue, in fact, that it was not the most important. If corporate raiders could borrow in order to take over a company, corporate management could borrow enough funds to buy their own company, and keep their jobs in the process. Dean LeBaron, who runs one of the nation's largest investment management companies and who headed an SEC takeover study committee in 1983, argued later that corporate management learned how to save their jobs in the next few years anyway. They imitated the raiders by restructuring their own companies, selling off pieces and borrowing heavily.

Boone Pickens had lost his bid for General American Oil when Phillips Petroleum swept in as a white knight. Mesa Petroleum and Boone Pickens's investment group was nearly $800 million richer when Gulf was bought away from them by Socal. In the fall of 1984, Boone Pickens started buying the shares of Phillips Petroleum, the nation's eleventh-largest oil company. He quickly acquired 9 million shares, at an average price of $42 a share, and threatened Phillips with a tender. Pickens wanted the company to sell assets, recapitalize, or otherwise produce more value for its shareholders.

By now, however, William Douce, Phillips's chairman, had long seen Pickens at work. If Pickens was indeed out to get the oil establishment, the establishment had formed an equally harsh opinion of him. Phillips also felt a close kinship to its employees. When Pickens made his overtures, townspeople set up vigils to pray for his defeat.

Pickens had prided himself on his unwillingness to accept greenmail. He would not take a higher payment for his shares, while the rest of the shareholders got nothing. He insisted that if Phillips wanted to buy him out, they had to do something for the shareholders as well. Pickens, with a large war chest, suggested that he would make a partial bid for the Phillips shares at $60 a share. The arbs thought they were off and running again. The stock rose to the mid-fifty-dollar range.

This time, Pickens would severely disappoint Wall Street, however. He and Phillips had come to an agreement and announced it on the day before Christmas. Phillips would buy out Pickens for $53 a share, insuring him a $90 million profit on his investment. In return, Pickens would not make an acquisition bid for Phillips for the next fifteen years. But to try to bolster the stock price, Phillips would radically restructure the company. It would buy back nearly 40 percent of the remaining shares for bonds whose face value was $60. And a very large interest in the company would be sold to the employees. Pickens thought he fulfilled his obligation to other shareholders.

When the stock opened for trading two days later, it plunged nearly ten points to about $45. The $60 bonds, the Wall Street pros figured, were probably worth closer to $45. And Pickens came in for a round of criticism for having accepted the proposal. To many, it was indeed greenmail—pure and simple.

In surely the most effective one-two punch in modern takeover history, Carl Icahn followed Pickens into the fray. It would be his biggest raid by far, and nearly raise him to Boone Pickens's status. In the first two weeks of January, rumors were widespread that Icahn was seeking to round up investors for a bid for Phillips. Blocks of stock were also trading in Phillips that were rumored to be purchases by Icahn. Ivan Boesky, who had taken a big position after the Pickens assault, had conversations with Icahn. In fact, Icahn had accumulated 7.5 million shares of Phillips and had approached Drexel Burnham to line up debt financing for a bid. Phillips's stock price began edging up, reaching nearly $50 a share. The Wall Street pros clearly believed enough in Icahn's ability to raise financing that they took even the potential for an Icahn bid very seriously.

On February 4, he sent William Douce a letter that Phillips made public the next day. It was a classic bear hug. He offered $55 a share, in what he termed a leveraged buyout. It was valued at more than $8 billion. He gave Douce two days to accept the proposal. Icahn planned to sell a substantial piece of Phillips in order to do the deal. He said that Drexel Burnham was "highly confident" that it could raise the cash needed to complete the transaction. Only a few years earlier, no one could have imagined that such a letter could have been written—no less have been greeted seriously. Icahn said he would step aside if Phillips came up with a package worth $55 a share.

If Icahn could raise funds against Phillips assets, certainly Phillips itself could. It was a matter of will—how far management was willing to indebt its company. It turned out that management would be willing to go very far.

The enormity of Icahn's proposition had been lost on a financial community that was very close to events. Only three and one-half years before, giant DuPont had struggled to raise $8 billion to buy Conoco. Now, Icahn, essentially an individual entrepreneur who controlled only two substantial companies with assets that were small compared to DuPont's, was threatening an $8 billion takeover. Phillips was a company that generated nearly $16 billion in sales. It had income that approached $1 billion a year. Carl Icahn, who commanded no huge lines of credit at a bank, or corporate assets against which to borrow, was about to bid for a company in what would have been the third- or fourth-largest merger of all time.

The key, of course, was the ability to raise money through junk bonds, and Icahn's banker was Drexel Burnham. Icahn's credibility, with Drexel's backing, was attested to when the stock of Phillips rose more than $3, to just over $50 a share, the day he sent the letter to Douce. Icahn's original plan called for a package that was half cash and half subordinated notes. It would add billions to Phillips's overall debt load.

The truth is that it never became publicly clear just how much financing Icahn had, and when he got it. Information dribbled out, because Icahn did not make a public tender offer for about a week. In court papers and SEC filings, it appeared that Icahn planned to sell nearly $4 billion of Phillips assets, compared to only $2 billion that were originally announced. Slowly, the structure of the financing also became clear. Only $1 billion of the $8 billion in financing was equity. Icahn's group would put up about 40 percent of that. The rest would be comprised of about half of senior straight debt, probably raised through the banks. The remaining half of the debt would be raised through subordinated debt—junk bonds with yields of 14 percent and almost 16 percent.

Phillips responded to Icahn's bear hug by raising the terms of its offer slightly, and by adopting a poison pill. The pill, designed by Lipton, gave shareholders the right to swap stock for new debt of Phillips should anyone acquire 30 percent or more of the company. The vast amount of new debt was designed precisely to stop a raider like Icahn, who had to borrow in effect against the target company's assets to raise the money. Icahn insisted he was coming for Phillips anyway.

Icahn now did not have much time to act. Shareholders were scheduled to vote on Phillips's proposed new capitalization (which it had agreed to with Pickens) on February 22. They would either approve or disapprove the plan Phillips worked out with Pickens to give shareholders more value. Without another offer, the shareholders might well approve the reorganization.

On February 12, Icahn at last came forward with his formal tender offer. It was a disappointment. Icahn raised the cash portion of his bid by $5, to $60 a share, but he reduced the value of the backend to $50 a share. The two-tier offer would run into a snag because Phillips had the year before adopted a fair-price provision. Unless an acquirer paid about an equal amount for the backend, either the board or shareholders had to give their approval to the merger.

But Phillips would receive a shock when it finally tallied the votes on its restructuring. The shareholders turned it down. They clearly wanted more money. It was an extraordinary event in the history of public stock companies. And it was a final testimony to the evolution of the takeover movement. Shareholders would now demand a sale of the company. A vote against management on such an issue was unheard-of a few years before.

Now, Phillips's back was simply to the wall. It knew the ultimate outcome of the vote on February 28. That weekend, it began talks with Icahn and came up with a more generous proposal that would raise the value of its shares, though it would also increase its debt load sharply. Icahn agreed to drop his bid.

Phillips offered a package of debt securities for half of the outstanding shares. The face value of the securities was $62 a share. It also raised its dividend, and threw in a preferred share as well. A look at the debt securities shows that it, too, included subordinated debt, as well as more highly rated securities. Phillips in effect borrowed against itself just as Icahn had intended to, issuing junk bonds, the subordinated debt. The market now valued the shares at about $55 apiece. But Phillips's debt had nearly tripled, to about $7.5 billion. That came to 75 percent of capital, making it the most highly leveraged major oil company in the business. Phillips planned to sell $2 billion in assets to help defray the cost. The company had won its independence, but at a very heavy price.

Icahn and Pickens would come up big winners, however. On Icahn's stock, he and his investors made a profit of $50 million. Pickens's Mesa already made that profit of approximately $90 million.

If it was true that Boone Pickens was a man driven to topple the oil establishment, it should also be true that he would not cease raiding the oil giants until he was stopped. One moneymaking raid after another should have turned Pickens's head. He had learned a way to make a lot of money for Mesa, his investor group, and himself. Wall Street, often understanding little else but the urge to make money, saw Pickens as a cynic who disguised himself as the protector of the small shareholder. But they would have understood him better not as a gladiator protecting the little guy but as one who enjoyed taking on the black-hooded knights of oil.

In February 1985, even before the Phillips Oil battle had run its course, Pickens was stalking his next victim. He announced that his investor group, called Mesa Partners II, had bought just under 8 percent of Unocal Corp., the Los Angeles–based oil company. It was a smaller target than Phillips, but still ranked as the nation's thirteenth-largest oil company, with sales of $11.5 billion. One attraction was its light debt, only some $1 billion in long-term obligations.

Fred Hartley, the strong-willed chairman of Unocal, may have understood Pickens better than most. Unlike James Lee, he seemed intent to fight to the death. This for him appeared to be a battle between two different kinds of men—one a member of the establishment and the other an interloper. Hartley probably thought of himself as having few illusions about the rhetoric of shareholders' rights, or even making money. He maintained that Unocal was better off with him and his team managing it. He wanted to defeat Pickens. Pickens wanted to defeat him. It was a naked contest of power and will. As happened so often before in this takeover movement, it would ultimately turn on a court decision.

Fred Hartley began working on his takeover defenses right away. He was certain that a bid was on its way, despite Pickens's insistence that this was just an investment. By the end of March, the Pickens group had bought more than 13 percent of Unocal, and Pickens suggested that he would consider a bid. Behind him stood Drexel Burnham, promising to provide up to $3 billion of financing through the sale of junk bonds.

In early April, Pickens unveiled his proposal. He offered $54 per share, in cash, for enough shares to give his group just over 50 percent of the company. The shares were trading for about $50. The remaining shares would be bought for debt securities after the company was taken over. The total value of the offer was just over $8 billion. Pickens claimed Drexel had raised $3 billion. Pickens also had a line of credit for $1 billion with the banks. In effect, Unocal woke up one day to find that Pickens had $4 billion to fight with.

Pickens did not make a formal bid, however. He chose first to try a proxy contest. But he needed a postponement of the annual meeting in order to have time to file the slate. Hartley refused, and Pickens took the issue to court. He got a postponement but Hartley would win the shareholder vote. Campaigning very hard, he narrowly defeated the Pickens proposal.

But Hartley was not about to wait for Pickens's next step. With Goldman Sachs and Dillon Read & Co. as his advisers, Hartley did what Pickens hoped to do. He borrowed heavily to buy up Unocal shares. Unocal's final offer was to buy back 29 percent of its shares for notes with a face value of $72. The cost to Unocal would be some $3.6 billion, quadrupling its outstanding debt. There was one very significant proviso: Mesa Partners II was not entitled to participate in the Unocal offer. It went only to other shareholders. Hartley was trying to strand the Mesa group.

The exclusion seemed ridiculous on the face of it. Certainly, a court would not uphold it. And in mid-May, the Delaware Chancery Court ruled that, indeed, the Pickens group could not be left out. The ruling opened the way for a possible settlement between the two parties. Pickens's own investor group started to have doubts about their own offer. Unocal had already publicly threatened that it would borrow more than $6 billion if necessary to buy back nearly half its stock if the Pickens tender succeeded. Moreover, Pickens stood to make almost $180 million if he could sell his shares under Unocal's tender offer.

Fred Hartley, despite an adverse court ruling, gave in little to Pickens during their meetings in Los Angeles. No agreement was reached and Pickens left for Amarillo. Hartley still hoped to win exclusion of Pickens's group from the Unocal offer on appeal. On May 17, he got his wish. The Delaware Supreme Court ruled that it was within the boundaries of the "business judgment rule" that Unocal could decide to exclude the Pickens group.

Eventually, even the Securities and Exchange Commission would urge that such a takeover defense not be allowed. And most take-over lawyers doubted whether others could use the defense. But Hartley had accomplished what he had set out to. He stopped Pickens and his investors. Now, Pickens was forced to negotiate. Hartley demanded a standstill agreement that would keep Pickens from acquiring shares for twenty-five years. Drexel also agreed not to finance any takeover attempt of Unocal. In return, Unocal bought one third of Mesa's Unocal shares in the tender. The remaining two thirds of the stock had to be sold over the years, and very likely at a substantial loss. Because of an obscure tax break, Pickens eventually claimed the group made about $80 million on the deal. But no one had any doubts. For the time being, Pickens had been stopped.

When oil prices plunged in early 1986, from $28 a barrel to nearly $10, a Wall Street analyst studied all the major oil companies. Two were in severe jeopardy of not being able to meet their dividends, he concluded. They were Phillips and Unocal. They had retained their independence, but they teetered precariously near the brink. Shareholders had been compensated very well, but equity was replaced with debt. Risk rose in the economy. And none of this money went to explore for more oil.

The times were very misleading. Some would argue that the

raiders had been stopped. In fact, they had not. The new raiders had become corporate management itself, now able to borrow heavily to buy out the public shareholders and keep their jobs. Companies like Storer Communications and Macy's would go private in billion-dollar leveraged buyouts. Others like Atlantic Richfield & Co. would restructure themselves through debt, and raise the share price, before the threat of a takeover. Then there were Phillips and Unocal. Boone Pickens got caught in one battle, but the war was still his.

     If anyone needed proof that hostile corporate takeovers would continue, Carl Icahn would provide it. In the spring of 1985 he believed that TWA looked like yet another possible victim. He bought shares, and provoked the search for a white knight. But TWA could only come up with Texas Air, run by Frank Lorenzo—and its unions hated Lorenzo for having helped bust them up. The bidding kept rising, but because the unions preferred Icahn to Texas Air, Icahn eventually won control. The TWA board turned down Lorenzo's latest bid and took Icahn's offer of nearly $360 million for less than half of the shares, and the promise of securities for the rest. In August 1985, the man who got rich by losing takeover battles finally won a big one.

     Icahn had apparently every intention of stripping TWA assets as he would other companies', and then financing a complete takeover with the help of junk bonds. But according to a *Fortune* magazine story, the junk-bond financiers of Icahn's LBO, Paine Webber & Co., balked at his plan to sell TWA's reservations system. If Icahn wanted to raise the money, part of which would go to bail out his investor group's $360 million contribution, he wouldn't be able to strip all those assets.

     The tables turned again on Icahn. He switched from Paine Webber to Drexel Burnham, which was now available for the financing. But Icahn was pushing even junk bonds too far. Among other things, airline competition was intensifying and profits had weakened throughout the industry. TWA was racking up losses far faster than anyone had anticipated.

Soon, Icahn realized he had to lower the cash terms of the offer. And TWA started searching for another buyer. Texas Air came forward again. Icahn felt an obligation to the unions, from whom he had won concessions. He decided to keep control of TWA. But he did not undertake a leveraged buyout for all the shares. That would have enabled him and his investor group to recoup some of its contribution. When he started, he probably fully expected to take out all the money once the LBO was consummated. But an LBO now would have hamstrung TWA with a very high level of debt. Icahn left his $360 million in TWA, and now he had to make that company run in order to get it out. He became chairman in January 1986.

In the spring of 1986, buried deeply in even more TWA losses, Icahn saw an opportunity to make a quick profit. He started buying up shares of Viacom, the New York TV syndicator and owner of Showtime, the cable movie channel. TV was now a hot takeover group and Icahn must have thought he could provoke another buyer. Vicaom ran very scared. Within a month, they were negotiating to buy Icahn's shares from him—a classic case of greenmail. When it was over, Icahn and his investors pocketed a $40 million profit. The takeover mechanism would go on. Icahn could still make companies—management and employees—tremble. And down deep, that is what the takeover movement of the preceding twelve years was all about.

Later that same year, Icahn raised his sights much higher. USX stock was now down as oil prices skidded, and Icahn saw a buy. He bought more than 11 percent of the $21 billion behemoth, lined up junk bond financing through Drexel Burnham, and threatened a hostile contest. Some would argue that Icahn dropped out in early January because Drexel, now threatened by the widening Boesky scandal, could not deliver the financing. In addition, USX fought back with the now-conventional restructuring plan to sell off assets and thereby raise the stock price.

What had clearly given Icahn the confidence in the first place was a turnaround he had engineered in TWA's profits. After sharp cutbacks, TWA was back in the black. Icahn also pointed proudly to high profits generated by his acquisition of ACF in 1983. He whittled the company down to its core businesses, and sold assets to pay off the debt he had taken on to acquire the company in the first place. He thought he could do the same for USX, but he would not get the chance. In effect, USX beat him to it. Target companies were simply emulating their raiders in order to keep those raiders away.

By the beginning of 1987, it was by no means clear whether Icahn's success at TWA would prove long-term. But if it did, it represented what he and others would claim was the takeover movement at its best. And that was its irony. Even at its best, the takeover movement produced very little compared to the extraordinary history of business development in the nation. In Icahn's wake were lost many jobs. In the whittling down of a company, there was seldom much building up. These were inconsequential achievements compared to the making of America's great, job-producing, ongoing corporations.

18

By the mid-1980s, the takeover movement had produced most of Wall Street's stars. Bob Greenhill had run the investment banking department of Morgan Stanley for years, as Joe Perella and Bruce Wasserstein now were at First Boston. Jay Higgins had been elevated to co-manage all of investment banking for Salomon. Steve Friedman and arbitrageur Bob Rubin were the heirs apparent to the throne of Goldman Sachs itself, and Geoff Boisi was co-head of investment banking. Drexel Burnham had risen meteorically to become one of the powerhouses on Wall Street, and Mike Milken was one of the richest young men in the world. Joe Flom now presided over not some newcomer law firm but one of the very largest firms in the nation. The second team of professionals behind these men had risen to the ranks of the envied and famous in their fields, and the reins were already being passed to third and fourth generations of bankers and lawyers.

On an informal list, compiled by *Financial World* magazine, of the highest-paid Wall Street professionals in 1985, those involved in takeovers easily dominated. Ivan Boesky was at the top with $100 million of annual income that year. The top twenty earners made at least $15 million each. Several partners of Goldman Sachs enjoyed annual incomes of nearly $10 million; and a handful, more than that. The proof of Wall Street's new status in America could be found on the college campus. One third of Yale's graduating class, for example, had applied to a Wall Street firm for jobs in the spring of 1986. Law firms complained that they were losing their best young attorneys to investment banks, and the best students were forsaking offers from these firms for more lucrative ones at brokerage houses.

The fashion on campus in the mid-1980s attested to the popularity of moneymaking on Wall Street, and most of that popularity—even glamour—was propelled by takeovers. These years also saw it become fashionable to wave a banner for so-called shareholder rights. In 1986, Boone Pickens, said by some to have political aspirations, formed a group dedicated to securing shareholders' rights. Institutional investors, including state and city pension administrators, had become in the mid-1980s active participants in an effort to influence corporations. When the SEC examined the poison pill, its sole criterion was whether it affected shareholders' rights to get the highest price for their stock.

For a vast and largely anonymous group of shareholders to be seriously compared to a single owner of a corporation in responsibility and governing foresight is extraordinary in itself. Surely a single owner has more sense of responsibility to employees and long-term growth and survival than thousands of shareholders who can look the other way. The good side of the shareholders' rights movement was that management and bureaucracies now had some kind of overseer. The bad side was that this overseer was most interested in short-term gains in the stock price. Nevertheless, shareholders' rights had become an accepted principle, ratified widely by the courts, and quick to roll off the tongue of many an investment professional.

In this environment, a young crop of eager men and women could not have had much perspective. "Many of these kids don't know what a bad market is," says Perella. To them, there had always been big profitable takeovers, and they could not understand the long gestation of the movement, the risks their illustrious bosses had taken, and the innovations they had made. What they did easily see was that the biggest rewards went to the boldest, and for the young, making money must have looked very easy. By the mid-1980s, it was.

The first wave of insider trading revelations in the spring of 1986 was greeted with a patronizing sympathy on the part of the pioneers of the movement. The elder guard was now looking toward their sixties. The generation of Greenhill and Friedman and

Boesky was entering its fifth decade. Boisi, Wasserstein, Siegel, and
Higgins were gathered around forty. But the men who were first
found guilty of insider trading that year were, for the most part,
closer to their early thirties. The immediate reaction was that they
had fallen victim to a growingly cynical attitude toward making
money. "We wanted to get rich," says one of the elders. "But we
weren't greedy. These kids are greedy."

On November 14, 1986, when the SEC announced that Ivan
Boesky had agreed to pay back $50 million in illegally earned profits
and another $50 million in fines, any talk of a generation gap
ceased. Few, if any, had believed the government would get a "big
fish." The combined penalty of $100 million sent Boesky to the
front page of most, if not all, of the nation's major newspapers. The
story was reported that night on all three television network news
broadcasts. By the next Monday, it was reported that Boesky
wore a tape recorder and had trapped others in the business,
enabling him to win a lesser conviction. He did agree to plead guilty
to only one felony count. Rumors circulated about who else had
been caught. Talk of reform was rampant in Washington and New
York. Stock prices retreated sharply in the immediate wake of the
revelations. And the scandal, added to other factors, led some to
believe takeovers would slow dramatically. The poison pill, for one
thing, had become an effective deterrent against some kinds of
raids. Managements had learned to restructure themselves to ward
off takeover attempts. The tax laws, once seldom invoked as a cause
of the takeover movement, had changed significantly with the tax
reform legislation. Now, depreciation would be less attractive for
LBOs. The interest deduction on all that borrowing became less
valuable, because the tax rate was down. Special loopholes in mergers were closed, especially those involving the subsequent disposi-
tion of assets. A rush of mergers took place near the end of the year.
Some would argue that 1987 was the beginning of the end of this
twelve-year movement. In all likelihood, they, too, like their predecessors in the early '70s, would be proved wrong.

The discovery of widespread insider-trading violations was not
the result of vigorous screening on the part of the New York Stock

Exchange or the SEC. As with many criminal cases, it came with a tipoff. In May 1986, an anonymous letter was sent to Merrill Lynch, stating that two Merrill salesmen in Caracas, Venezuela, were trading on inside information about prospective takeovers. A Merrill investigator, Richard Drew, had discovered a connection to a former Merrill employee, William Campbell, whose biggest client was Bank Leu of Switzerland. Drew then turned over his findings to the SEC, unable to discover where Bank Leu was getting its information.

It turned out that the unusually prescient trading by Bank Leu had its source in a fast-rising investment banker, Dennis Levine. Levine had worked on several major deals, including the Martin Marietta–Bendix imbroglio. He was now rising into the ranks of young banking stars, having just been hired by Drexel Burnham Lambert for a reputed $1 million annual compensation. What the SEC would discover was that the apparently persuasive Levine had attracted several colleagues into his small ring of information trading. A handful of bankers and lawyers, more or less of his own generation, supplied him information on forthcoming deals. He would buy shares of those companies, before the announcement, through his Swiss account. The SEC accused him of trading in fifty-four stocks since 1980 and earning $12.6 million. By June, Levine pleaded guilty to four felony counts and agreed to pay back profits of $11.6 million. Five of his cronies at other investment banking and law firms were also to plead guilty, though their profits were far lower. That spring, Wall Street was grieving over the lapse in judgment of these young men, each of whom had at least good careers before them, and some of whom perhaps brilliant ones. What no one had known yet was that Levine in turn had been providing information to Ivan Boesky on a systematic basis.

It cannot be said that Ivan Boesky was the victim of an increasingly cynical system. He was one of the pioneers, and the evidence is that the man approached every objective with obsessiveness. The easy argument that he reflected his times does not explain what happened, and underestimates the man. He made his own opportunities, and did not depend on a popular ethic for his own drive. Nor did he make all his money through inside information. Apparently, however, he was willing to take many an advantage, including the ones Dennis Levine would provide.

On the other hand, it is fair to speculate that Levine and the others looked up to Boesky in a way that would not have occurred in earlier decades. There were many reports that Levine bragged frequently about his relationship and access to Boesky, for example. Boesky, always controversial, and well known as a very aggressive arbitrageur, had indeed won himself considerable dignity in a time that increasingly measured so much by the money one made.

One other speculation is probably justified. As the takeover movement became more institutionalized, more a way of life, the ends began to obscure the means. The reason for making an acquisition became increasingly secondary to getting the deal done. The young generation must have deduced, and been sent clear messages, that doing a deal was typically the fastest way to get ahead, not ruminating about whether it was all that good for the client. There is little doubt that the business justification for deals had frequently taken the back seat by the 1980s. And they may well not have been able to separate the ease with which their superiors made so much money from their own right to make money as well. Criminals always seem to think they are only doing what everyone else is doing, only perhaps a little more aggressively. And finally, information reigned supreme on Wall Street. Word of prospective targets, and potential acquirers, traveled through the relatively small Wall Street circle all the time. Most knew better than to act on it, at least not explicitly. These men unabashedly traded on what they knew.

Apparently, Dennis Levine had been feeding Ivan Boesky information, in order to gain his confidence, for some time during early 1985. In the spring, they made an agreement that would prove Boesky's undoing—and shock Wall Street as well. Boesky would pay Levine 5 percent of any profits he made if Levine provided him with the information on which he, Boesky, made the investment. He also came to an agreement to pay Levine 1 percent of profits on mergers for which Levine provided additional information when Boesky already had a position.

Once caught, Levine was inevitably going to name Boesky. The SEC alleged that "in or about" April 1986, Boesky agreed to pay Levine $2.4 million based on the formula described above. The SEC also cited several explicit cases in which Boesky used the information provided by Levine. The year before, for example, Nabisco

Brands Inc. hired Shearson Lehman to represent it in a possible merger with R.J. Reynolds. Ira Sokolow was a banker at Shearson and a friend of Levine's. Between April and May, according to the SEC, Sokolow passed on information about the merger to Levine, who in turn disclosed it to Boesky. With that information, Boesky bought 377,000 shares of Nabisco in about a week in late May. When talks of the merger were formally announced on May 30, Boesky sold his position for a $4 million profit. The SEC cited two other specific cases in which Boesky made a total of $5 million in the same way, and mentioned a handful of other stocks in which Boesky took positions based on Levine's information. These examples, plus the agreement to pay Levine $2.4 million based on a formula, led the SEC to determine that Boesky had made at least $50 million in illegal profits this way. The SEC could have fined Boesky up to $150 million, but fined him only $50 million.

What stunned many on Wall Street, including several former employees who had worked closely with Boesky, was his blatant, undisguised use of the information. Many thought that even the controversial Boesky was more ethical. And those who doubted his ethics at least thought he was more clever. To buy shares immediately on receiving inside information, and in such large amounts, and then to sell out an entire position on the very day a possible deal is announced, was as explicit a violation as there could be. That a man who had already made probably $200 million would pay for such information by agreement—even if, as some reports had it, Boesky was having a tough year—struck older pros as extraordinary. But, Boesky always demonstrated that he was determined to get the edge if he could. Maybe more to the point, Ivan Boesky may have believed there was nothing really wrong with a foot fault. And speculation rose over whether he had paid off others in his history as an arbitrageur, and whether other arbitrageurs and investment bankers, at still higher levels than Levine, could also have been involved.

A takeover movement that had become so widespread, with so many profitable opportunities, in a time when making money had become so cherished, many would say, would inevitably result in such a scandal. But it was not at all clear that the scandal got to the heart of how and why deals are done on Wall Street. The SEC did not uncover the Boesky transgressions through careful investigation. They were tipped off. Shame in itself would not bring this merger movement down. Making money was as exalted after Boesky as before, and probably more so than at any other time in the postwar period.

A scandal that touched the highest levels of Wall Street was not the only irony of 1986. Harry Gray, after a long fight to stay on top at United Technologies, at last left the company. The year before, he had passed the chief executive position over to Robert Daniell. And in December, United Technologies announced the undoing of some of Gray's mergers. They would reduce payrolls by 11,000 and take a loss of nearly $500 million.

At that same time, Ed Hennessy, once Gray's number two and by now his rival at Allied, looked to have stumbled over his recent merger of Allied with Signal. In 1986 he took a $750 million write-off when he sold a group of companies to Michael Dingman's Henley Group. In the same week that United Technologies announced its cutbacks, Allied also announced the sale of several more companies. *The Wall Street Journal* concluded in a headline late in December: ALLIED-SIGNAL MERGER YIELDS FEW BENEFITS.

In 1986, Transworld Corp. would arrange to sell Hilton Hotels. Carl Icahn already owned TWA, of course. So the holding company had indeed followed the course Leon Levy had suggested, and its management had opposed, back in 1983. Avis, as an article in Long Island's newspaper *Newsday* pointed out, had changed corporate parents for the fourth time since 1981. In the round robin that in many ways captured the bottom line of the merger movement, Avis was moved into Norton Simon's hands in 1977 in an intense battle described earlier. Eventually, Esmark took over Norton Simon. Then Beatrice Foods acquired Esmark. In 1986, Kohlberg Kravis Roberts arranged a $6 billion leveraged buyout to acquire Beatrice. As part of its plan to reduce debt, they sold Avis to Wesray, run by former Treasury Secretary William Simon. The takeover movement increasingly looked like a board game, with its participants about as remote from the reality of business as children sitting around playing Monopoly.

*   *   *

It is difficult to justify this merger movement that was now twelve years old. Its protagonists argue that it was directed at entrenched management and bureaucratic decision-making. In some cases, acquisitions and, indeed, raids did produce more business efficiency. The oil business did take more care because of Boone Pickens. But in the longer run, tidying up a business is not the equivalent of building a new one. Here, the merger movement could claim few credits.

What men like T. Boone Pickens and Carl Icahn claim is that they helped move assets into the hands of people who could manage them better. Icahn says that the stock market only recognizes earnings and that these managements were not managing their assets well enough to produce profits. They should then be moved into other hands. But the efforts of these raiders, even if their case held true, were small by comparison to the long course of the merger movement. A close look reveals little improvement in management. Quite the contrary. For the most part, companies were bought because they were well managed. Harry Gray still states emphatically that he did not believe in buying companies to turn them around. He bought good companies at good prices, and wouldn't pay more than they were worth. T. Boone Pickens makes a somewhat similar claim: "We saw bargains, and like any other business, we went after them." On the face of it, there is nothing wrong with this. The final argument in favor of an unobstructed takeover movement is that corporations should be allowed to make their own mistakes: that in the long run, it is better to let the market run free.

But the true measure of the takeover movement's achievement is whether the money spent was well utilized. And on these grounds, justification is hard to come by. An enormous amount of debt was created to make these acquisitions, replacing equity in the process. The period since 1980 is notable in that debt outstanding in the United States actually rose faster than overall gross national product, the total income generated by the economy. In the past, it had only risen as fast. One significant contributor to that was takeovers. Moreover, in a time of low inflation, taking on debt makes much less sense. When inflation is rising, it is rational to borrow because you pay back in dollars of lesser value. With inflation subsiding over this period, debt should have grown much more slowly.

Given that, the effective utilization of this debt took on even greater importance. No one can adequately tally the good mergers and the bad. For many, the clock is still running. But what does stand out clearly is that the preponderance of dollars was spent on natural resources, especially oil, and the assumptions made were that the prices would be increasing. In fact, prices dropped sharply. Virtually every oil acquisition made in the 1980s looks suspect. Even those that managed well—and as of 1986, Chevron gets high marks for its takeover of Gulf—probably need substantial jumps in the price of oil to make these investments pay off. Chevron disposed of Gulf Canada quickly, which helped it get its debt under control. But companies such as Phillips and Unocal, as well as those that restructured for fear of being taken over, such as Atlantic Richfield, may now be more efficient but they are burdened with debt.

Pickens argues that he would have sold assets far more quickly at Phillips had he taken it over, and that managers hesitate only because they want to maintain their turf. But that raises another issue. The divestiture of assets into other hands presumes that the assets will now be managed better. The good side of the argument is that smaller companies are assuredly easier to manage than large. But those who bought the pieces of a company—an Avis divestiture, for example—may well have overpaid for it. It became the fashion during the latter part of this merger movement to think that these pieces were very valuable.

The final question is whether all this money could have been better spent. Big business in America did seem to run out of many profitable opportunities in the '70s and '80s. Some restructuring, as it became called, was inevitable. But in the end, economic theory tells us that it does not matter that U.S. Steel was able to preserve itself by transforming itself into USX, an oil company. For the economy as a whole, that may be no net gain, even a loss. Had U.S. Steel been able to build more competitive steel plants, that would have added to the economy. The net effect of raids and takeovers in the oil industry is that much less money is spent on exploration for new oil, or oil substitutes. There are fewer companies, for one thing. And those that remain are so heavily indebted that they cannot afford to do much but reduce their exploration budgets. Time Inc., which in the 1970s developed *People* and *Money* magazines, reduced significantly their expenditures on magazine development in 1986, partly for fear of being acquired. So, too, reacted much of corporate America to the fear of takeovers.

In 1986, some positive grumblings were being heard about reform. The most productive new development was the growing body of academic opinion that claimed the antitrust leniency had gone too far. The changes in tax laws also would do less to encourage unproductive acquisitions and leveraged buyouts. The Boesky scandal might induce some correction of potential abuses on Wall Street. While such changes might be the hardest to develop fairly, they might cut down on the outsize profits that unduly encourage mergers.

But what surely became clear as this takeover movement progressed, and what is its final criticism, is that it lost touch with business's first principles. The achievements of longstanding companies were reduced to such measurements as book value and market share. Standing assets, whether they were plants or name brands or franchises, took precedence over the new and undeveloped. But by the mid-1980s, people were forgotten, for in the restructuring that was necessitated by takeovers, thousands lost their jobs.

Even during the Boesky scandal, media attention focused exclusively on the star players. The story of Boesky's employees went untold. When the scandal broke most of them were shocked. Maybe more to the point, they could not find jobs once the firm stopped doing business. No one knew whether he was tainted. In fact, the employees themselves, people who worked behind the cage or in accounting, did not know whether they could be incriminated. "We thought he was a god," says one mid-level employee. "If he called at three in the morning with a question, you'd break your back to get an answer. We'd come in for meetings at six. It hurts to give somebody so much faith and confidence, and have it come back in your face. They talk to us on the Street now like we have a disease. We don't know what will happen next. Every day we come in here shaking. You feel like your whole career is taken away from you. He wrecked a lot of lives, let me tell you."

AUTHOR'S NOTES

Most of the participants in the takeover movement who are referred to in this book were interviewed by the author. Unless otherwise noted, all direct quotations in the text are based on these interviews. Many of the participants were interviewed several times, and a large number had been interviewed by the author for other articles and stories during the years of the takeover movement. Observations and conclusions are based on all these interviews. In addition, numerous interviews were conducted with participants and government officials who preferred to remain anonymous.

The information obtained from the interviews is typically used throughout the book, not isolated to individual chapters. For this reason, I list the key sources for the book below, rather than according to the chapters in which they appear.

Participants in interviews include R. Port, E. Dwyer, E. Grubb, C. Baird, E. Carter, J. Flom, M. Lipton, R. Kent, L. Driever, R. Greenhill, H. Gray, S. Payne, F. Petito, W. Sword, Y. Johnstone, A. Fleischer, S. Fraidin, F. Schaeffer, R. Cheney, S. Friedman, G. Boisi, R. Hurst, T. B. Pickens, W. Chatlos, F. Murphy, E. Large, T. Drohan, E. Hennessy, R. Rubin, M. Siegel, J. Higgins, J. Perella, B. Wasserstein, F. Rohatyn, I. Harris, C. Icahn, L. Pollack, L. Levy, D. LeBaron, H. Goldschmidt (law professor), R. Rosenthal, G. Kellner (arbitrageur), D. Margolis (through public relations counsel), W. Weinhold (business analyst), H. Geneen, I. Boesky, G. Wyser-Pratte, L. Sheriff, P. Hallingby, J. Morgan, A. Amster, J. Bierwirth, H. McGraw (when author was a *Business Week* editor), M. Dingman, P. Montrone (Henley Group), W. Douce, M. Boyar (securities analyst), T. Forstmann (principal in Forstmann-Little, on leveraged buyouts in general), P. Drucker (management consultant), oil analysts at Merrill Lynch & Co., C.J. Lawrence & Co., Carl Pforzheimer & Co., and John Herold Inc.

Public relations counsel for many corporations were also generally courteous and quick to provide necessary information.

Original documents, such as Securities and Exchange Commission filings and corporate press releases, were relied on as far as practical to establish the dates and ordering of events during takeover contests. Daily newspaper accounts were also used to supply such information, and the author is grateful for the accuracy and energy of his colleagues in reporting these events.

Overall data on the aggregate number and volume of takeovers is based on the annual reviews compiled by W.T. Grimm & Co., in Chicago.

The book depends, to as great an extent as possible, on personal interviews and original observations. The following chapter notes record only those secondary sources that were especially valuable in providing accounts of events, or in supplying ideas to the author. Quotations or accounts taken from books, newspapers, or magazines are cited in the text where important.

CHAPTER 1

The history of Inco was drawn from newspaper and magazine accounts, as well as from personal reminiscences of the principals. In particular, a *Fortune* magazine article on Inco (by Lansing Lamont, January 1975) and a *New York Times* account on ESB (by Leonard Sloane, July 26, 1974) were valuable.

Stock prices are taken directly from Dow Jones & Co. and Standard & Poor's Corp. quotations. Inflation statistics are always drawn from the Commerce Department's consumer price index.

CHAPTER 2

The history of tender offers is summarized in many legal publications. Of particular interest in a 1967 article by Arthur Fleischer, Jr., called "Corporate Acquisition by Tender Offer" (Philadelphia: University of Pennsylvania Law Review, January 1967). Two legal texts on this and related subjects were invaluable. *Tender Offers: Defenses, Responses and Planning,* by Arthur Fleischer, Jr. (New York: Law and Business Inc. /Harcourt Brace Jovanovich, 1983) and *Takeovers and Freezeouts,* by Martin Lipton and Erica Steinberg (New York Law Publishing Co., 1978).

For the history of Skadden, Arps, an interview with a longstanding partner, Barry Garfinkel, was very helpful.

Frank Petito (since deceased) and William Sword were valuable sources for the history of Morgan Stanley's involvement in takeovers.

CHAPTER 3

The recounting of these events is largely based on personal interviews.

The chronological summary of the United Aircraft bid that begins on page 41 is based on a detailed diary kept by one of the participants.

CHAPTER 4

The history of the battery business is based on trade journal accounts. Lawrence Driever was of special help in the account of the closing down of ESB.

CHAPTER 5

The history of takeovers: Of special importance were *Financial Performance of Conglomerates,* by Harry H. Lynch (Cambridge, Mass.: Harvard Business School, 1971); *The Rise and Fall of the Conglomerate Kings,* by Robert Sobel (Briarcliff Manor, N.Y.: Stein and Day, 1984); *Concentration, Mergers and Public Policy,* by

Yale Brazen (New York: Macmillan, 1982); "Merger Trends and Prospects for the 1980s" by Malcolm Salter and Wolf Weinhold (Cambridge, Mass.: Harvard Business School, 1980); "Merger Policy and Legislation in the 98th Congress" (Congressional Research Service, 1984). I am particularly grateful to Mr. Sobel's book for his account of the major conglomerators.

"Conventional wisdom" is first given its rightful place in business and economic thought, as far as I know, in *The Affluent Society*, by John Kenneth Galbraith (Boston: Houghton Mifflin, 1958).

The discussion of the evolution of antitrust policy is a distillation of discussions with several antitrust lawyers and scholars.

CHAPTER 6

Mark Boyar, an investment analyst who runs Asset Analysis Focus, provided useful insights into the cash-rich position of corporations over this period.

A profile of Felix Rohatyn in *The New Yorker* magazine (by Jeremy Bernstein, January 24, 1983) was especially useful, as was a *Business Week* cover story on J. Ira Harris (June 25, 1979).

The history of First Boston's participation in takeovers is almost entirely based on personal interviews.

CHAPTER 7

Peter Drucker was interviewed on the subject of diversification.

The details of General Electric's offer for Utah International depends significantly on an account in *Fortune* magazine (by Louis Kraar, August 1977).

Wolf Weinhold, a researcher at Harvard Business School, did a thorough analysis of GE's investment in Utah International, on which these conclusions are based. (He is also cited above as the co-author of a Harvard Business School research report on merger history.)

CHAPTER 8

The Ivan Boesky material is based on personal interviews. The author edited *Merger Mania*, by Ivan Boesky (New York: Holt, Rinehart and Winston, 1985). He also served as a paid consultant to Boesky in 1980 in search of entertainment and media investments.

The basic material on the history and practice of arbitrage and risk arbitrage is derived from *Merger Mania* and from two monographs by Guy Wyser-Pratte that were published by New York University in 1971 and 1982 respectively. These were supplemented by interviews with arbitrageurs, tax accountants, and lawyers.

Numerous biographical articles have appeared on Boesky. But of particular use was an account in *The Atlantic* (by Connie Bruck, December 1984). A *Fortune* magazine article (by Eleanor Johnson Tracy, October 1977) supplied biographical information on several other arbitrageurs. All the key arbitrageurs mentioned were interviewed separately as well.

CHAPTER 9

Biographical information in this chapter is almost entirely derived from personal interviews.

Many investment banking firms did surveys on the number of target companies that either survived or succumbed to a takeover. Most of the surveys arrived at a similar conclusion, which is that only about one out of five remained independent.

CHAPTER 10

The events of Eaton, Cutler Hammer, et al., are partially documented in Fleischer's book *Tender Offers: Defenses, Responses and Planning,* cited above under Chapter 2.

The remarks cited in the Royal Dutch Shell offer for Shell Oil are from the record of the Court of Chancery of Delaware.

The dawn raid for Becton Dickinson is well documented in *The Takeover Barons of Wall Street,* by Richard Phalon (New York: G.P. Putnam's Sons, 1981) on which much of this account depends. The key events were substantially corroborated by several of the participants.

CHAPTER 11

The account of events in this chapter relied on personal interviews and daily newspaper articles entirely.

CHAPTER 12

The giant battle for Conoco was very well chronicled in an article by Steven Brill in *The American Lawyer* (November 1981). The author is very grateful for the details provided, though Brill should not be held responsible for any conclusions in this book.

CHAPTER 13

Stock data is based on Standard & Poor's indexes.

Again, the author is grateful to *The American Lawyer* for information on the Conoco deal, in particular about the legal roadblocks Flom tried to throw up at the last minute. Fleischer's *Tender Offers* (see notes on Chapter 2) also provides valuable information on the acquisition.

CHAPTER 14

The comparative value of the Mesa and Cities Service offers is taken from *Forbes* magazine (by Priscilla Meyer and Tony Mack, July 5, 1982).

The Martin Marietta–Bendix confrontation is very well documented in two books: *3 Plus 1 Equals Billions,* by Allan Sloan (New York: Arbor House, 1983), and *Till Death Do Us Part,* by Hope Lampert (New York: Harcourt Brace Jovanovich, 1983).

The author corroborated the record of many of the events with several of the participants.

CHAPTER 15

Again, aggregate data on takeover volume is taken from W.T. Grimm.

Leon Levy wrote a personal account of the Transworld events in *Fortune* magazine (June 13, 1983).

The citations concerning the valuation of Getty Oil are taken directly from court testimony.

CHAPTER 16

Drexel Burnham Lambert provided a comprehensive history of the growth of junk bonds—which it refers to as high-yield bonds—as well as its own studies of the risk.

The description of Mike Milken was taken from those who know him. He was not interviewed by the author.

The Gray Memo was obtained by the author.

CHAPTER 17

An article by Steven Brill in *The American Lawyer* (May 1985), concerning the Phillips takeover, is of particular interest.

The details of Carl Icahn's financing plans for TWA are dependent on an article in *Fortune* magazine (by Carol Loomis, February 17, 1986).

CHAPTER 18

All charges cited against Dennis Levine and Ivan Boesky, including details of trading, are based on Securities and Exchange Commission documents and press releases.

INDEX